The Body Politic

Writings from the
Women's Liberation Movement
in Britain 1969-1972

Compiled by
MICHELENE WANDOR

Stage 1

Publisher's note

We hope that this book will be read by many women who are
not yet involved in the Women's Liberation Movement. To
make it as widely available as possible, it is being distrib-
uted commercially, through bookshops, as well as through
the Movement itself. We have produced the book as cheaply
as possible, using cheap paper, binding, etc; however,
commercial distribution absorbs over 50% of the cover
price, so this is inevitably higher than we would like it to
be. Reduced bulk prices are available to groups through the
Women's Liberation Workshop, 3/4 Shavers Place, London
SW1 (phone 01-839 3918). Royalties and a percentage of any
profits from the sale of the book will be going to the
Movement.

ISBN 0 85035 013 1 paperback
ISBN 0 85035 014 X hardback library edition

Published 1972 by stage 1, 21 Theobalds Road, London
WC1X 8SL

Cover design by Ian Escott, based on a poster designed by
Carol de Jongh for the first national Women's Liberation
demonstration in London on March 6th 1971

Printed in Great Britain by S.W. (Litho) Ltd. (T.U.),
6 Cottons Gardens, London E2

CONTENTS

APPENDIX

PREFACE

This collection of writings has been put together over the last two years. It is intended to be both a minimal historical account of the Women's Liberation Movement in Britain during the last three years and an introduction to the vast spectrum of issues and ideas which concern us. Everything in the book has been written by women out of their own experiences in the Movement; some pieces have already appeared in Women's Liberation publications, others have been written specially for this book.

The amount of publicity accorded to the Movement since its beginnings in 1968-1969 has been enormous. Most of it has been misleading, derogatory or downright hostile. More recently our ideas and activities have received more serious treatment, generally from women journalists who have themselves become involved in the Movement. However there is still an enormous gap between the political experience of involvement and the reports of meetings, discussions and demonstrations which appear in the press. The Movement has published its own literature right from the start, but although the output and scope is increasing rapidly it still only reaches a relatively small number of women. One of the aims of this book is to make some of that writing more widely available to other women who may be sceptical of the reports they read and perhaps unaware that there is a growing amount of Women's Liberation literature.

The book has many gaps, and is rather London-orientated; but it has never been intended as a definitive guide either to the Movement as a whole or to any one group. Some of it will be dated by the time it appears in print, but the living experience of a heterogeneous movement is always ahead of the written material which records it. The book is not definitive, but part of an ongoing process of development, discussion and action.

Although I have worked on the book throughout, a number of other women have been involved at various stages of its compilation. Where relevant, each piece is followed by a short reading list; I hope people will use this book as an initial point of reference and go on to other sources to find out more. The book ends with a list of Women's Liberation Groups all over Britain, and of other existing organisations useful to women.

Michelene Wandor

THE FOUR DEMANDS

At the first national women's conference at Ruskin College, Oxford, in February-March 1970, the following four demands were formulated.

EQUAL PAY

We have to understand <u>why</u> we don't have equal pay. It's always been said that a woman's place is in the home. We don't want to do equal work and housework as well. We don't want to do equal work when it's shitwork. Equal pay means not just the same money for the same work, but also recognising how many women work not because they want to, but because they <u>have</u> to, either for money or for friends. Equal pay is the <u>first</u> step not just to more money, but to control over how, why, and for whom we work.

EQUAL EDUCATION AND OPPORTUNITY

We don't want to demand an education equally as bad as that of men - we want equal resources, not equal repression. We want to fight for real education, to make our own jobs and opportunities.

24-HOUR NURSERIES

We need somewhere for the kids, but we have to choose as to whether the kids will be kept out of the way or given their own space, and whether, freed from children, we just manage to survive through working or make the time to discover who stops us from living.

FREE CONTRACEPTION AND ABORTION ON DEMAND

We want to be free to choose when and how many kids to have, if any. We have to fight for control over our own bodies, for even the magic pill or (in the case of mistakes) abortion on demand only gives us the freedom to get into a real mess without any visible consequences. We still can't talk of sex as anything but a joke or a battle-ground.

(Women's Newspaper, issue no. 1, March 6 1971)

WOMEN'S LIBERATION AND THE NEW POLITICS

Sheila Rowbotham

(Sheila Rowbotham is a member of London Women's Liberation Workshop)

Introductory note

This was written in June 1969, when there was no Women's Liberation Movement in Britain, only a few small groups. This means that there are many things left out which I would have included now. My own preoccupations have changed now too, and the questions I would ask about the women's movement have shifted somewhat. However, I think the concerns of this article are still relevant to us. How do people come to a new consciousness of themselves in the world? How does a new concept of what it is to be female come about? How are new ideas made social through the practical activities of a movement? How is social transformation communicated to the individual psyche? I didn't know the answers in 1969 and I don't know them now. But they seem to me questions which the particular context of the women's movement helps us to shape, and which are vital for the revolutionary movement as a whole. I have made a few cuts in the article and added some new notes. If you want to compare this with the original edition, see Spokesman Pamphlet no. 17, of the same title.

The so-called women's question is a whole people question. It is not simply that our situation can only be fundamentally changed by the total transformation of all existing social relations, but also because without us any such transformation can be only partial and consequently soon distorted. The creation of a new woman of necessity demands the creation of a new man.

Recently E. E. Evans-Pritchard pointed out that the position of women and the relationship of the sexes called into question also those between parents and children, brothers and sisters, teachers and pupils, managers and workers, citizens of one country and citizens of another.

"In so far as the problems of the relations of the sexes are not those just of sex as such, but of authority, leadership, control, cooperation and competition, they are problems which occur in every sort of society; and they cannot be solved by an insistance on absolute equality but rather by recognition of differences, exercise of charity and acknowledgement of authority. " (1)

The case is most beautifully put. The domination of women is at once the most complex and the most fundamental of links in the chain. Accordingly in moments of acute social unrest the question of our position leaps to the surface.

Consistently from the Right comes the implicit commitment to the smothering of the women's revolt. Our upris-
ing is the most terrible to the conservative, precisely
because it is so important for the revolution. The opposition to the women is always more intense than that towards
any other group, and it is always expressed in the most
hysterical terms. The imagery too becomes sexual almost
immediately. (2)

Now while the Left has always included 'the women problem'
and 'equal rights for women' on the agenda, it has placed
them rather far down. There is a hesitancy and a hopelessness about the issue, a tendency to 'if' and 'but' and 'of
course'. This is expressed in a curious fear that the subject is 'diversionary'. Of course it is diversionary. It is
one of the largest diversions that could possibly be made -
the diversion of one half of the human race towards social
revolution. Partly the matter is very concrete. It is about
25p an hour and the suicide rate, about nursery schools and
legal discrimination. All these need to be studied. But
there is another important aspect to 'the women problem' -
how it feels in the head. If the external social situation
subdues us, it is our consciousness that contains us.

The attempt is here to explore the nature of women's containment, to examine the ways out and to see how these
ways out relate to a total social transformation. At the
same time it is necessary to try and understand the awk-
wardness with which marxism has touched upon the situation of women, which of necessity involves questioning the
emphasis of some species of marxism. To think of providing final answers would be absurd. But hopefully it should
be possible to begin enquiry.

On containment

The first question is why do we stand for it? The oppressed
are mysteriously quiet. The conservative answer is 'because they like it like that'. But the revolutionary can't afford to be so sure. He has learned to be doubtful about the
'happiness' of the exploited. He knows that containment
cannot be directly related to quietness. The subordination
of women only achieves perspective when it is seen in relation to the mechanism of domination. The way in which we
are contained only really becomes comprehensible when it
is seen as part of the general situation of the oppressed. In
order to understand why those in control stay on top and the
people they use don't shake them off it is necessary to
trace the way in which the outward relationship of dominat-
or to dominated becomes internalised.

"But they are happy like that."
"Can't you see they enjoy it."

Superficially there is a complicity between the subordinated and the authority figure. But this is in fact the mutuality of whore and pimp. They associate because of the way the game is rigged. She continually keeps back a percentage, he continually steals her clothes and beats her to survive. Deceit and violence are the basis of their relationship, and continue to be so until the external situation is changed. However the conception of change is beyond the notions of the oppressed. They are confined within the limits of their imagination of the possible. For the dominated without hope the relationship is habitual. There is neither the memory of a different condition in the past, nor the possibility of difference in the future, but an always world of dominating and dominated without moral belief in change or the means of effecting it.

The oppressed in their state before politics lack both the idea and practice to act upon the external world. Both coherent protest and organised resistance is inconceivable. They do not presume to alter things, they are timid. Life is cyclical, weary, events happen, disaster impinges, there is no rational order in the universe, to the authorities properly belong the business and responsibilities of government. They play dumb and the superior people assume they have nothing to say, nothing to complain of. Those in power conclude their 'inferiors' must be a different order of people. This justifies their subjugation. The impression is confirmed by their inability to take the advantage offered to them, by the shrugging off of responsibilities, by the failure to take initiatives. They refuse to help themselves, they are their own worst enemy. But meanwhile they survive. They are skilled in collaboration and subterfuge. They do not compete, they resort to indirect, sly methods. Like Brer Rabbit they lie low.

All these characteristics can be detected amongst oppressed groups before they have created a political movement. They are also most common among those women completely dependent on men. The same mistake has been made about these traditional women as the rest. Because they do not articulate their complaints in terms recognised by those in control, they are presumed to be happy.

Women have been lying low for so long most of us cannot imagine how to get up. We have apparently acquiesced always in the imperial game and are so perfectly colonised that we are unable to consult ourselves. Because the assumption does not occur to us, it does not occur to anyone else either. We are afraid to mention ourselves in case it might disturb or divert some important matter he has in hand. We are the assistants, the receivers, the collaborators, dumb, lacking in presumption, not acting consciously upon the external world, much given to masochism. We become sly - never trust a woman - we seek revenge, slighted we are terrible; we are trained for sub-

5

terfuge, we are natural creatures of the underground.
Within us there are great gullies of bitterness, but they do
not appear on the surface. Our wrapped-up consciousness
creeps along the sewers, occasionally emerging through a
man-hole. After death, hag-like spirits roam the earth,
the symbols of frustrated unfulfilled desires. But in life
our spirits are contained.

On the language of silence

The revolutionary who is serious must listen very carefully
to the people who are not heard and who do not speak. Unless attention is paid to the nature of their silence there
can be no transmission of either memory or possibility and
the idea and practice of transformation can accordingly not
exist.

Movements develop in the process of communicating themselves. The forms of communicating consequently define
considerably their shape and direction. Communication for
people who have no name, who have not been recognised,
who have not known themselves, is a difficult business.
For women it is especially difficult. We have accepted for
so long man's image of himself and of ourselves and the
world as his creation that we find it almost impossible to
conceive of a different past or a different future. MANkind
is his, WOMANkind is his, huMANity is his. We have not
even words for ourselves. Thinking is difficult when the
words are not your own. Borrowed concepts are like
passed-down clothes: they fit badly and do not give confidence; we lumber awkwardly about in them or scuttle off
shamefacedly into obscurity wondering whether we should
do our/their flies up for us/them.

First there is the paralysis. Their words stick in your
throat, their setting caused you to flounder. This is of
course not peculiar to women. It is part of the common
condition of the subordinated. In the 1848 revolution in
France the people stormed the Assembly. A fireman adjusted his helmet and leapt onto the rostrum as if it were a
roof. The people cheered him and told him to speak. But
he stood there dumb, unable to cope with the constructions
of those who had been his masters for so long. He was
dragged down in shame and disgrace. (3)

There is not only the paralysis, there is the labour of making connections. Theory and the removed language in
which it is expressed presents a means of going beyond the
immediate. It crystallises innumerable experiences, it
puts a canopy over the world which enables it to be regarded as a relating whole. It makes reality intelligible. But
this theory is constructed from the experience of the dominators and consequently reflects the world from their point
of view. They, however, present it as the summation of the
world as it is, their model of existence, ideology, to

6

reaffirm their position. Thus the struggle to take hold of definitions, the tools of theory, and to structure connections, model-building, is an essential part of the politicisation of the oppressed. Without this it is impossible to shatter the hold of the dominators and storm their positions of superiority.

But the struggle becomes a kind of agony. In the making of the working class in Britain the conflict of silence with 'their' language, the problem of paralysis and connection has been continuous. Every man who has emerged through the labour movement expressed this in some form. The embarrassment about dialect, the divorce between home talking and educated language, the otherness of 'culture', their culture. It is happening now in the relations between teacher and pupil in every working-class school. The intensity of the degree of accommodation has varied. It has meant sometimes a stilted borrowing from the culture of the ruling class, even at the point of denouncing their political and economic hold most fiercely; or it has resulted in a dismissal of theory as something contaminated by belonging to the rulers. The persistent elevation of understanding through direct experience has become both the strength and the weakness of British working class politics. It provides security in the defence of existing strongholds, and weakness in the creation of an offensive strategy.

Similarly relevant is the understanding of the movement of Black America. (4) For an oppressed group to successfully challenge those who control them they have to be able to create, to construct a total alternative kind of being. Such an alternative does not drop neatly from the sky. It has to be hewn out through suffering, in struggle, over time, and with thought.

In order to see how this relates both to the situation of woman in a traditional state of complete social dependence and to the situation of the woman in the process of casting off this dependence, it is necessary to consider the ways in which these women understand the world, and the ways in which they communicate their understanding. While such a study requires, in fact, volumes of empirical research, some impressions will have to do for us now. The first mistake of superior people is to equate the silence of the oppressed with stupidity. The second is to assume the 'inferiority' of experience-knowing to theoretical understanding because the former has been associated with those lower down. Those few who rise from the ranks before any cultural or political movement exists tend to fall into a similar misconception. This is not surprising because it was that very instrument of the oppressors, removed language, that enabled them to 'make' themselves. It is necessary both to understand how the oppressed refine and develop their capacity to apprehend directly what is going

7

on, and at the same time to see how this reinforces their
defensive outlook on the world.

Most important is observation. If you are safe and sound
you don't need to keep a sharp look out and if you have absolute power you don't need to take into account the feelings
and reactions of those you control. Consequently the self-
consciousness of a dominant class or group increases as
they become less confident. As for the weak, they excel in
perception. The traditional woman who knows the ways of a
man, who can meet him with flattery, who can delight him,
will be successful. Her ability to succeed is inseparable
from her capacity to excite his desire and to entangle him
in obligation. This woman-lore is a delicate art, half im-
parted by other women, half learned from experience. She
attunes herself to him, she picks up the slightest quiver of
resentment, nurses his vanity with tenderness, follows the
flow of his speech, responds to his rhythm. She accordingly is able to distinguish precisely and exactly the difference
between what is said and what is meant - intention does not
exist for her in the word alone. After all, what he says
with his pants on invariably does not relate to what he does
with them off, and the consequences are very real for her.
Not surprisingly the weakness of her position makes her
unwilling to state exactly how she feels; she takes refuge in
ambiguity, cultivates mystery. In response to forthright
questioning she becomes devious and dumb. She avoids
direct and open confrontation, preferring to get her oppon-
ent in the dark. Her tactics are manipulative. She takes
pride in her sublety and her ability to get things from the
man deviously. We women have our ways.

To locate this more exactly, think of three characteristics
especially associated with women and often regarded as
marks of inferiority: giggling, gossip, and old wives tales.
All three make considerable sense in the environment of
the dominated. Girls giggle at the moment of taboo. It is a
way at once of making a point and of avoiding the issue. It
precludes criticism and does not give the game away. A
guerrilla tactic rather than a head-on encounter, it irri-
tates in moments of weakness. Gossip provides another
important way of perceiving and describing the world.
an underground and rather subversive way it communicates
through anecdote the reflection form it has become to the
novel. For the woman dependent on men it provides also a
powerful form of social control over the behaviour of other
women. Gossip can determine who is within the protection
of society and restrict other women from moving over into
self-determination and giving the game away. It is specifically directed against any manifestation of liberation, sexual or otherwise, and is designed to prevent women scabs
taking on some of the powers of the men. Not surprisingly
it is most common amongst the older, more established
women and is aimed at the younger ones yet to find a

settled place. The greater the institutional bondage, the more gossip becomes a fine art. Related to gossip is the old wives tale, which presents a series of myth warnings within which forbidden subjects can be contained. This satisfies curiosity and restrains young girls from wandering out of the protected territory of dependent womanhood.

Experience-knowing is thus characterised by symbol, myth, allegory. The dominated can tell stories, they can fantasise, they can create Utopia, but they cannot devise the means of getting there. They cannot make use of maps, plan out the route and calculate the odds. The dominators continue to hold ideology. Thus while the traditional woman is able to defend herself, she is unable to create the conditions which would make such defence unnecessary. Moreover she has no separate identity because she has no way of defining herself or her condition. Experiencing herself in isolation she can only know herself in the situation in which she is put, as object. She has only article awareness. Her highest aspiration can be to become merely his most elaborate commodity, clothes-pegging the proof of his wealth about, or playing intellectual foil to his thinking, her leisure the confirmation of his ceaseless striving to accumulate, her passivity the proof of his ability to subdue the world. This fragmentation, isolation and lack of identity makes it impossible for her to relate her own situation to that of any other oppressed group, or to seek a way out. Trapped, she turns round and repeats the process of domination within her own group. She translates the outer authority inwards, repeating what is done to her by men to other women. The woman of the upper class despises the working woman, the married distrust the unmarried, the old suppress the young. The conflicts between women are well-known, the war between wife and mother-in-law, or in polygamy between the wives, or between wife and concubine. Most venemous are the feelings of the dependent toward the emancipated. This causes the free woman to view the rest with a mixture of contempt and fear; she feels at once superior, ie more like the man, and insecure, accused of being incapable of being a woman. While feeling more able to fend for herself, she has shed many of the traditional defences, and in a society structured for men can become suddenly very defenceless. If the traditional feminine woman presents no alternative and exhausts herself in internecine conflict, those who become 'free' are at once uncertain of their position and inclined to rush off down blind alleys.

The anxious object (5)

The girl who for some reason breaks away intellectually is in a particularly isolated position. She finds herself straddled across a great gulf, which grows wider, while she is pulled both ways. A most perilous and lonely condition, comparable to that of a black or working class

militant. In the process of becoming interested in ideas,
she finds herself to some extent cut off from most other
girls and inclines naturally towards boys as friends. They
do more interesting things, discuss wider topics. She
really defines herself as a boy. Other girls appear curious
and rather boring, passive and accepting. She has little to
say to most of them. The social contempt in which women
are held confirms this. She is constantly being told she is
'quite good for a girl'. Femininity becomes synonymous
with frivolity, stupidity and narrowness. It seems obviously better to be a man. Doesn't she feel like a man, do their
things, talk their talk? It is natural for her to define her
situation in terms of a kind of sub-manness.

The image is constantly reaffirmed. The books she reads
and the films she sees are almost invariably by men. The
women characters created by them, however sympathetic-
ally and with whatever intuitive understanding, must of
necessity be the projection of their responses towards
women. One is simply not conscious of men writers or men
film-makers. They are just writers, just film-makers.
The reflected image of women they create will be taken
straight by women themselves: these characters 'are' women.

Throughout this process the educated girl probably takes
her 'emancipation' as being beyond question, not worth
even stating or discussing. The suffragettes happened a
long time ago.

Men will rapidly accept her as different, an exception, an
interesting diversion. She lives in fact as a man. There
might be a hint of strain over her virginity, a flicker of
doubt, the discovery of a strange duplicity lurking still in
men. But no connection is obvious. She cannot see a condition of women. It is not until she becomes older, grows
less decorative, has babies, that the rather deep cracks in
the gloss of 'emancipation' appear. She has the rest of her
life to explore the limits and ambiguities of her 'freedom'.
And what a spurious freedom. We walk and talk and think
as living contradictions. Most of us find the process too
painful and, not surprisingly, settle for limited liberated
areas. We give up struggling on every front and ease into a
niche of acceptance. We become the educated housewife
desperately searching for dignity and fulfilment through
ever more elaborate cooking recipes or constant redecor-
ation schemes, suspicious and defensive about women who
are unmarried or women who work. Or the occupational
variant of this Proopism: doing a womany womanness to a
very male style. These two responses are described as
mature integration. They are of course simply avoiding the
issue in a peculiarly complicit and false way.

Obversely we become the popular (distorted) image of the
suffragette. A tweedy, sensibly-shod battle-axe with a sev-
ere hair-style and a deep voice, advancing aggressively on

the male world and the board room. The sexual corollary of this is the retreat into lesbianism. Both share a profound distaste for the male. Emancipation is doing without men.

Our other retreat is into sexuality. Because women have traditionally been deprived of the power to make 'free' choices, our bodies have been part of somebody else's belongings, we prove that we have control, that we are liberated simply by fucking. But if the definition of our constraint is not extended beyond sexuality we are only entrammelled in a greater bondage. We may not be choosing but reacting, ironically under the compulsion of our real subordination. We could be expressing in our sexual life the very essence of our secondariness and the destructive contradictions in our consciousness, through the inability to meet and communicate and love with a man on every level. The same 'free' woman could still expect men to pay for her, buy her expensive presents. She must of necessity be excessively preoccupied with her appearance and regard other women's men as fair game. After all she needs constantly the reassurance that she is wanted and beautiful, because only through these is she capable of defining her freedom.

We shelter as well as retreat. We take refuge behind the privilege of class and education, using the manner and accent of the rulers to secure respect and serious consideration: a protected dignity at the expense of the working class, and a protected liberation based on the underpaid labour of an au pair. Most of us live a combination of these or run the whole gamut knowing them for subterfuge - at certain moments struggling through and beyond them all. However they are peculiarly stultifying, peculiarly paralysing. They present neither the possibility for the individual woman nor for women as a group to emerge in a redefined and whole way. They never go beyond confirmation or denial of what men say we are, and they ignore the infinite acceptability, the infinite absorbability of exceptional individuals and privileged elites, from an oppressed group with no real effect on the position of the rest. In their existing form such 'emancipations' can no more provide a means of transforming the situation of women than the dreams of the traditionally dependent women. Consciousness is atomised, the situation is met at the moment of psychological aloneness. The free woman merely exchanges fantasy for neurosis. Schizophrenia and psychosomatic illness are the real expression of her condition. Not surprisingly, too, such a false freedom is never attractive to the vast mass of women, even those whose position of class privilege would attain to it. They see the emancipated woman as a kind of fake male, as someone playing at being a man. They feel a certain revulsion and do not trust her.

In reality the simple 'abstraction' between 'unfree' and

11

'free', 'traditional dependent' and 'emancipated' cannot be maintained. Under closer examination such polarization dissolves. Rather like the innocent idea that there are girls you can sleep with and girls you marry, clearly defined categories can only be observed from a distance. Individuals weave between the two poles in an infinitely complex manner, but the freezing of reality in this way helps to indicate what is happening.

On men

Amidst such ambiguity and confusion it is not surprising that men are unsure how to act. There is the assumed superiority but there is also the suspicion of the traditional dependent woman. They notice most women seem incapable of behaving like men and quite naturally assume this implies inferiority. They feel the dependent woman clings to them, that she cannot relate to them in certain ways. They turn to the 'free' woman, expecting to find at once a kind of forbidden fruit and a decent chap. Few women can sustain these roles together. Even if they could there would still be dissatisfaction and unease. The free woman seems to switch from their game back to the behaviour of the traditional woman or she brings competition into bed. He wants her to be independent, but fears she might outstrip him. Such anxieties make even the most benevolent of men unwilling to let go of the certainties retained within their external control of the traditional relationship. The origins of the fears would seem to be partly sexual, partly the terror of dissolving identity - with nothing fixed in the world - but also the whole social pressure within capitalism to compete, to prove yourself by subduing nature, by grappling with existence and in the process dominating others. Men as the makers of the world are subjected to these pressures most intensely. The emergence of women thus creates a tension. Any breakthrough must occur dialectically. As women's situation becomes more defined, the conditions will be created in which men can clarify more exactly the nature of these fears. At the moment of clarification such anxieties begin to dissolve, and a new process of release will begin for both men and women.

While individual men and women are obviously engaged in this now, in order for there to be a significant shift in the social sense, the beginning of a new series in the process of change, there has to be the intensification of experience which takes place when individuals combine and collectively create their consciousness together. In other words there must be some kind of interaction - discussion and action - interlocking-organisation. If this is not to defeat its own purpose the initiative must come from the group most immediately concerned - women themselves. A movement is thus an essential form of group expression. It is the means of finding a voice.

On breaking the silence

There is nothing like learning from example, apart from doing it yourself. We are fortunate to live in a time when all manner of people who had previously been trodden in the dirt, people with no place in society, people with no right to speak have audaciously lifted up their heads and taken power into their hands. (6) We are thus able to learn from their audacity.

It is possible to trace a dialectic in the breaking of silence. Most important at first have been those amongst the rulers who cut themselves off from their own kind to take up the cause of the 'inferior' people in an ideal or moral sense. For instance, the enlightened aristocrats before the French Revolution, the intellectuals in the Russian and Chinese Revolutions, the white liberals in America. They are able to communicate possibility to the oppressed. Not all of them can withstand the time when the dominated use the tools they gave them against them. Some of them retreat. Then there is that section of the subordinated who break away under their encouragement. At first they will be only a few isolated individuals, immediately absorbed within the dominant culture. However, as the rate of migration intensifies, entrance becomes limited, and under certain specific conditions the possibility of a mass movement from below emerges. Such a dialectic can be seen working in the making of the proletariat, in the struggles for national liberation, in the history of the black people of America. An important speeding-up process is the relating of one struggle to another. To know someone else has made it, however far away, can be a most powerful encouragement.

Various phases of consciousness can be observed. First there is the simple moral protest against oppression, as against religion or common humanity. Secondly there is the more material demand of the privileged among the inferior to be allowed to compete equally with the dominant group. This is conceived as equal rights. The oppressed are still able to define themselves only according to the terms of the domination. The black man must still want to be white because white represents power over the world. Thirdly there is the realisation that the real liberation of the oppressed group can only be achieved through the transformation of the economic base and of social relations - ie that it consequently affects others who are dissatisfied. This is the discovery of marxism. Fourthly and closely related is the realisation within marxism of the inter-locking nature of oppressions and the significance of hegemonic control.

In order to locate the situation of women more exactly, it is necessary to examine what kind of movement has been created in the past, what relevance it has now, in the present, and, finally, how marxism relates to our liberation.

On feminism

It is most important to be clear about the way in which we use 'feminism'. There are two possible interpretations, one ideal, the other historical. Feminism can be seen as the conception of a society in which the roles of dominator and dominated are reversed, and in which women take over the superior status of men. It can also be seen as the demand for equality for women made on religious or ethical grounds: this feminism wants to compete more fairly with men and is expressed in the struggle for equal rights.

Feminism in the first sense is utopian - ie it exists in the realm of stories and visions, not as a political movement. Detailed study of the myths would be illuminating. There is for example an Anglo-Norman poem, Des Grantz Geanz, probably composed in the mid thirteenth century. Thirty daughters of the king of Greece plotted to murder their husbands. None of them wanted to have a master and to be in subjection. Each wanted to be her own mistress. Their plot discovered, they were punished by being set adrift in a boat, and arrived very sea-sick on a desert island. Albine, the eldest, took posession of the land, which was called Albion after her. The sisters learned to trap animals, they grew 'big and fat' and began to want human company. Incubi or bad fairies came to satisfy their needs. These incubi were both invisible and undemanding. Together they bred giants, who flourished until Brutus conquered the island and called it Britain. (7) Again in a Chinese novel written in 1825 by Ju-Chen a hundred fairy folk turned into women and oppressed the men, binding their feet and generally holding them in subordination. (8)

Utopian feminism found an existential gesture when Valerie Solanas tried to shoot off Andy Warhol's balls because 'he had too much control over my life'. Her S. C. U. M. Manifesto (Society for Cutting Up Men) is a kaleidoscopic vision of the ways in which modern capitalism crouches in the inner crevices of the psyche, combined with an acutely myopic political perspective. S. C. U. M. could never get mass woman appeal. For a start S. C. U. M. can't cope at all with sexuality. The S. C. U. M. female has to 'condition away her sex drive' in order to be 'cool', 'cerebral' and 'free'. Nor can S. C. U. M. present anything but the reversal of domination and the elimination of first men and then women. Not much to make a social revolution for.
S. C. U. M. gives women the chance to cut off men's balls to fuck up our own cunts. (9)

What about the more sedate kind of feminism? It is possible to trace two phases: the emergence of the religious and moral idea of the individual worth and dignity of women, and the movement for specific reforms, legal, educational, the vote, etc. To relate this more precisely to Britain, the first glimmering assertions were expressed not surprisingly

14

in religious terms. Religious mysticism undoubtedly provided a shelter in a situation where it was impossible to conceive any alternative. For example, Margery Kempe, a 14th century mystic, saw devils after a difficult childbirth, communed with heaven, and subsequently 'never desired to commune fleshly with her husband, for the debt of matrimony was so abominable to her that she would rather have eaten or drunk the ooze and muck in the gutter than consent to any fleshly communing save only for obedience'. (10)

It was no coincidence that the effect of man's questioning his relationship to God created an element of doubt about the nature of his relationship to women. All were, after all, equal in the eyes of the Lord. Within the puritan sect women could find a certain degree of self-expression. But the division of loyalty produced some confusion. Women not only preached and prophesied as handmaidens of the Lord, they divorced their husbands for spiritual deviation. (11) However, the puritan woman was as yet incapable of feminist justification. The women petitioners of Parliament against popish lords and superstitious bishops reassured the gentlemen of the Commons in 1642: 'We do it not of any self-conceit or pride of heart as seeking to equal ourselves with men, either in authority or wisdom'. (12) But by the late 17th century on the 'authority' of 'reason and good sense' the case that woman was 'as good as the Man' was being argued. (13) The grounds were now that given a similar external environment women would prove themselves intellectually as capable as men. Not surprisingly this took the form of demanding education. 'Had we the same literature they would find our brains as fruitful as our bodies'. (14) Richardson's novel Clarissa Harlowe marks a further stage in this moral revolt. Clarissa resists an arranged property marriage, remains 'pure' despite being raped, and is able to extend her experience with the generalised reflection on 'one half of humanity tormenting the other and being tormented themselves in tormenting'.

Corresponding with Richardson a woman brought the radical nature of his position home to him. Lady Bradsheigh declared the laws of society were made by men 'to justify their tyranny', argued for equality in sex relationships, and said of the views of the Old Testament Patriarchs, 'if they took it into their heads to be tyrants, why should we allow them to be worthy examples to imitate'. (15)

Mary Wollstonecraft's Vindication, often taken as the 'beginnings' of feminism, was really the important theoretical summation of this moral phase. Along with William Thompson's One Half of the Human Race in 1820 it put the case firmly on the secularised basis of equal rights, though Thompson's work is more radical in emphasis because when Mary Wollstonecraft wrote it was still necessary to justify the woman's right to self-development on the grounds that it would make her a better mother.

While radical theory played an important role, there were
good economic reasons for the development of the movement in the second half of the 19th century which tried to
improve the legal status of woman and enable her to be
educated and enter the professions. The increasing prospe-
rity of the middle class released many women from housework into aristocratic leisure. But it also deterred men
from marrying young, as the conspicuous display of the
household increased. For the unmarried gentlewoman on
the capitalist labour market the only hope was to become a
governess. The vote seemed the obvious way of carrying
into effect a general improvement in the position of women.
(16)

There were two crucial weaknesses in feminism in its
liberal-radical political phase. First it could not come to
terms theoretically with social class. Secondly it could not
define itself except in terms of the dominant group. The
New Woman was in fact merely the upper middle class man
in a peculiar kind of drag. These weaknesses made the
split with Sylvia Pankhurst and the patriotism of World War
1 inevitable. It was a case of anything they can do we can
do better. There was no alternative social vision.

The feminist movement at this stage consequently failed to
produce any prospect for a real social emancipation which
could include all women, or to create a consciousness
through which women could appreciate their identity as a
group. (17)

Now

Liberal-radical feminism expressed the way in which
women could see themselves in a particular context. But it
obscures the real contradictions of the woman's position
now. It cannot contain within it the possibility of real
change for the woman with a family, it cannot speak for the
exploitation of the working woman, it cannot comprehend
the process of objectification. It cannot break the silence.

Certainly the struggle phrased in terms of equal rights eff-
ected a vital and necessary exposure. It laid bare one level
in the structure of domination. But like a snake's skin, as
one idea system is peeled off another forms beneath it.
Liberal-radical feminism is now only the shrivelled skin of
a past reality shed on the ground. It is no good waving
cast-off skins. We are concerned with the living creature.

Because of the inadequacies in the liberal-radical feminist
approach there has been a tendency to dismiss 'emancipation' as such, to conclude that there is something peculiarly immutable about our position. Instead of course we
should examine the real conditions from which change could
develop. It is necessary to look more closely at the situation

of the housewife in the family, at the position of the woman at work and the means by which women are thingified in the head, here and at this moment, in order to begin to find out what can be done. Such a separation is for convenience only, in fact they are completely intertwined.

Housewife

The housewife is not considered much except by those who want to make sure she stays put. Yet here social secondariness is experienced most intensely. It is here that the real contradiction in the woman's situation is most clearly expressed. Susanne Gail in the Penguin Work describes this.

'It was never a burden to me to be a woman before I had Carl. Feminists had seemed to me to be tilting at windmills; women who allowed men to rule them did so from their own free choice. I felt that I had proved myself the intellectual equal of men, and maintained my femininity as well. But afterwards I quite lost my sense of identity; for weeks it was an effort to speak. And when I again became conscious of myself as other than a thing, it was in a state of rebellion that I had to clamp down firmly because of Carl. I also grew very thin and I still do not menstruate. '

The pregnant housewife is not only unable to escape from her femininity, she is economically, socially and psychologically dependent on the man - from this point 'free' choice becomes impossible. Think of the social position of the housewife with a family. In order to clear up the confusion it is necessary to place the housewife socially. There is much conservative cant about the respect due to motherhood. Imagine these benevolent gentlemen if all mothers demanded a wage from the state for their important work and threatened a general strike if this was not granted. A hairdressing day-release class, using the criteria of cash and respect, created a model of social stratification:

The Queen
pop singers (various grades)
employers
principal of college
vice-principal of college
teacher
hairdressing students
black people
mothers

It is no coincidence that mothers came at the bottom. Firstly consider the housewife as a producer. Rather than producing marketable commodities her function relates to the development and sustenance of people. Those who make people rather than things are not valued very highly in our society. The relationship to production is connected very closely to the relationship in distribution. This is obscured because the housewife who does not work receives money from the husband. In other words the society pays him to pay her. If the housewife wants to 'improve' herself, she has in fact to 'improve' the situation of her husband. She has to translate her ambition into his person. Thus the respect due to her is delicately adjusted by the respect due to him. The more of herself she pours into her image of him the more she loses herself. The relationship is at once that of economic, social and psychological dependence. It is exploitative: in terms of cash she undoubtedly puts in much more than she receives back. The individual man will vary in what he demands or extracts from the woman in labour, as will her ability to bargain with him personally.

But the exploitation of women at home only becomes clear when it is seen in a social way. The individual man acts as a kind of middle-man or channel through to the rest of society. The domestic work of the housewife is socially vital: recognition is shown by paying the woman through the medium of the man. Any individual man - especially the working class man - is unable to avoid this, whatever his private intention. Both the work situation and social assumptions are too rigid for him to experiment with a different division of labour. Essentially the woman gives her labour to the community and the community gives her nothing in return. She is a social attachment.

In the situation of poverty such reflected 'exploitation' is clear and apparent. In the case of many working class women it is easy to locate the way in which the family situation reflects in microcosm the deprivation of the man at work. He translates the alienation and frustration he finds in the external world into the home. The woman experiences a reflected alienation. But it is a mistake to conclude that the alleviation of poverty will solve this. Increased affluence merely enables the less immediate problems to emerge. After two centuries of conditioning, teaching us to value worth in terms of money, we are now having to learn that it is possible to have enough money to live comfortably and have no sense of worth. Production for waste does not apply to things, it applies to people. As modern capitalism devises ever newer and more ingenious waste-disposal schemes a great revolt of the useless begins. Student unrest is only the anticipation of the malaise of vast numbers of lower managerial, white collar and skilled workers who receive high material 'rewards' but who have little fulfilment or control at work. They spend their time in tasks which do not seem whole, which they do not believe in and cannot take hold of. Such expenditure of self cannot be measured neatly. It is close to the situation of the middle class housewife. She will actually seek for more and more tasks. She will lose herself in work - either inside or outside the home. This loss of self is the only way in which she can achieve a sense of virtue, of worth. The more she puts of herself into the objects around her, the more the objects come to dominate her. Such alienation will also be experienced by the working class woman, especially after her children grow up. So far 'welfare' capitalism can only shovel aside the useless who express their futility in neurosis, by putting them into cold storage until they emerge tranquillised.

The woman at home is thus a victim of the reflected alienation of the man's work situation and also of an alienation of her own. Only significant structural changes can radically affect this. The production relations of the man would have to change, the woman would have to be paid directly by the community, and the social division of labour would have to be transformed. Such changes would necessitate social ownership as well as control.

No such total immediate solution can be envisaged yet, but there are specific, concrete ways in which the sheer drudgery and monotony of housework can be alleviated, and possible means by which women could have more sense of fulfilment and more control over their external environment. There are firstly particular improvements like more nurseries, launderettes, good cheap municipal restaurants in all areas, better housing and imaginative architecture which takes the needs of the people as a prime consideration (look at the space considered necessary for the working class, compared to the space in middle class areas, as though being working class meant you needed less air to breathe), cheap council flats for teenagers who want to live away from home. Eventually we should make detachable, enlargeable dwellings, because while most people settle in a relatively stable way in couples to bring up children that doesn't mean they want to be falling over one another all the time. Under socialism it should be possible to build for much greater personal flexibility, so the environment would be quite literally both living and moving.

Meanwhile though, 'improvements' are not enough. The important way in which reforms become a means to more substantial transformation is when they are consciously made by the struggle of the people who benefit from them. When women take part in tenants' campaigns, in squatting, in sit-downs for zebra crossings, in demonstrations with dirty washing for more council launderettes, when they organise co-operative play-groups in their street or flats there are the beginnings of the possibility of breaking the silence. It means that people in groups are creating and controlling aspects of their immediate environment. At this point socialism can make sense as the natural and necessary development of such control.

The way in which the family has developed in capitalism is

so closely related to the system of production which has emerged through the private ownership of capital and the growth of factories, that certain changes are bound to appear under a system of social control. As the society takes over some of the functions of the individual family this makes possible a changing relationship between men and women. Most important is the independent social security of the woman.

Although we have the advantage of the experience of the socialist countries, these indicate more the compexity of the family relationship and the primitive level of our thinking about it rather than a clear guide. In order to replace it by a more honest way of living we should remember the reasons for seeking to transform it, rather than making a fetish of its form. The objection to the bourgeois family is the necessary dependence and isolation of the woman, the internalisation of the competition and struggle for dominance, the tension and the possessiveness of man and woman directed towards the children. Rather than presenting only the institutional form of the state nursery school, which is by no means a complete answer, we should agitate for innumerable ways of reducing the drawbacks to the family. We should produce a multiplicity of practical schemes for social living, some of which we can achieve immediately, which would at once liberate individuals and enable them to see that a socialist society would mean more choice and would allow people real alternatives. (18)

Worker

It would seem then that any real change for the woman at home would have to be social. It would involve a fundamental recreation of the structure of society and the ways in which people relate to each other. When the position of woman as worker is considered the case becomes conclusive.

Here again the contradiction between the 'role' as woman and the 'role' as sub-man is most marked. The woman has to run the home and go out to work as a sub-man. The more privileged can avoid this by hiring other women, but the working class woman is forced to carry the double load. An immediate way of lessening this, apart from a determined campaign for better facilities in the home situation, is for the unions to press for a much more flexible attitude to part-time work, convenient hours, for more creches at work (why not for men as well as women, with time off work to play with the children so the child would have continuing contact with parents of both sexes). As for the future, when we talk about work in the socialist society we should consider in a positive way not simply the breakdown of the specialised division of labour between men and women. It is simply no good to avoid any positive thinking

about these things and trust to some magic 'revolution' to
create completely new forms of living; the depth of revolutionary change will be considerably dependent on the conscious conceptions and struggles formed in the old society.

The working woman is subordinated both as a woman and as
a worker. Her demand for equal pay (19) carries profound
economic and social implications. Firstly, it's going to
cost someone a lot of money - anything between £600 and
£1000 million. The question is, of course, who? Within the
terms of the Labour Party's incomes policy 'equality'
would mean a readjustment between men and women workers, ie it would be contained within a struggle between two
groups of workers divided only by the intensity of their rate
of exploitation. It is apparent that equal pay must be phrased
in terms of the social redistribution of wealth. Even so the
securing of equal pay alone won't solve the problem unless
the whole social subordination of women is challenged. This
is summed up in the phrases 'women's work', 'girl's work'.
When men and women are not working side by side it is
possible to define work customarily done by women as work
which does not require skill. The other aspect of this is the
refusal to admit women int᷊ the more highly graded and
paid jobs. At Fords in 1968 the Court of Enquiry into the
dispute revealed that whereas one man in four was on grade
C, only two women in 900 amongst the machinists were
receiving pay at this rate. Yet when they went for the job
the women had to pass a test on the three machines. If they
failed, they weren't employed. Indeed at Fords the real
issue was over the question of grading.

The assumption is really that women exist through their
husbands, and the whole work situation is geared to this.
Consequently innumerable attendant secondarinesses arise.
Women on the buses are not only not allowed to drive them,
they have to wait five years before they can get sick pay.
Men get it after only one year. Similarly the inequalities in
training opportunities - only 7% of girls enter apprentice-
ships (predominantly hairdressing), compared with 43% of
boys. Very few girls get day release in Colleges of Further
Education. Employers are reluctant to let clerical workers
have day release, partly because they can't be spared from
the office, partly because they leave quite soon to get
married.

Equal pay then is a vital demand, not because it will solve
the situation of working women, but because it will expose
more clearly the nature of their oppression. The inequality
of women at work is inseparable from our inequality in
society as a whole. Given our real situation, we have to
demand UNEQUAL rights, ie the concept of equality has to
leave the realm of moral abstraction and become concret-
ised in the existing social situation. Fords employers
justify discrimination against women on the grounds that

women have to take time off to have children. Unequal rights has to take this kind of thing into account.

Even when the class disadvantages don't exist, the middle class women experience a special and peculiar secondariness. The socialisation, education and opportunity for development and expression of women is a preparation for a complementary role. In terms of work there exists great difficulty still in securing jobs which require considerable initiative and responsibility and at the same time are not just extensions of the familial role. Even more significant is the fact that women won't apply for such jobs even when they have a chance of getting them. Part of secondariness is the assumption of it.

Nor is this something that is confined to work. It penetrates right inside the labour movement. There are only 5 women amongst 151 men trade unionists on the industrial training boards. Half the members of U.S.D.A.W. are women, but only an eighth of the executive. When Lil Bilocca and the fishermen's wives campaigned against the unsafe conditions on the trawlers they met considerable hostility and ridicule. (20) Girls who are students are not at work and relatively free drom the domestic situation, but the assumed subordination remains. Glance at any Left theoretical journal or go to any large meeting, you won't find many articles either by or about women and you won't see many women speaking. Think of the way women relate to the Left groups. Very largely we complement the men: we hold small groups together, we send out reminders, we type the leaflets, we administer rather than initiate. Only a small number of men are at once aware that this happens and take positive steps to stop it. In fact in some cases they positively discourage women from finding a voice. Revolutionary students are quite capable of wolf-whistling and cat-calling when a girl speaks; more common though is tolerant humour, patronising derision or that silence after which everyone continues as if nobody had spoken. The girl in the process of becoming interested in socialism is thus often treated as an intruder if she speaks or acts in her own right. She is most subtly once again taught her place. She drops back again, lets go, settles into a movement as somebody's bird. None of this develops confidence. Ultimately this 'politics of the gang-bang' cannot secure deep commitment from most women. (21)

In terms of organised power, the militant action of women at work is obviously crucial; the demand for equal pay would be merely paper resolutions unless there was the possibility of grinding things to a halt. But there is also the need for a political campaign for equal pay. This would be most effective if it acted as a means of co-ordinating industrial activity and circulating information about the various struggles. A respectable main body working through traditional channels would be accompanied by less orthodox action by a smaller group. In the short run, by struggling on specific issues which express the ways through which we are contained, it will be possible to generate a confidence and enable more women to act consciously to change the world... It will also be possible to make reforms of a social nature which will make more obvious the potentialities of a fundamental social transformation. Ultimately this social transformation must be a revolution in both the domestic and the work situation of women. Marxism has customarily gone this far. In the experiments with house communes, the discussion of attitudes to sex in the 1920's, in the real improvements in the position of women in the Soviet Union, in the communes in China, and in the general raising of women's position in Cuba it is possible to see some of the potentialities. But there is still very much to be done.

Structural changes will interact on the way the woman can see herself and call into question the assumption of social secondariness. But unless the internal process of subjugation is understood, unless the language of silence is experienced from inside and translated into the language of the oppressed communicating themselves, male hegemony will remain.

Without such a translation, marxism will not be really meaningful. There will be a gap between the experience and the theory. This will make a movement impossible, it will lead people to say 'women are reactionary'. By this they mean only that the revolution has proved itself unable to relate to what is happening. Marxism will prove incapable of speaking for the silence in the head, for the paralysis of the spirit. If women are to be convincingly mobilised it is necessary for marxism to extend into unexplored territory. The struggle is not simply against the external mechanisms of domination and containment, but against those internal mechanisms. It is the struggle against the assumption that men make and define the world, whether it be capitalist or socialist. Unless this is made explicit and conscious, revolutionary politics will remain for most women something removed and abstracted.

Really because the movement which demands at once social revolution and the possibility of creating a new woman is still politically embryonic it is difficult to visualise clearly the means of effecting this. This recent brief experience of revolutionary women's groups provide some clues. Discussion is vital. At this stage this is the way in which the individual woman is able to stop experiencing her situation as neurosis. The confidence is essential too. The decision to exclude men should be made on the basis of the experience of each group. It may be necessary in the early stages for women to discuss the situation without men because their nervous hostility or benevolent patronage are precisely the points at which we become hysterical or dry up through lack of confidence as a group. However there are considerable dangers in continuing on a separatist basis. Some women may simply drop into the 'male' aggressive role. Also the interaction between our situation and that of men under capitalism can be forgotten. The way is not open for men to redefine themselves. This can create a polarisation. Most dangerous, too, is the tendency for us to see our struggle as proving we are as good as men.

This achievement of consciousness is obviously a problem for both the working class and the black people, but if it becomes predominant it can eat a movement away. All the competitive and egotistical characteristics of capitalism penetrate the attempt to transform it, and the same authoritarianism, the same projection and elevation of individuals starts to happen. There is danger too, however, in dogmatic opposition to groups which consist only of women. There can be considerable dishonesties at work here. A refusal to explore the real situations of women, a desire to straitjacket our consciousness by a talmudic obsession with the 'correct' texts taken out of their particular historical context. Such a response is frequently one of fear. It is the deep-seated feeling that people have to be school-mastered/mistressed into socialism. Such paternal maternalism is misplaced. A marxist approach to the situation of women can be justified only on its ability to illuminate our position and the way out, not as some kind of moral imperative.

It is necessary not only to learn more about our social position and the means of changing it: to communicate we have to find the symbols which express our oppression. The Spanish peasants destroyed Virgins in the churches; the Chinese put paper hats on the local gentry; in a more abstract way the exam is a symbol for the student movement. The symbol has to carry a whole complex of experience within it. Thus women in the States located Miss America as a symbol; in England we located in a tactical way the Ideal Home Exhibition, the ICA women's exhibition, the Nelbarden swimwear campaign which is based on women experiencing themselves as objects. These express in a fragmentary way some aspects of thingification, women as sex-objects, as consumer dustbins, as rarefied art objects, woman as unreal unless she is being regarded by men. (22) Such spheres of consciousness are both intangible and complex. This means they need to be thought out more, not less. Object-consciousness is the common condition of all women, it is our normal state of mind.

A peasant woman in yellow Fan Shen said, 'Our husbands regard us as some sort of dog who keeps the house. We even despise ourselves'.

A West Indian woman in Dalston, London said, 'We women are just shells for the men'.

24

An English woman in Guildford said, 'When I'm in the bath it's the only time I'm myself'.

An American girl said, 'Really being a groupie is like borrowing a series of lives from people and thinking you can be them. It's not something you can do'.

It is not a question of simply rational enlightenment. Intellectual awareness of what is going on does not mean object-consciousness dissolves. When I go out without mascara on my eyes I experience myself as I knew myself before puberty. It is inconceivable to me that any man could desire me sexually, my body hangs together quite differently. Rationally I can see the absurdity of myself. But this does not mean I experience myself in a different way.

The naive belief that institutional change will automatically penetrate the concealed pockets of the psyche, that it is not for marxists to be bothering their heads about such airy-fairy nonsense, still prevails. Not only does such myopic mechanicalism screen itself from understanding what has happened in the countries which have made revolution, it ignores the explicit warnings of innumerable marxists. Of course no single idealist liberation is capable of personal-ising this object-consciousness, of course revolutionary changes in the fabric are essential. The way sexual 'freedom', despite its liberatory implications, has been grot-esquely distorted under capitalism is the most convincing proof of this. There is a cruel irony in the way the assert-ion of the dignity and honesty of sexual love has become the freedom for the woman-object to strip to sell the object-commodity, or the freedom for the woman-object to fuck her refracted envy of the dominator man.

But this doesn't make transformation simple. Modern capitalism beguiles with flickering lights, it mystifies with a giant kaleidoscope. We lose ourselves and one another in the reflected images of unrealisable desires. We walk into a world of distorting mirrors. We smash the mirrors. Only pain convinces us we are there. But there is still more glass. Your nose is pressed against the glass, the object suddenly finds herself peeping at herself. There is the possiblity of a moment of illumination. The feminine voyeur finds her identity as pornography. The 'emancipated' woman sees herself as naked buttocks bursting out of black suspenders, as tits drooping into undulating passive flesh. WHO ME? Comprehension screeches to a halt. She is jerked into watching herself as object watching herself. She is being asked to desire herself. The traditional escape route of 'morality' is blocked. She can either shut off the experience or force some kind of breakthrough.

Revolution must relate to both the means and the nature of this breakthrough. There must be the acceleration of collective demystification accompanied by the conscious dismantling of the external framework, there must be the connection with the experience of the other oppressed groups, there must be a political alternative, a way out which relates to all the groups. Object-consciousness cannot be shattered by individual rationality, it cannot be simply eliminated by external change, it cannot be bypassed by psychological or cultural concentrations. It demands social revolution and it demands it whole. It demands release from the inner and the outer bondages. It is not to be fobbed off with an either/or. Which brings us all back again to marxism and the whole people question.

On the whole people question

Well, here we all are then, millions of us, our situation demanding a fundamental redistribution of wealth, a profound social transformation in the ways people relate to each other and an end to alienation. Communism is the necessary condition of our freedom. A communist society means having babies in a state of social freedom. It means you don't starve when you're helpless to fend for yourself or have to be a dependent. It means the possibility of such communication that human beings share the pains of labour and the ecstasy of creation. Real comradeship involves the end of subjugation and domination, the explosion of sado-masochism and the climax of love.

However, there are a few inescapable points to be considered before we make it.

The subordination of women cannot be reduced simply by reducing our exploitation either as a class or our exploitation at work. These exploitations are only part of the oppression of some women. The full extent of our oppression is not fully revealed by the isolation of these particular forms of exploitation. The woman question is not comprehensible except in terms of the total process of a complete series of repressive structures. Thus the particular form of domination changes but the process operates in both pre-capitalist and post-capitalist society. The function of revolutionary theory is to keep track of the moving shape of these subordinations. Such a revolutionary theory is compelled to be continually reforming and recreating itself. It has to understand the way capitalism subdues us as consumers as well as workers. It has to follow the particular experience of domination not only of the worker but also of the student. It has to understand the condition of blackness as well as the condition of womanness.

Thus while the working class is undoubtedly the most crucial force in modern capitalism for creating a new society, this does not mean that the specific experiences of other oppressed groups are in any way invalidated. It does not imply they must relate to socialism simply as an abstract idea or merely project their own situation onto that of the working class. Every group has a particular struggle coming directly from the position in which it finds itself. It accordingly has a particular consciousness of oppression.

Not only is it consequently possible to mobilise many more people, it is possible to mobilise them at several levels. Capitalism has to be resisted not only at work but in the home, not only in the institutional apparatus of government but in the head. The revolutionary struggle is thus extended and sustained in a multi-structural, multi-dimensional way. As well as the macro-theory, which is about systems at war, about a mass movement for political power, marxism has to explore the way human beings relate to one another. This means noticing all the little unimportant things which revolutionary theory tends to regard as not worthy of attention. Like how we live with one another and how we feel and regard each other, how we communicate with each other. We are contained within the inner and outer bondages and unless we create a revolutionary theory of the microcosm as well as the macrocosm we shall be incapable of preventing our personal practice becoming unconnected to our economic and institutional transformation. We will consequently continually lose ourselves in the new structures we have created.

In order to comprehend this it is necessary to replace a mechanical model of social change (base/superstructure) by a complex and interrelated self-regulating revolutionary model. It also means that some forms of action will be directed specifically towards transforming people's perception and comprehension of themselves and the world, as well as being concerned with material change. The so-called women's question is thus a whole people question not only because our liberation is inextricably bound up with the revolt of all those who are oppressed, but because their liberation is not realisable fully unless our subordination is ended. Nor does the particular experience of women speak only for itself. Like the consciousness of all the people who are kept down it brings its own species of implication for the revolutionary struggle. Trotsky's comment on the complaint of Russian working women, 'You only think about yourselves', is more apt. (23)

"It is quite true that there are no limits to masculine egotism in ordinary life. In order to change the conditions of life we must learn to see them through the eyes of women."

Such a leap in consciousness would undoubtedly shatter whole layers of comfortable paternal authoritarian assumptions within the revolutionary movement.

But that, comrades, is another story...

Footnotes

1. E. E. Evans-Pritchard, 'The position of women in primitive societies and other essays in social anthropology', 1965, p. 56.

2. Edith Thomas in 'The women incendiaries', 1963, describes this in connection with the Paris Commune. Wilhelm Reich's 'The sexual revolution', 1967, contains an account of the hostility to the Women's Club after the Russian Revolution as well as the whole dilemma of the Bolsheviks about their approach to sexuality. Helen Foster Snow's 'Women in modern China', 1967, mentions similar hostility in China.

3. E. J. P. Mayer, 'The recollections of Alexis de Tocqueville', 1959, pp. 132-3.

4. See Karl Mannheim, 'Ideology and Utopia', 1965, parts 4 & 5. F. Graus, 'Social utopias in the middle ages' in 'Past & present', 1967, no. 38. Any biography of worker students, eg Thomas Bell, 'Pioneering days', 1941; Thomas Cooper, 'The life of Thomas Cooper written by himself'; Gwynn A. Williams 'Rowland Detriosier, a working class infidel 1800-34'; University of York, 'Borthwick Papers' no. 28, 1965.
See also E. P. Thompson, 'Education and experience', Fifth Mansbridge Memorial Lecture, 1968.
Frantz Fanon, 'The wretched of the earth', and Black Power literature in general, especially Stokely Carmichael in 'The dialectics of liberation', ed. David Cooper, and Eldridge Cleaver's 'Soul on ice'.

5. This section is taken from my article, 'Women, the struggle for freedom', Black Dwarf, 10 January 1969.

6. Mao Tse-Tung, 'Investigation of the peasant movement in Hunan: the movement of the riff-raff', 'Selected readings' 1967.

7. Beryl Smalley, 'English friars and antiquity in the early XIVth century', 1960, pp. 17-18.

8. Simone de Beauvoir, 'The Long March', 1958, p. 139.

9. Valerie Solanas, 'S. C. U. M. Manifesto', 1968.

10. W. Butler-Bowden (ed), 'The book of Margery Kempe', 1954, pp. 15-16.

11. See Thomas, 'Women in the Civil War sects', op. cit.

12. Ellen MacArthur, 'Women petitioners and the Long Parliament', 'English Historical Review', vol. 24.

13. Roger L'Estrange, 'The woman as good as the man, or the equality of both sexes', 1677.
For a strong dose of anti-feminism see 'The women's fegaries showing the great endeavour they have used for obtaining of the breeaches', c. 1675.

14. Hannah Wooley quoted in M. S. Storr, 'Mary Wollstone-craft et le mouvement feministe dans la literature anglaise' 1932.

15. Christopher Hill, 'Clarissa Harlowe and her times', in 'Puritanism and revolution', 1962, pp. 367-394

16. See J. A. & Olive Banks, 'Feminism and family planning', 1964

17. See David Mitchell, 'Women on the warpath', 1966, and George Dangerfield, 'The strange death of liberal England', 1961, for accounts of the suffragettes. For a contemporary criticism of bourgeois feminism see A. M. Kollontai's 'Critique of the feminist movement' in R. A. J. Schlesinger, 'Changing attitudes in Soviet Russia', 'The Family', 1949.

18. See Juliet Mitchell's 'Women: the longest revolution' in 'New Left Review' no. 40, Nov-Dec 1966, for a brief account of socialist and marxist approaches to the family and the reaction. The literature is voluminous, but apart from Engels, 'The origin of the family' see especially A. Bebel, 'Women in the past, present and future', 1887; Alexandra Kollontai, 'Communism and the family', 1920; Lenin on 'The emancipation of women'; Alexandra Kollontai, 'Free love'; Leon Trotsky, 'Problems of life', 1924.

19. Since Barbara Castle's Equal Pay Act in 1970, employers have already begun to find ways round an increased wages bill. They have introduced job evaluation schemes and re-defined skills. They have also considered replacing labour-intensive female work by machines, or keeping men's wages down in order to pay for the women.

20. See PEP Report, 'Women at work'; 'Women's wages' in 'Labour Research' Aug. 1968; Sabby Sagall, 'Interview with Rose Boland', 'Socialist Worker' Sep. 21 1968; Audrey Wise, 'Equal pay is not enough', and 'Lil Bilocca and Hull trawlers', 'Black Dwarf' Jan. 10 1969; 'Working class girls', 'Black Dwarf' May 2 1969; Sabina Roberts, 'Equal pay, the first step', 'Socialist Woman' Mar-Apr 1969; Kath Fincham & Sabina Roberts, 'The struggle for democracy - who says women can only do unskilled work'; Sue Pascoe, 'Conference of London and Westminster Trades Council on equal pay for women', 'Socialist Woman' May-June 1969; 'Woman's Rights: account of equal pay demonstration and information about the various women's groups which exist', 'Black Dwarf' Jun. 1 1969.

21. Since this was written there have been a few changes - although they've been painfully slow. Women's Liberation has made open contempt impossible. But there is a new danger now. Men on the Left can pigeonhole certain questions as 'women's lib' without examining how ideas in the women's movement mean they must reassess their own politics.

22. I. C. A. Woman, Women's Liberation Workshop, 'Black

Dwarf' Jun. 14 1969. Nelbarden swimwear, 'Shrew' no. 3, July 1969.

23. Trotsky, 'Problems of life', op. cit. p. 99

'Socialist Woman', Summer 1972

WOMEN AND THE FAMILY

Jan Williams, Hazel Twort and Ann Bachelli

(This paper was written by members of the London Peckham Rye group, Women's Liberation Workshop, and presented at the Ruskin College Women's Conference, Oxford, March 1970. It was also printed in 'Shrew', February-March 1970.)

This paper has been written by three women, each with two kids. We talked and wrote together as a group. We are oppressed and have been from the moment we were born. Our families have squashed us into roles because our mothers wanted daughters in their own image, and our fathers wanted daughters like their submissive wives. We each had a girl-hood instead of a childhood and are only now beginning to be conscious of what that means in terms of what we are now. Now we feel we are martyrs. Martyrdom that has, over the years of being housewives and mothers, become almost enjoyable. The family exists on martyrdom. This is generally getting less but only since we have glimpsed how we live from outside. We have found it extremely difficult to look at ourselves - as through a window - and most of all it has been a sheer impossibility to imagine ourselves being involved in change of any sort. Our window on the world is looked through with our hands in the sink and we've begun to hate that sink and all it implies - so begins our consciousness. We need to work, work is a dignity, or should be, we know that most work is not, but at least at worst it involves you with other people, ideas and a struggle. Women are still told that they are oppressed because of capitalism: get rid of that and it'll all be alright. But this serves no purpose at all to women who don't feel part of anything, it just pushes them further away from ever feeling anything. The oppression every woman suffers is deeply in her, she first has to realise this and then to fight it - with other women helping. Men will not generally help with this, they need passive, ignorant, decorative women. We are, therefore, talking about that 65% of women who do not work and who are presumably housewives.

The 'family', as it is experienced, is the woman and the children in the house, the flat or the room and the man who comes and goes. The space that the family occupies is essential to its own image of itself, its own way of living, its self-expression. The woman who goes out to work goes out of her family if only for that period of time: however drab the work routine, children are temporarily forgotten, housework ignored. In the home the woman is in the family, and the two are disturbingly synonymous. Housework cannot be separated from children, nor the children from the four walls, the food you cook, the shopping you do, the clothes you wear. How you, the house, the children, look may not be how they are, but reflects what you want them to be. It is not just that every pop-psychologist's 'mum' lives in a Woman's Own dreamhouse, where the material solution to any problem is immediately on hand; it is that in our society being a mother is being a housewife: the security of the family is the stability of the walls - the image of the family home is the image of the family, but not in any simple way. The folk-lore has many permutations - from happy secure family in new semi, to poor but happy slum dwellers, to the 'broken home' of the 'juvenile delinquent' who comes from both.

There is little to be said about housework on its own. An endless routine, it creates its own high moments of achievement and satisfaction so as to evade not monotony - the feature of many jobs - but futility. The bolt you tighten on the factory floor vanishes to be replaced by another: but the clean kitchen floor is tomorrow's dirty floor and the clean floor of the day after that. The appropriate symbol for housework (and for housework alone) is not the interminable conveyor-belt but a compulsive circle like a pet mouse in its cage spinning round on its exercise wheel, unable to get off. Into this one inserts one's own saving peaks: 'happiness is the bathroom scrubbed down'. But even the glorious end of today's chores is not even an anti-climax as there is no real climax - there is nothing to fill the 'joyful moment'. But the routine is never quite routine, so the vacuum in one's mind is never vacuous enough to be filled. 'Housework is a worm eating away at one's ideas.' Like a fever dream it goes on and on, until you desperately hope that it can all be achieved at one blow. You lay the breakfast the night before, you have even been known to light the gas under the kettle for tomorrow's tea, wishing that by breakfast time everything could be over with - by 8am the children washed, teeth-cleaned and ready for bed, tucked-up, the end.

And yet there is nothing tangible to force you to do it. A job is compulsory: either you go or you don't have a job. The pressures of housework are more insidious: neighbours criticise and compare; grandmothers hand on standards; within you and without you is your mother's voice, criticising and directing. Their overriding criterion is cleanliness: a dirty house is a disintegrating person. The compulsion to housework, then, is not economic or legal: it is moral and personal. And the housewife sees it in moral and personal terms. Hence her description of this structure of her oppression assumes querulous and complaining tones, the tones of a private neurosis to express a social fact - the imposed isolation of her work. For emancipated women to attack the complaint and ignore the whole socialising force which produces it simply reinforces the position.

Like every other form of social activity, every other aspect of social relationships, housework cannot be pinned down to a neat descriptive formula. The more we examine it, the more aspects it reveals, and the more we become aware of its contradictions and paradoxes. Isolated, the only adult in a private house, the housewife is yet crowded, by the emotional and physical demands of her family, by the unseen pressures of society. But although isolated, the housewife is never alone: her domain is the kitchen, the most communal room, and even the possibility of sleeping alone is denied her. To have the right to sleep alone is essential. People in permanent relationships do not do this. A woman needs time alone - after a day of being a public servant to the rest of the family, of giving out all the time, of being open to all demands - and in ordinary families the only time of the day this feeling of aloneness is possible is during the few moments before she goes to sleep after getting into bed. To then have to touch, caress, console yet another person is too much. The hatred of the man and sex begins - it is the beginning of such sayings as 'Oh God, he wants his rights again' or the husband saying 'you can't have a headache every night'. So that eventually she has no identity, no specificity, no privacy - she is defined by the demands of others. The only escape is the daydream, turning-in-on-oneself is the only way out. It is a journey from a body which is always being touched - the mother must always allow herself to be open to physical contact - to an area which cannot be touched, to an area of total privacy, where one's body is one's own again. Ironically, housework is often seen as being self-determined labour - 'your time is your own'. In fact, in order to 'keep up', in order to be 'a good housewife', one has to work to a pre-determined routine. The 'freedom' of the housewife is in fact the denial of her right to a job. Even the division work/place of work, leisure/home does not apply to the housewife: her place of work is also the place of leisure and further it is her work which provides the basis of other people's leisure.

The 'rationalisation' of housework is held out as a future prospect - better technical equipment means less work. But even if this different equipment were made easily available to all classes, the situation of the housewife would be essentially unchanged, and problems would remain. Indeed some would be exacerbated. The only social world most housewives have is the shopping centre - hence their 'irrational' tendency to shop every day rather than once a week. Deprived of this they would lose one way of keeping up their morale. Being literally house-bound, afraid of leaving the house and being seen is a typical woman's syndrome. Developments in technology on their own cannot change women's position in the home. We must be quite clear about this.

Unless we can discuss through the implications of the role of the housewife - the institution of the housewife, if you like - and work out the reasons why this institution survives so tenaciously, we will be unable to combat the various levels of oppression. Moreover, it is not enough simply to command women out to work - particularly since we all know that means that women usually end up with two jobs, one monotonous, the other futile.

We would like at this point to make clear that we do hold our children very dear. We love them passionately and care deeply about them. We feel it is because of this, or at least with this as one of the main reasons, that we have become immersed in working for the liberation of women.

Women are brought up for marriage and motherhood. The essential time spent in this is five years - five out of a lifetime of seventy years and more. The discrepancy between the time spent and the importance given to it is understandable - the human infant does need much care and attention. But from the viewpoint of the woman the discrepancy is absurd. Her whole life seems to be one long 'before' and 'after'. Children go on being children beyond their first five years, in fact often until they produce the grandchildren which can replace them in their mother's eyes. But what does being a mother mean? In modern mythology it means a consistent being, untouched by the moods which the child exhibits, always forgiving, understanding, and certainly never violent or moody. The tyranny of consistency undermines both mother - she must never give way to anger or even to sudden affection - and child - whatever it does the superior adult can cope. It sets in motion a circular pattern. Consistency eventually means monotony; inconsistency leads to guilt; both cover suppressed feelings which can erupt into violence - which itself once more produces guilt and the struggle for the elusive and magical consistency. The smooth, unruffled exterior is simultaneously a masking of and a cause of conflict. Modern notions of the perfect and well-adjusted mother must be questioned and challenged. It may well be that they are designed not only to produce a compliant child, but also to produce the mother who, by turning a serene and contented face to the world, gives it an alibi for ignoring her problem.

Guilt and anxiety always weave their way through one's happiness. The guilt of giving birth is endorsed by the constant notion that you are responsible for the child's personality. The first months of a baby's life are full of difficulties - the lack of sleep, the fear (particularly with the first child) that you are not doing the right thing, the appalling ignorance and one's amateur status. The only answer to these problems appears to be total dedication to the child. Furthermore, this dedication can be seen as an investment in the child's future - at least one might prevent future neuroses. Even more, your anxiety can cover up feelings of violence and hatred towards your child. The mother of the battered baby acts out the fantasies of many mothers. And however anti-authoritarian the mother hopes to be in the future, or for that matter in the present, she still wants the children to do what she wants them to do.

For some families, one route out of the problem of the all-embracing mother and the pressures upon her has been a shifting of roles. The father has entered more into the life of the child. But this shifting of roles has also been a subtle reversal of roles. Instead of the comforting mother, whose ultimate threat was always 'I'll tell your father', and the punitive father, the father has become the source of amusement, and the mother has remained the person ultimately responsible for the child's psychological and emotional future. Although the roles have changed, the ultimate responsibility has remained unchanged.

For this reason we should not be misled into thinking that the simple extension of woman into the man's role and the man into the woman's is the solution of the problem. Man as mother as well as man as house-slave is no answer. Obviously men can, and should, (and in rare cases do) perform domestic tasks and bring up families. This is not the point at issue. In the end the demand for complete reversal is the demand to extend oppression - understandable, but leading to a dead end. Our perspective must be different.

The demand for communal living must be understood in this way. The commune offers obvious advantages - at the minimum it helps to spread the load, to share work and thus to allow us time which is really free. But we must be careful not to turn it into an extended family, turned in on itself, where all are enclosed in increasing domesticity.

We must also be aware of its limitations. Living communally can only change the lives of the people in the community. It can help people to become less obsessed about their possessions and help them to regard their children in a less possessive way. It could help people out economically and offer them a less competitive home environment. It can free women a little to pursue their own work by sharing the practicalities of daily living. What it cannot do is be anything more than an individual solution to an individual's neuroses. The causes of these neuroses will still be present and real to all around her and thereby to her. Living in a commune must not be envisaged as a resolution of the housewife problem. The crucial point is that however women live in this society, their militant work must be governed by the imperative need to rouse the consciousness of their silent, submerged sisters. Women must realise the deadly effects of their passivity and overcome them by working together for their liberation.

Footnote   'The myth of motherhood' by Lee Comer (Spokesman, 8p) discusses sources of popular ideas of motherhood.

THE FAMILY : A CRITIQUE OF CERTAIN FEATURES

Michaela Nava

(Written by a member of the London Women's Liberation
Workshop, and given as a paper at 'A radical critique of
sociology', a one-day conference at the London School of
Economics in December 1971)

I want to make it clear from the start that I do not want
simply to 'abolish' the family. However, I do feel that the
family in our society needs to change very radically, that
certain features have very destructive consequences, both
for the individual and for the wider society. In this paper I
propose to isolate those features I consider most negative,
which are: (1) the sexual division of labour, and (2) marriage as a long-term monogamous institution. I want to examine the effects of these, and suggest a possible alternative
way of living.

The sexual division of labour

The sexual division of labour within the family was initially
determined by the woman's biological function. Usually
pregnant or nursing, she was clearly less capable ot hunt-
ing and doing strenuous work away from the home than was
the man. Childcare and work in and around the home then
logically became her domain.

In spite of the fact that women in our society no longer
spend the whole of their adult lives pregnant or nursing
young children, in spite of the fact that in the last fifty
years there has been a tremendous increase in opportunities for women to participate in the productive and political processes of life outside the home, within the family
the division of labour based on sex has hardly been challenged at all even by women themselves. (Your sociology
books claim that fathers increasingly participate in child-
care and housework, but this in fact means no more than a
little assistance at weekends. Wilmott and Young in their
study of the family in East London claim that the responsibility for the housework is increasingly shared. As evidence for this they point out that almost two-thirds of the
husbands in their survey had washed-up at least once during the previous week. Big deal! That still leaves the women
having washed-up at least twenty times as often. In John
and Elizabeth Newson's study on patterns of infant care,
61% of fathers never bathed their babies, 50% never got up
at night, 43% never changed nappies.)

The situation now is that women are still the main socialisers of young children. Many see this as their main function in life; others, who have additional expectations of
themselves, still expect to give up work outside the home
until the youngest child is five and starts school. Most

women still consider it 'natural' that they should have to choose between children and a job, that they must sacrifice the satisfactions of one or the other. They take for granted the father's 'right' to both.

Woman's biological function still determines her social role. This fact has been allowed to persist because girls and boys are brought up to believe that mothers are uniquely capable of looking after their babies, and that their babies will suffer if they do not. I suggest that this assumption is a myth. We must examine what it is based on.

Rationalisation for the myth

It is assumed that mothers possess some special unverifiable quality called 'maternal instinct'. In fact, there is no physiological evidence for this at all. Some mothers get great pleasure out of their children and feel very protective towards them when they are young, but then so do fathers. Others, in spite of intensive socialisation to that end, feel very little. Female monkeys reared in zoos, in isolation, are unable to breast-feed their babies. They have to be taught how, by their keepers, in order for their infants to survive.

Bowlby's hypothesis that young children separated from their mothers are likely to suffer extreme deprivation resulting in nervous disorders, instability of character, apathy, regression, and in extreme cases even death, has had a major impact on child-rearing practices in our society. Although his initial observations were derived from children in institutional care (many of whom had experienced traumatic incidents in their earlier lives), his theories were generalised to cover all separation of children from their mothers in the first five years. They were subsequently widely popularised by people like Dr Spock. They have also provided a major rationalisation for the ideology that a woman's place is in the home. Much of the widespread guilt that working mothers experience today must be attributed to Bowlby and his hypothesis, in spite of the fact that it was subsequently proved to be inaccurate. Bowlby himself later withdrew certain claims and differentiated between partial separation in a stable, stimulating environment with adequate care and total separation in impersonal institutional care.

However, the damage was done, the myth was maintained in spite of evidence to show that what is necessary for healthy development in the child is stable, sensitive care from loving and friendly people in a physically and intellectually stimulating environment.

There has been no evidence to show that the person to provide this environment and care need be the mother rather than the father. Nor is there evidence that in order for the child to develop healthily this care must be provided by one person rather than several. Margaret Mead points out that whether the biological mother is the principal socialise of her child or not is a socio-cultural question, not a biological one. Other studies have shown that whom the infant chooses to become attached to, and how many people he selects, depends on the social setting; 'in certain societies multiple object relationships are the norm'.

Functions of the myth

Women who stay at home to look after their babies are, in addition, available to carry out the important job of unpaid cook and housekeeper for their husbands and school-age children, ie workers and future workers.

When there was an increased demand for women's labour power, as for example during the second world war, nurseries were made available. However, when women were no longer needed as a work force these day care centres were closed down. Yudkin and Holme point out that 'Bowlby's hypotheses continue even now to provide both official and unofficial bodies with supposedly irrefutable evidence in favour of such money-saving projects as closing down day nurseries'.

Effects of the myth

Now I would like to look at some of the effects of woman's chief role being regarded as that of wife/mother/housewife and all others being subsidiary to this.

Outside the home, repercussions are that inevitably women have only nominal equality, if that. At school, they are educated if not overtly (Newsom recommendations), then more subtly with the expectation that their main functions will be mother/wife/housekeeper. If they manage to overcome this and do become sufficiently educated (only $\frac{1}{3}$ of those receiving higher education are women) to qualify for work requiring more than minimal skills and commitment, they are often not employed because they are not expected to 'last on the job' - ie it is expected that when (not if) a woman has children she will leave to care for them. If she does this and takes ten years away from the labour market, she is reintroduced at a lower level of pay and responsibility. At a professional level, the man has had time to 'get ahead'. If she attempts to work while her children are young, in addition to having to resolve problems of day care she will find many employers reluctant to give her work. The woman editor of 'The Economist' recently said that she would not employ the mother of young children. Fathers of young children are not asked if they have made adequate childcare arrangements. They have no dual role.

Women make fewer demands in a work situation, do equal work for less pay (scab) and remain a largely ununionised and relatively reactionary section of the labour force because they have been socialised to see work outside the home as subsidiary to their 'true' role of mother/housewife.

However, Hannah Gavron has pointed out that almost all mothers would like to do some work outside the home (only 10% showed no desire at all), and that the main reason for not doing so was the feeling that their children might be deprived if they did. The quality of the work itself made little difference; unskilled work in factories was still preferable to the isolation of the home.

In the home, women who do no productive work outside and have no other roles often glorify the role of motherhood and pursue it with a kind of manic zeal. Having and bringing up children becomes highly competitive and a substitute for productive work, often at the expense of the children themselves. There now exist the recognised syndromes of over-mothering and over-control, when children are not allowed to experience themselves as autonomous persons. As the child grows up and attempts to break away, the woman who has invested everything in motherhood, who sees her child as some kind of possession, finds it very painful to relinquish her hold on it. She is forced to recognise that without her child she no longer has an identity.

Women without other work often develop an excessive pride in the home which is mercilessly exploited by advertising and big business. Some women resent their husbands' increased participation in the home and see it as an intrusion into the one area where previously they held some autonomy.

Because women's work in the home is unpaid, they are forced to be economically dependent on their husbands. The implications of economic dependency are tremendous: this dependency is the traditional source of the power and authority of the man, and entails compromise, submission and lack of self-respect on the part of the woman. Most importantly, it makes the woman a prisoner of the situation, there are no viable means of leaving an unsatisfactory relationship, particularly if there are children.

Women in the home are isolated and deprived of adult company. Fewer satisfying relationships outside the home can lead to an intensification of emotional dependency and demands on the husband. Women who repress their own work needs become ambitious for their men.

Juliet Mitchell points out that the alleged freedom of women in the home is illusory - it is simply freedom to work unsupervised and in isolation.

The effects on kids : how the myth perpetuates itself

The mother who believes the myth will inevitably socialise her children into the same old stereotyped sex roles. Girls are brought up to be nurturant, passive, dependent. They are supposed to inhibit aggression and overt displays of sexuality more than boys are. Achievement at school is not greatly encouraged for girls because their ultimate object- ive is wifehood and motherhood anyhow. Studies show that girls who have been brought up in this traditional way have a greater concern for security and a greater fear of change. In fact they are generally more conservative, both politic- ally and psychologically.

Boys are expected to suppress feelings of dependency and strong emotion, they are encouraged to be assertive and daring. Too much concern with child care and the household is considered unmanly. (Cissiness in our society is more socially ostracised than is the converse concept of tomboy. The identification of the girl with the 'top dog' is better understood.)

The mother as the main socialiser of her children will ine- vitably perpetuate the myth, even if she is conscious of its disadvantages. It is naive to expect children to take much notice when mothers tell them that housework and childcare should be the equal responsibility of both parents if they see that their fathers are still only helpers (ie they help when they want) and that only at weekends. Studies show (10) that sex roles in children are more sharply differentiated when the mother plays an exclusive role in child-rearing than where there is equal parental care.

Monogamous marriage

Engels pointed out that monogamy developed along with the establishment of private property. It was based on econom- ic factors: a man needed to be able to identify his own chil- dren in order for them to be able to provide a workforce for him and ultimately inherit his wealth. Since the purpose of monogamy was to ensure the paternity of the children, this, in effect, meant monogamy for the woman only.

The concept of marriage as exclusive and permanent has persisted until the 20th century. It is these ideals of perm- anence and exclusiveness that I particularly want to challenge.

Some effects of failing to live up to the ideals

Although over a third of marriages in the USA (and many here) end in divorce, this is seen not as a failure of the in- stitution but rather as a failure on the part of the individuals themselves. Trying to hold together an empty marriage is seen as commendable. A marriage that has lasted for only ten weeks or ten years as opposed to a lifetime is seen as a failed marriage, and by implication a failed relationship - almost a waste of time.

Marriage is expected to be both sexually and therefore

40

emotionally exclusive, so when it isn't we feel threatened
(because we may be left), humilated (our pride - what will
people say - something must be wrong with me), excluded
(guilt often making the transgressing partner temporarily
incapable of continuing the ongoing relationship), anxious
(the secrecy surrounding the other relationship prevents us
from knowing where we stand). If we got rid of all these and
isolated what was left of jealousy, there probably wouldn't
be very much.

To what extent is jealousy culturally determined? Where
alternative relationships are institutionalised, as in polygamy, there is very little jealousy. Parents can love three
children equally, why not three lovers? Secure, autonomous
kids are not always threatened by their parents' love for
their siblings. Why are their parents threatened by their
partners' love for a friend?

Some effects of succeeding in living up to the ideals

There is absolutely no evidence that one person necessarily
remains desirous of and responsive to one other person to
the exclusion of all others for up to sixty years. On the contrary, there is ample evidence that they do not. Therefore,
living up to the ideal entails sexual repression. The possible
consequences of transgressing cultural norms (having alternative sexual relationships) are more serious for women
than for men because of (a) women's economic dependence
on her husband and consequent vulnerability, (b) greater
societal intolerance. (Adulterous mothers are sometimes
denied legal custody of their children.)

These factors, combined with woman's own need to be able
to identify with the wife/mother image, demand greater
sexual fidelity on the part of the woman, resulting in a correspondingly greater sexual repression.

Some results of sexual repression

On a micro level, sexual repression creates a kind of indi-
scriminate blanket repression. You can't choose what you
want to repress. Sexually repressed parents are obviously
likely to instil sexual repression in their children, particularly in their daughters who must be brought up to adjust
to their adult role.

On a political level, Wilhelm Reich, in 'The mass psychology of fascism', claims that one of the reasons people do
not rebel when the objective political situation appears to
demand that they do is because of the kind of character
structure that the repression of sexuality creates. He says
that 'suppression of the natural sexuality in the child...
makes the child... shy, obedient, afraid of authority,... it
paralyses the rebellious forces because any rebellion is
laden with anxiety, it produces, by inhibiting sexual curiosity

and sexual thinking in the child, a general inhibition of thinking and of critical faculties. In brief, the goal of sexual repression is that of producing an individual who is adjusted to the authoritarian order and who will submit to it in spite of all misery and degradation. ... The result is fear of freedom and a conservative, reactionary mentality.'

Thus anxiety associated with forbidden sexual activity becomes part of the anxiety associated with all rebellious thoughts and actions. The ruling class has not been blind to these associations, it has traditionally had an intuitive understanding of Reich's thesis. It is generally recognised that OZ was prosecuted not for its sexual perversions but for its sexual freedom. The Conservative party has consistently opposed bills aimed at creating a less repressive sexual environment in this country. Fascist Greece has banned mini-skirts. Sexual repression increased tremendously in Germany during the thirties, and in the USSR the rise of stalinism was accompanied by reactionary repressive measures denying individuals' previously held (post-revolution) autonomous exercise of their own activities. Religion, particularly the Catholic church, is also instinctively aware of the importance of sexual repression in maintaining its authority.

Conclusion

Alright, so the family as it exists now has many destructive features, although it can also provide love and security. The destructive features described earlier are perpetuated by the isolation of the family. How do we overcome the problems? How do we change things? The problems are obviously not soluble within the context of the nuclear family, since the institution is too limited and limiting. Obviously group living is one possible alternative. What are the implications of living in a group of about, say, 10-30 people? How do I visualise the new ideal?

The family would be liberated, not eliminated - biological parents and children would continue to identify with each other and perhaps, not necessarily, continue to have a special relationship with each other. But the importance of the collective would be stressed at the expense of the small family unit. The traditional isolation of the family would be broken down, and with it would go its individualistic, competitive features.

Housework and childcare should be shared as equally as possible between members of the group. Certainly there would be no sexual division of labour.

Marriage should be abolished. Traditional marriage defines people by their relationship to each other (ie Mrs Brown, 'my husband', etc). People in groups should be seen as autonomous individuals and not as half a couple, or father,

42

mother, etc. If permanent couple relationships do exist, the individuals in them are less likely to invest all their emotional energy in their partners because of the increased importance and intensity of other relationships in the group. We must question the romantic idealisation of love which involves concepts such as 'two selves merging' and 'losing oneself' in the other person. R. D. Laing suggests that 'love lets the other be, but with affection and concern'. Tension and hostility are likely to be decreased in a group situation.

As for kids, why should mothers - or even fathers - be the only socialisers? Margaret Mead has pointed out the advantages of several caretakers. She also suggests that the biological mother as the only socialiser of her child might well be the most efficient way to produce a character suited to lifelong monogamy, if that is what we want. 'Clinical and anthropological studies support the relationship between strong attachments to single individuals in childhood and the capacity for a limited number of intense exclusive relationships in adulthood'. If a child is attached to several adults and one leaves, this would clearly be less hurtful than if one out of two leaves. Studies of child-rearing practices in kibbutzim point out that the curtailment of parental obligations towards the child seems to create more positive attitudes between children and parents. Particular emphasis has been given to the advantageous effects of increased peer interaction. Personality studies have shown kibbutz children to have less inclination to conformity and greater personal maturity than children outside (although the sexual division of labour persists in the kibbutzim).

On the economic side, children should not be economically dependent on their parents, but on the group: this would immediately alter traditional authority relationships. All money and property should belong to the group. Group living could radically alter consumption patterns. Three or four traditional nuclear units would need only one TV, one washing machine. Those who choose to work at home should do so; their work should be recognised and paid for by the state. Women who have babies get paid maternal leave: fathers of new babies should get paid paternal leave, in order to be able to care for their wives and older children. This measure doesn't need group living in order to come about, and it would probably benefit women in nuclear families more than those in groups, who can in any case rely on the support of several people.

There are of course other things that would have to change. Among these are (a) the legal position of the family and (b) architecture - most houses today are built with only two or three bedrooms.

What chance is there for any real change? On a personal level the way we actually live lags far behind our theories. We may have new ideas, but the old responses and resistances persist. Our emotional responses are determined by our earliest childhood experiences, by our parents, whose values were determined by their parents. To what extent are we capable of breaking the cycle of unquestioningly accepting these values and patterns of response? Are we capable of acting upon and changing not only our ideas and environment, but also our feelings?

Marx pointed out that 'the family contains within itself all the antagonisms and contradictions which later develop on a wider scale within society'. Ultimately, the important questions are:
How far could radical change within the family structure affect the larger structure?
What are the political implications of non-stereotyped sex roles, communality and sexual liberation,
Are these possible without a change in the economic organisation of our society?

MUM: What do you want to be when you grow up then, pet?

DAUGHTER: A nurse.

MUM: You don't want to be a nurse! All those sick people! And terrible pay. You've got to have a real vocation.

DAD: Money isn't everything, you know.

DAUGHTER: Maybe I'll just be a Mum, like you.

DAD: That's the trouble with girls. No ambition.

Dinah Brooke, 'Shrew', vol. 3, no. 4

IDENTITY

Dinah Brooke

(Written by a member of the London Women's Liberation Workshop, and presented as a talk to students at Hornsey College of Art in Summer 1971, as part of a series of seminars on Women's Studies)

Who are you? Who am I? I'm Dinah Brooke. I'm a writer. No, I'm not. I'm Dinah Dux, wife of an American, mother of twins. Well, I'm both. Anyway, I'm Dinah. Brooke is my father's surname. Dux is my husband's surname.

Of course, it doesn't really mean anything when you change your name when you get married. It just means you've promised to obey somebody. A man. You chose him though. You chose who you were going to obey, so that makes it all right really. It was a free choice. Oh, it also means you can't buy a house unless he signs the papers, or have the coil fitted without his written consent, and things like that, because after all he's a man, and he's responsible for you.

But these are external things, nothing to do with your real identity, are they? I mean, you know who you are really. You feel who you are. You are what you feel. But then you feel different at different times. If you've been to a cousin's wedding, perhaps, or seen a sentimental film, you might suddenly be overwhelmed by a sentimental desire for white veils and orange blossom, and a little log cabin, and home-baked bread, and a babe on your knee. Or perhaps it was a different sort of film and you feel irresistably attractive and doomed. Or perhaps you have been working well, and people like what you do, and you feel a great surge of power and energy, or perhaps you feel utterly depressed and hopeless and dull and empty. Whatever feelings you have about yourself you are not what you feel at any one moment, but a mixture of all the things you ever feel about yourself, even if they are totally contradictory. Your identity is made up of all the things you have ever felt about yourself. Even if you haven't felt them for a long time, they have still left their mark on you.

Of course there is another side to your identity too, and that is the way you appear to other people. Your parents probably have a fairly clear idea of what you are like, and could describe you quite easily. Maybe you would agree with their description, and maybe you wouldn't even recognise it. Your friends too know, to a certain extent, what you are like. They know who you are. And one of the first things they know about you is your sex. That's also one of the first things your lovers are likely to know. It was probably the first thing that was said about you when you were born. 'It's a boy', or 'It's a girl'. Your identity was first defined by your sex.

As you grew up you didn't just grow up in a vacuum. You grew up into a series of expectations. Other people's expectations about you. These are very important. Infants who are brought up in institutions where noone has much time to expect anything from them have a very high mortality rate. Children are expected to walk when they are about one, talk when they are about two, and go to school when they are five. There's a law about going to school when you are five. There isn't one about walking when you're one, but most people do it anyway. On the whole little girls are given pink baby clothes and little dresses to wear, and little boys blue baby clothes and shorts or trousers. On the whole little girls play with dolls and little boys with cars and guns. They may want to anyway, but certainly if you go into a toyshop and ask for a toy suitable for a girl you will be shown a doll, doll's house, nurse's outfit; and for a boy planes, cars, guns and cowboy suits. That's what grand-parents expect of them. That's what it says in the magazines.

In school girls will probably be expected to do cooking and needlework, and boys woodwork. Girls will play hockey and rounders, boys football and cricket. When they are about fifteen most girls will probably leave school. After all, there's not much point in them getting any more education because what'll they do with it? Just get married. They might as well be earning a bit of money. They need money for clothes because boys expect them to look nice. If they stay on at school their friends will think they're right twits for still wearing some kind of horrible uniform, and never having time to go out with boys because of their homework. And as for staying on and trying to get a place at university, well, they'll have to be very bright, because the people who run the universities don't expect that many girls will want to go, so they don't provide so many places. And of course all the ones who do go are probably all doing the same sub-jects, English literature, or history, or art, and making things even more difficult for each other. Because when they started to specialise at school the teachers probably thought the art s were more suitable subjects for girls I mean why would a girl want to do mathematics or physics unless she was absolutely determined to be a doctor or a scientist, and not many people really know what they want to do at that age, or know what to do in order to do what they want.

Well, whether you've been to university and got a BA or to typing school and learned to be a secretary, you'll probably get married after a couple of years, so it really doesn't much matter what sort of job you have in between. Of course men have to get married as well. I mean obviously you can't have women getting married without men getting married. When he gets married he has to have a steady job, and a house, and be capable of supporting a wife and kids. He's got a lot of responsibilities. He'd better stick to his job and work hard at it. When she gets married she has a man who has a job and a house. She'd better work hard at keeping the house clean, and cooking tasty meals, and buying the right things. She's his wife. That's how she's identified. And then she has a kid and she's a mum. She has another to keep it company, or by mistake, or because she can't think of anything else to do, and she's still a mum. That's her identity.

What I've been trying to show in this oversimplified life history is that our identity is not decided or created entirely from within ourselves. To a very large extent it is imposed on us from outside. By other people in particular, like our parents and schoolteachers, and by other people in general. By society. Look through the advertisements in any magazine and you will see what society expects women to be like. Pretty, sexy, silly, childish, inefficient. When they are mums they know how many cans of baked beans to buy. They know about Oxo cubes. They have the whitest washing in the street, and they are always there.

You have made it as far as being students. You are probably thinking I'm different. I'm not that sort of woman. I'm intelligent and free, and my life is not going to be like that. It's quite possible that all your life you've been different from other girls. Boring, unambitious girls. Stupid cow-like women. Probably your friends and relations, fathers and boyfriends have agreed that you are different.

But the inescapable fact is that you're a woman. For people who don't know you and know that you are different, people in shops for instance, or men who whistle at you in the street, the one thing that they do know about you is that you are a woman.

So you're put in a very difficult position when you think about your identity. You are a woman. But you are not like most other women: women in advertisements for instance, or in magazine stories, or perhaps friends of your parents. You are not that sort of woman. You probably rather despise them. But what exactly is the difference? What was mum before she was identified as a mum? What was a wife before she was identified as a wife? Those words surely can't describe their real identity, their true selves, their whole selves. They are fitting into roles which society has prepared for them, and it's easy to feel rather contemptuous of them because the roles are so narrow. But it's not very pleasant to feel that people are contemptuous of you. It's a bit frightening, especially when you can see no way out of your own limited role. You probably envy the freedom of women who are not yet wives and mothers, but you daren't even admit it to yourself, so you probably react by feeling contemptuous of them and pitying the loneliness of their lives. So here are two groups of women despising each other. One for being cows and cabbages, the other for being, perhaps, promiscuous bitches, or hard and cold.

But let's go back for a moment to students. Art students in particular. She was probably good at drawing when she was a kid. Perhaps she just drifted into art school because she could do it, and because she liked the life. (And she probably found it easier to get in if she was pretty.) Or perhaps she really wanted to be an artist. Probably when she was eleven or twelve she read the lives of painters and imagined herself being a great painter. Genius triumphs over all. She looks at her own life and tries to relate it to the lives of other painters. Giotto was a poor farm boy looking after the sheep, wasn't he, and some papal legate came by and saw him draw a perfect circle. It doesn't matter if you're poor, so long as you have talent. You have to have luck, too, admittedly. And the ability to persevere. Well, we can all have that. Gauguin had that. Van Gogh had that. We all identify with people we admire. People who are doing what we would like to do. That's how our adult characters are formed, by a continuous process of identifying with other people and trying to be like them.

The trouble is, most of the great painters you read about are men. I know there have been women painters, but I don't remember reading about Angelica Kaufman and Berthe Morisot in books on the lives of painters when I was a kid. Maybe I don't even want to paint like them anyway. Maybe I'd rather paint or sculpt like Michaelangelo. But the thing is that if I want to identify with him, in my own mind, I have to forget about the awkward fact that I am a woman. It's perfectly possible to forget about it in your own mind, but it's less possible to ignore it in your life. After all, everybody knows you're a woman. Michaelangelo didn't have much time for women. He even wrote his love poems to boys. Most painters loved women though, and painted lots of pictures of them. Modigliani, for instance. After he died his wife threw herself out of the window. It's a very romantic story. When you read it, if you want to become a painter, you find it hard to know who to identify with. With Modigliani, who was a painter, or with his wife who was also a painter (I think) and who loved him so much that she threw herself out of the window.

And then there's sex. Does it seem odd that there should be problems of identity in the act of fucking? To start with, somebody's fucking and somebody's being fucked. It's interesting, by the way, that the American expression 'fucked over' can be translated by the English expression 'buggered about'. In the active sense they both mean messing about, manipulating, exploiting, using a position of power in an unscrupulous and unpleasant way, not taking into account the needs and feelings of the person being fucked or buggered.

Sexual freedom means that you can make love whenever you want to. That you're not uptight about sex. That you can read pornography and enjoy it. Let me suggest a piece of porn to look at. This is the bit from Henry Miller that Kate Millett quoted at the very beginning of her book, 'Sexual politics'. Ida, the wife of the friend with whom Henry the hero is staying, is ordered to bring him breakfast in bed (against her will) and then they have a silent fuck. The hero, we gather, had wanted her for some time, mainly because she doesn't like him. Now who do you identify with in that story? Ida? 'If she had a soul at all', says Henry. If anyone was being fucked up, buggered about, manipulated, exploited and insulted into the bargain, it was certainly Ida. Aha, you may say, she enjoys it. So he says. Ah, but there she is at his feet, gobbling his prick, and it was her idea, not his. Fair enough. There's a certain amount of physical pleasure that's almost automatic, maybe she did get pleasure out of it, always assuming that such a situation existed. But psychologically she's getting what she can out of being a slave. It's quite possible for a woman reader to get sexual satisfaction from this passage, but I think that while reading it she has to split herself into various parts. Part of her knows that she's a woman, like Ida. But the pleasure, as I see it, in this particular fuck lies more in the ordering someone about and making them submit to your every whim than in the actual fucking. So unless the woman reader is a real convert to masochism, like Ida, she's likely to identify with the hero, who's a man, as he bullies and plays with the puppet woman. She's not really a person you can admire, Ida. In fact she's despicable. The hero despises her. And if you identify with the hero you despise her too. And yet you are a woman.

What I have been trying to illustrate is that in this present society, and in most of the societies we know about, most men despise all women, and most women despise most women as well, and that includes themselves. A woman's identity is formed in fact in ways which are almost a prescription for schizophrenia. The conditioning processes of society, advertisements, magazine stories and articles, films, novels, TV, and the expectations of people around her, expressed in the educational and legal systems, insist that she needn't bother to be a person, but should find her true fulfilment in being a wife and mother. If she tries to fight this conditoning process and find models to identify with in order to grow into an independent and creative person, most of the models she finds will be male, which means that in order to identify with them she has to shut her eyes, for the moment, to the fact that she is female, which does not help her to develop feelings of sympathy and solidarity with other women, which in turn means that it is all the more difficult to fight the conditioning process.

INTERVIEW : "I'VE ALWAYS BEEN WORKING FOR
WOMEN'S LIBERATION"

(This interview appeared in 'Shrew' September 1971, in the
issue produced collectively by the Notting Hill group of the
London Women's Liberation Workshop)

MURIEL
age: 49   left school: 14
born: Nottingham   occupation: factory worker
mother: housewife   father: engineer, instrument maker

How would you define yourself?

I don't really know. I doubt I think about myself as an individual at all. I would say I was a member of the working
class. As far as work is concerned I'm part of the engineering industry. I don't think of myself as anything outside the
trade union movement. I suppose really that would be my
life in a sense.

What did your father do?

He was an instrument maker. He was a victim of the depression, but I suppose he was a victim of capitalism really.
He didn't work at his trade from 1921 after the first world
war until he went back into the rearmament programme in
'37.

What did your mother do all that time?

She was just a housewife. She did very little. She did the
odd cleaning job when my father was unemployed but there
wasn't work for women in those days. And she would have
thought it was beneath her to have gone to work.

What did they want you to do when you left school?

Originally - it was just kid's talk - I wanted to be a teacher.
That meant I had to go to grammar school, but of course I
never got there because my father said he didn't think it
was worthwhile making sacrifices and if it had been a boy
it would have been different. A girl was going to get married
and stay at home. The war changed that attitude. My first
job was in the offices of Boots the Chemists. And I stayed
there until the government got hold of me during the war.

Certain age groups, at a certain stage in the war - I suppose
it would be '41, '42 - they started to call up women. You had
a choice of going into either industry or the services. I
chose industry. So I was sent to a government training centre which I quite enjoyed. I was there for six months to
learn basic engineering and after that I got quite interested
in it, and did a course on my own initiative so I could go on
to aeronautical inspection. In '46 I thought, I've had enough
of factories. So I went back into accounting work. I did it
for three years and then decided I'd had enough of office

50

types. I preferred to go back to a factory.

I've always been fairly active - I think since I was about 17 - in the Labour Party. And I really got a little tired of being the odd one out. They were all Conservatives and snobbish with it. 'I vote Conservative because the Boss votes Conservative'.

What do you spend most of your hours doing?

I start work at 7. 30 in the morning and I'm there till 4.30. That's most of the day gone, isn't it? Then I get home, do a bit of tidying up, make a meal and at least two nights a week I'm out at a meeting. I try to fix up a certain amount of time for housework.

What do you spend most of your time thinking about?

Sometimes about women's lib. Sometimes I get very irritated about the position of women. Things that happen at work now and again. For instance they won't allow me to do certain jobs because they're men's jobs, you see. At the moment one of the men is on holiday so this one man's got it to himself, you see, doing the whole job himself. And even if he's busy I daren't offer to help him. Understandably, you see, he'd say I was lowering the rate of pay. Because I'm getting considerably less than they are.

How much less?

About £5 a week. And of course if they did let me do the job they would pay me more than I'm getting but not as much as they pay him.

Do you feel that you and N are equal partners?

Well yes, we're equal partners. If you mean equal partners in the amount of housework that's done, no, then we're not. But yes, I think we have a good relationship. And he would agree that I should be able to fulfil myself. I must say though that I myself have always taken a back seat. When there are things to be done invariably I've said, oh well, you can do the job better than I can. Political jobs, jobs in the Labour Party. Because he's got greater experience. Of course he's held me back to some extent. It's only really in the last two or three years that I've attempted to sort of do anything on my own.

Why do you think you changed?

Partly because N himself - he's quite a bit older than me - thinks he should be taking a back seat. And he has a tendency to push me. One of the things that changed me was being on our district committee in the union. Two branches elect one delegate to the committee. And we just couldn't get any man to do the job. I volunteered. There are 18 delegates, mainly men, and I'd always felt they knew so much more about the union than I did. But going and listening to them I thought, god, I know a darn sight more about it than they do. And these are the leading elements in the trade unions in the district. I mean, why the hell had I thought they were so superior all this time?

What do you think your husband spends most of his time thinking about?

I think almost certainly the trade union. He's a convenor at work, and the district president. Almost all his spare time is taken up with the union.

What difference does it make, do you think, to people you deal with that you are a woman?

At work the machinists have a tendency to think that women can't do the job of engineering, though it was proved during the war. And they invariably say that women have more time off than men. Which is definitely untrue. In the trade union branches it helps being a woman. You've only got to put your hand up to speak and they say, let the woman delegate speak. It's a little bit patronising sometimes, but you can use it. In general we're second class citizens, aren't we? All women.

How does it come home to you that this is true?

Money. 90% of the time it's money. I think if we got equal pay we'd be a long, long way towards general equality. The other thing I resent very much is that the mother is generally the guardian of the child. My sister particularly gets upset about this because she can't sign any paper for the child to go on a school holiday or anything. It's always the husband who has to sign. So we're appendages, aren't we, of the male. If you're attached to the male you're all right, if not you're just nothing.

Has it ever made you regret being a woman?

No, I don't think I ever thought I'd rather be a man.

Do women you know discuss sexual relations with their men?

I think the younger ones do, with their own men and with men in general. But I don't think my age husbands and wives discuss it among themselves very much. I suppose when we were first married we did, and before we were married. But not now.

And have other women spoken to you about it?

A few, not many. And I have to know them very, very well. I think my sister's the only person I've discussed this very much with on a sort of personal basis.

Do you meet women who tell you that they don't enjoy sex?

A lot. They put up with it, yes. They say, well you can't always be saying no, you know. Sometimes they feel very guilty about it too. They think they ought to, and they ought to make the men happy and satisfied. A lot of the younger ones enjoy sex more than my age, for instance, but I was lucky in that I had a father who believed that you should all be told everything you want to know. So I didn't get any sort of false ideas. I wasn't frightened of it. But I think if it had been left to my mother I would have, because she didn't like sex and she would say, it's something you got to put up with when you're married but you'll never enjoy it.

In a relationship whose responsibility do you think birth control should be?

It's something that should be decided between themselves. I think if I'd been 20 now I would probably take the pill. But of course it wasn't there at the time I got married. So the simplest way was for N to take precautions. I'm afraid all the other sorts of devices are too mechanical for me. By the time I got organised, I'd have lost all interest.

Why don't you have children?

Because we decided not to. Not originally, consciously. We used to talk about it but we'd say, next year, you know, the time might be right next year. But it never was right. I don't think the desire could have been all that strong really. N already has a daughter, so he had no particular desire to have any more, and he said it was up to me. I decided when I was about 30 that I didn't want to start a family after that. I suppose if I'd found I was pregnant at that stage I wouldn't have minded so much, but I certainly would have minded after I got to 40.

Do you regret not having children?

Not really. There are occasions when I look at teenagers and I think, I could have had a son or a daughter that age. But it's a very passing thing. And I must say that I look after children now and again, for friends, and I'm very glad to get rid of them at the end of the day. People assume you don't have children because you couldn't. To a certain extent they probably feel sorry for you. I just let it go. I don't feel any pressure, not really. Although I think some people might.

You don't go along with this idea that the ultimate fulfilment is having children?

I've heard a lot of people say this of course, and I feel like laughing at them. I think there are a lot of things in life for men and women. It's not an essential for somebody to have children. I think it's an excuse for some women. Women will complain about not being able to get out of the home and not being able to do a job, and I think they're very pleased that they can't because they have a child.

Do you think it's necessary for a woman to have a permanent relationship in order to have a child?

I think it might be better for a child to have both male and
female close to them. But if a woman wanted to have a
child, I would say, go ahead. The trouble with a woman on
her own having a child is a financial one, isn't it? She's on
the poverty line straight away. The man who loses his wife
gets all the help in bringing the children up, home helps,
income tax allowance and all. A woman bringing up a child
alone doesn't get anything. She's just got to do two jobs.

What do you remember about your parents' relationship?

They had a most unhappy marriage. They used to say they
stayed together for the sake of the children, which is a very
wrong thing. It's rather ironic that when my father had got
both his daughters off his hands he thought, I'm going to get
out of it. But my sister and I said, no you're not, not now.
You can't leave Mother alone at this time of life. Maybe we
shouldn't have done it, but we couldn't see our mother and
the kind of person she was ever making a life of her own at
that age. He accepted that position.

What did they argue about?

90% of the time I think about money. It's a terrible thing,
money. Sometimes I think if there are happier marriages
since the war than before it's because money's been much
easier. When I think of the families I knew as a child they
always seemed to be rowing and it was invariably about
money.

How much do you live on a week?

I have no idea, not really. Money's joint. In general I use
my wages for keeping the house going - food, my own
clothes, all the bills. Whatever we've got left we bank or
spend now and again on something important.

How much do you earn?

Before taxes, £19.10. I know I'm being exploited. Well, aren't
we all? Women more than men. I think I took £14.33 today.
£5 gone. Isn't it terrible! £3 on income tax. I won't work
overtime. I'd ban it. Wouldn't allow it, overtime.

How much do you think you spend on food and clothes?

For two people about £8 or £9 a week. I'm very extravagant.
Clothes, not an awful lot. Maybe £50 a year.

Entertainment and holidays?

On holidays it probably works out at about £3 a week over
the year. And entertainment, well, we seldom go to the cinema. I'm always amazed at the price when I go. Maybe we
spend 30 bob on the occasional drink.

How often do you eat out in a restaurant?

Three or four times a year at the most.

How many women are there in your industry and how many in the place where you work?

Where I work, BOC Welding, there's about 200. About 20, 30, maybe 15%, women. In the engineering union there's 141,000 women members. The total membership is about 1,300,000. So it works out at 14%, 15%.

Could you describe your job?

I'm officially called a print store assistant. What I actually do is keep files of all the drawings for the components, the parts they make, in the factory. The men come to me, give me a drawing number and I find the drawing, give it to them and keep a record of where it's gone.

Do you get anything out of your job besides money?

No, only companionship, I think. The enjoyment of working and talking with people. The job itself, no. Nothing at all.

What do you think about women's liberation?

Women's liberation or women's liberation groups?

How do you distinguish between the two?

Well, I've thought that I've always been working for women's liberation within the trade union as far as possible. I'm always on about equality and it's time that women were doing more jobs in the union, in everything. The groups - it's only something I've taken notice of recently. On the Miss World thing I thought, there's really somebody bothered. I was very pleased. Although I must confess I couldn't see myself actually disrupting the Miss World contest. It's not my sort of thing. I admire the ones who did tremendously. And I think it's been brought to the notice of a lot more people that women do think that they're second-class citizens because of the liberation groups.

Are you against disrupting or would you be embarrassed to disrupt a beauty contest?

Well, I would have less embarrassment about the Miss World contest than about Vic Feather. But that's my upbringing; I've probably got more respect for them even though I might not agree. Whereas the Miss World contest, yes, I think it's a terrible thing anyway. How on earth a girl can take part in it I really don't know.

What was your impression of us when we first met?

My main impression was enthusiasm. In a sense it made me feel a bit old. And I was surprised to a certain extent, at your understanding of women's liberation. But you all struck me as being not my kind of people. Which is a wrong impression of course. The middle class and the working class. And this is the impression that most women have got in the trade union movement. That it is basically a middle class organisation. I'd like to get over it, but I don't know how you're going to do it.

Were you ever taken in when the newspapers called us bra burners?

No, I never thought that. Just as in the same way they talk about them being homosexuals very often. They say this to me sometimes. So I say I'm in women's liberation - I'm damned if I'm a homosexual. And even if I were, so what? Sex is unimportant. It's the ideas that are the important thing.

What do you think was the most important event in your life?

The biggest personal event was meeting my husband. The biggest social event was the war. It changed everybody's life. And I think all to the good.

How are you different from young women in your attitude to work?

Well, they don't like work, do they? They've always been able to move from job to job so they haven't got the fear of being out of work. Which I think anybody who has lived through the depression can't help having. And that is good. Why shouldn't they tell the boss off and say, you can do what you like with your job. I wish I could be more like it.

What do you think can be the connection between women like yourself and women who are always at home?

I don't know. I do sometimes talk to them in queues, at Tesco's or Sainsbury's. I have a natter about prices and women. I'm always on at the branch meeting to men about bringing their wives more into it. Somebody said to me last Monday night, of course my wife's not like you, she's not interested. And I said, have you ever tried to make her interested? And unfortunately men don't. Then they complain that the woman's not behind them when they're on strike.

If you had real power what would you do?

I can't conceive of having real power. It's so sort of abstract. One of the things I'd like to do is at least do away with the racial tension in the world.

What about abolishing your job?

You couldn't, could you? Somebody has got to work. You could make jobs more interesting. And I'm quite sure all the work necessary in the world could be done in about 20 hours a week.

TWENTIETH-CENTURY SERVANTS

A secretary

(This piece appeared in the revolutionary paper 'Black Dwarf', in an issue in Summer 1970 which had a section on women's liberation)

Secretaries, like housewives, are isolated, 'private', they don't work with other secretaries, but usually for one or more men. Even if the boss is a woman the odds are that the secretary isn't going to be a man. This situation confuses: like the housewife who might feel - and we'll certainly be induced by the office structure to feel - that our frustrations are individual maladjustments to a well-tried system. But when we talk to each other we soon find that our experience is a shared one. Only by clarifying the common area and by working out its rationale can we begin to have a basis for concerted action.

To some extent we are losers even before we get to work. The tube ads showing 'the most desired woman in the world' after her $7\frac{1}{2}$ hours of super-typing must be set against the 'hints for comportment' promulgated in the dingy secretarial manuals. Job expectations begin - and end - here: 'Do not have preferences. If you have preferences among the staff or customers, it means you have dislikes also... Outside the office you can let yourself go, but inside you must keep steady'. Even though devoid of feeling, we must present a 'neat, tidy, polite and genial impression' to that strange and awesome creature, the Boss. In this context the same manual's subsequent gentle warning against 'perhaps presenting a false exterior' can only be taken as a joke. False to what? The ideal secretary has no interior - ie no feelings.

It is difficult for a secretary to have a rational goal; for her there is no finished product. The men we work for have deals to put through, manuscripts to finish, and so on. Our routine work, however, has no such structure and, like the labour of Sisyphus, it can never be completed. And since there is usually no possibility of promotion out of being a secretary, the only goal we can have is to be more efficient secretaries. The ways in which we try to personalise our work are indicative of the destructive and alienating nature of secretarial jobs. I think most secretaries try to personalise their work by reifying time: by alotting a certain amount of time to each task - eg doing six letters by lunchtime, making lists of things to do and trying to cross everything off by the time you go home.

The secretary is, however, different from other mechanical labourers who are forced into machine-like roles by their jobs. The difference is her relationship to her boss. This is not - despite the mystifications of the secretarial manuals and advertisements - either strange and awesome, or even individualistic, since it is patterned by the structure of the work situation. Compare this structure to the bourgeois family structure: it fits exactly. The paternalistic boss (male) and the inferior secretary (female) doing the drudging chores, always on a collar and lead lest she should stray too far.

A brief description of my own experience will illustrate what I mean - and this experience is not unique. The two of us who work as secretaries for a small group of men have different backgrounds and we react - in some details - differently to the situation. Anne left school at 15, is married and has two children. What she resents most are the extensions of her housewife role forced on her: she is the one who has to make the coffee, buy the biscuits and lavatory paper, and see that the place is tidy. She says she does enough charring at home. What oppresses me most - this being my first job since leaving university - are the strict boundaries of my job. I don't have ideas; I only type out other people's. If I point out a spelling mistake that's just about the limit of my territory. A suggestion for a more substantial change is ignored. Consequently, although what we have to type out is often absorbing, our relationship to it is purely mechanical; and something that we do 'on our own', like banking the cheques every week, becomes far more creative.

We both resent feeling that we should look nice every day, be cheerful, sympathetic, etc. It is the limbo area of semi-personalisation which we hate most. Being sympathetic and so on is characteristic of a person, and yet at other times we are treated as non-existent - arguments and confidences proceed as if we weren't there; the situation is straight master/servant. This sort of semi-personalisation produces very nasty kinds of exploitation. Secretaries can easily be flattered into doing more of the chores: even though we know the man can type as fast as we can, that answering the telephone is not a specific skill they don't have, it is difficult to refuse when you are told 'you set the letters out so nicely'. Like a servant's, our protest can only be petty and frustrating - Anne and I play games, forming a (perhaps subversive) bloc, with secret jokes, and at one time even a secret language. It's what used to happen below stairs in the nice nineteenth century middle class home.

There is a further, more sinister dimension to this in offices such as ours, which is a political left-wing set-up. By a strange contortion our politics can be used against us: we have the same political goals as our employers and want to work for the same revolutionary ends; yet the structure of the work situation remains divided up in the old bourgeois stratifications. This has dangerous implications for the men in the group, for how can a left-wing organisation be anything but bourgeois while its internal structure is run on these lines, when, as employers, they resort to bourgeois patterns and bandy about those mystery words 'efficiency', 'division of labour' - words effectively designed to preclude flexible discussions of role and so on. We are told by the men we work for that division of labour is necessary in all work situations; but this answer would seem to attribute a beautiful arbitrariness to the system that invariably allots the women the inferior jobs. As Anne pointed out, things would be slightly different in the office if we made the divisions. Employers who know about exploitation simply make better exploiters.

FRIEND: What's that?

HUSBAND: Violets for the little woman. Wedding anniversary.

FRIEND: Romantic.

HUSBAND: Don't know what I'd do without her. Marvellous housekeeper. Great mother. Does all my secretarial work too.

FRIEND: Do you pay her?

HUSBAND: What for? She's my wife. She doesn't need money.

Dinah Brooke, 'Shrew', vol. 3, no. 4

TELEVISION AND WOMEN

Lis Kustow

(Written by a member of the London Women's Liberation Workshop)

I was married and 23. It was the early 60s. Having been supported by the state through university and drama school, it was now time to find a job. Although people were still talking then about the vexed question of girls combining a job with marriage, it was assumed that an Educated Wife would have the good grace to find herself a rewarding full-time occupation for two or three years before embarking on Educated Motherhood. For my generation of women, education was a golden halo which brightened the kitchen and playroom and shone at the marital dinner table. The girl who regarded her work as the most important part of her life was thought unnatural, sexless, humourless, worst of all ambitious. Her male counterpart doing the same thing was considered to be bright, creative, witty, desirable, best of all ambitious. Having obtained a degree in modern languages and a husband, and walked steadily along the path of liberal middle class conformity, I felt no impetus to do anything which wasn't expected of me. Arts graduates were automatically assumed to sail into 'interesting work' commensurate with their degree status. I didn't feel any strong voice inside urging me to be anything and after a little experience I rejected the idea of staying in the academic world or becoming an actress, two possibilities at that time, which symbolised the seemingly unresolvable conflict between reflection and action. When I heard about television through a male contemporary who was already making programmes shortly after leaving university, I thought this would provide the answer. He suggested I applied to become a researcher and I immediately conjured up pictures of studying in a glamorous library through which the world passed hot-foot. This sounded like a job to meet all requirements so I wrote a letter to the head of a BBC department asking for work. It so happened they needed a researcher for a languages programme, and after an informal interview in which I was asked if I thought I could cope with a husband and working in the BBC, I was selected in preference to three men who were after the same job. I couldn't for the life of me imagine why, and assumed that Fate had mysteriously intervened.

A few weeks later I passed through the lofty foyer of the BBC Television Centre at White City, terrified, numb and unconfident at the thought of having landed myself a 'serious' job and working in a huge, daunting organisation. There was a whole new language to learn, a new code of behaviour. Anxious not to put a foot wrong or prove myself unworthy of my heaven-sent job, I meticulously observed every nuance around me, and tried to do twice as much as was required to show devotion to hard work. It took quite a number of weeks to acquire the authoritative BBC telephone voice (it took years to try and lose it), to learn my way round the building and know precisely the limits and status in the fine job-grading system so I wouldn't tread on the secretary's toes by typing my own letters, for example, or put responsibility onto someone who wasn't paid to take it. For several months I spent my time checking, double and triple checking word captions for the programme, and progress-chasing armed with sheaves of different coloured forms. My work was basically limited to the office plus an appearance at the weekly studio recording session. I had very little contact with anyone not connected with the programme I was working on and I never questioned what I was doing or how bored I was. My efforts were concentrated on keeping my job, which, from what I observed around me, meant I had to be noticed. If I was noticed, I thought, that would prove I had enough personality to stay in my personality job. When I was noticed it was usually because of my legs. The logic seemed to be: show legs, wear short skirts. It worked for a time. Men talked about programmes, I listened, they bought me drinks, noticed my legs, and everyone was happy. However, I must have overdone it, because one day the producergod told me discreetly to lower my hemlines.

The next step up from being a researcher is to direct programmes. I noticed that the few women I came across or heard of who had 'made the grade' as directors were without exception subjected to a battery of personal criticisms. A was an old battle-axe who should have retired years ago, B was emotional and impossible to work with, why couldn't C do something about her appearance, D was alright at her job but then she hadn't managed to get a husband. The one girl researcher I knew who fought for promotion was consistently criticised for being 'neurotic and difficult'. Encouragement was given to many mediocre men to move upwards, but women had to fight for every inch. As far as I could see, the jungle fight for promotion wasn't worth the agony, and there wasn't much sweetness and light once you got there, so I stayed thankfully put.

One day I learnt that I was now being considered 'potential director material' by the heirarchy, as the confidential reports on me had apparently been favourable. Although flattered to be considered in the running for higher things, if I thought about it for a moment, I felt sick. I could hide my feelings of inadequacy under the charade of the superior secretary, but I thought it would be like standing unarmed in the front lines to expose myself to the perils of direction. Men could approve of your legs, but would they approve of your programme? Thinking about directing was rather like postulating how I'd behave under torture. If I could find the guts to stand out against Them (experienced producers and technicians) it would be a way of proving myself, of saying 'I can do it'. The final accolade of proving myself would be a small caption appearing for approximately half a second on the screen, saying directed by me. Once that had happened, I thought I could die, give up television, retire to oblivion. My mark would have been made which both proved my existence and would allow the anguished struggling to prove myself to cease. Directing a programme became a single milestone like marriage. Once you've done it, you don't have to do it again. I decided I'd direct one programme. After that the future was a blank.

Early in 1964, I was sitting in the Hot Seat of Gallery Five with clammy hands watching the second hand of the large clock in front of me with terror. Directing for the first time is like a dumb man being asked to address a Nurenburg rally. You sit in the director's seat which marks the middle of a row of chairs facing complex dials, buttons and monitor screens. To your right is a production secretary who attends to physical as well as mechanical needs, calls shots, makes timings and hands out directors' comforters (boiled sweets). The rest of the row is made up of the producer, technical operations manager, lighting supervisor. In the next-door room of the gallery, another row of more active technicians is making sure that pictures appear on the screen with the right kind of dimensions and contrasts and that sounds are coming from the studio floor with requisite clarity.

As a woman, I had one mammoth hurdle to jump at one go. The Director is always Right. Your voice is heard all over the studio below as well as upstairs in the gallery. For the duration of the rehearsing and recording of a programme you are God, pronouncing, all-controlling, with a ready answer for all occasions. As women are usually wrong, this meant giving the lie to one's whole existence outside the claustrophobic world of the studio gallery. The corollary to 'the Director is always Right' is - 'the Director takes the can'. If things go wrong, you can't call down a plague of locusts but have to prove they can go right in your next programme, providing you get one.

In three hours I had to have a transmittable programme, come what may. Then the unspeakable happened. I did manage to get out one sentence to muster the crew to start rehearsal: 'Are you with me, everybody?' Then I dried. Completely. My head felt like a mass of cotton wool and I was paralysed in my chair. Luckily for me, the producer had moved to sit right behind me, and he whispered instructions for me to give to the cameramen sentence by sentence. I, zombie-like, repeated them as loudly as I could over the microphone. Miraculously the rehearsal started moving. After about an hour I was managing to give a few instructions myself. At the end of the morning there was a programme. I felt as though I had given birth to someone else's child. It had nothing to do with me. A completely alienated achievement which I drowned with drink in the bar immediately afterwards.

In television, one programme inexorably follows another. It was assumed that I was now on the way to becoming a director and I passively and uncomfortably accepted this fate. The road to self-fulfilment (a phrase that runs through the English education system with hollow, repetitious familiarity) seemed to lie with Aunty, the nickname given ironically enough to the most male-dominated, chauvinistic institution imaginable. In the following few years after the first ordeal I wrote, produced and directed film and studio programmes of my own and then went freelance to work in ITV. Once established to a certain extent as a director, I found out that I was considered in my profession by people who didn't know me as: hard, ruthless, man-eating, dangerous. In my own eyes I was timid, confused and as lacking in self-confidence as ever. I took it for granted that as a woman director I was a rare, isolated creature looked upon as a curiosity, and I tried to hide the fact that when it came down to it there was any difference between me and my male counterpart.

As a reward for having positions of responsibility, women are forced to do their work, and to be seen to be doing it, better than equivalent men. They also accept more, complain less in a world which is happier with feminine wiles and guile than feminine honesty. Who can blame the woman who finds going to bed with a man helpful in getting her a more responsible job when the sexual language is often the only one of communication between men and women, in an industry where, at its lowest, sex offers some kind of relief to the constancy of mechanical demands? Who can blame the woman who turns herself into a carbon copy of the 'efficient' male when being efficient is the only way she'll find approval or justification for holding down her job? Here, too, she is a victim of the dual criteria by which men and women make their careers, but which are never openly acknowledged. In an aggressive industry, men are allowed to be aggressive. In a competitive industry, men are distinguished by their 'talent' and encouraged if they are thought to possess the magic 'it'. In this same industry, women can't afford to show aggression, otherwise they'll be considered 'masculine'. Nor are they referred to as 'talented', because this is a male prerogative, deriving from the argument: to make good programmes, you must be creative... artists are creative... to be creative you must have talent... women are not artists... women are uncreative therefore they don't have talent. So much for creativity. As for aggression, men are singularly concerned for what happens to women when they act 'against their nature' aggressively, as though that too was a male prerogative. Thus the two characteristics whatever you may think of them, which advance a television career, are condemned in women.

So many of the major tensions of working in television are shared by both men and women that it is easy for men to dismiss accusations of discrimination as 'having a chip on your shoulder'. The pressures of getting programmes off the ground within schedule and within budget occupy every minute of the day and many evenings. Because salaries are relatively high compared with other industries, compensation in over-work (at researcher level and above you're not paid for overtime) is taken for granted. The pace of television often staggers newcomers, but it is, after all, a constantly devouring and regurgitating machine. This frenzy of production is seen most clearly in the current affairs and drama departments. Even if it does not need to exist, the desire for urgency becomes a disease, so that, for example, you often find yourself on two telephones at once, writing memos, dictating letters, checking and double-checking arrangements without stopping to think if it is necessary. (It often is, as the bigger the machine, the more parts to supervise.) Perhaps due to the single-track obsession with programmes, there is little intercommunication at production level in television and little discussion about ideas in general. This concentration on the processes of production easily ends up by effecting the same kind of alienation experienced by a worker in a large factory. Many producers and directors have lost interest in their programmes the moment they are completed, thus making it difficult to maintain a real continuity and growth. 'You're only as good as your last programme' is a well-known TV cliche.

Television is a world eaten up by the 'token woman' syndrome. From my observation the 'successful' women fall into two categories. Those who make a name for themselves in front of the camera by exemplifying femininity first and carefully controlled intelligence second, or those who prove by years of devotion and demonstrable obsession with the problems of television that they are capable of holding their own with men at an executive board meeting. In interviews given to the press, these women are usually at great pains to point out how competently they manage their domestic lives and how much they appreciate their children, although conceding the indispensability of their au-pair. Because they have 'made it', they often hide the sacrifices that making it in this way may have entailed. The biggest sacrifice is to adapt themselves totally to the male world which has adopted them like prize pets and isolated them from other women with whom they had at least some contact before their rise to fame.

As a few women have managed to hold some of the higher-paid jobs in television, they are often used to hiding what is really going on. 'If Mary has managed it, why can't any girl?

But then, women lack ambition.' Lack of ambition is hardly
the problem. When the Broadcasting Section of the Women
in Media group started finding out where women were employed in television (no official figures were available), they
discovered that many jobs were specifically closed to
women. Here are some of the technical posts that are not
open to women in the BBC (the situation is similar in ITV):
film cameramen and assistants, sound recordists and assistants, lighting assistants, dubbing mixers, film project-
ionists, film despatch clerks, studio cameramen, boom
operators, floor assistants, gram and tape supervisors,
racks operators (in lighting gallery), technical managers,
videotape editors, telecine operators. Some of these jobs
do need physical strength, but only very few as much mobile
equipment is mechanised. Most require technical knowledge
and training skills only, but what impetus have women to
enter technical colleges when they cannot be employed in
what they have been trained to do?

In non-technical jobs at production level, women are again
conspicuous by their absence. In the BBC Presentation
Department, women are excluded as newsreaders and network announcers as a matter of policy. Their meager participation in Current Affairs can be seen from this breakdown of production posts: producers and assistant producers: male 32, female 3; production assistants: male 15,
female 3; research assistants: male 6, female 14. The
research grade is the lowest of those listed. However, in
'The Times' in July 1972, following a reorganisation in the
Current Affairs Department of the BBC, it was stated:
'Women will contribute to current affairs programmes on
a larger scale than before. 'Nationwide', which has been
extended from three to five nights a week, will have Miss
Esther Rantzan in its team from time to time.' Robin Scott,
controller of BBC 2, interviewed in the 'Daily Mirror',
commented on women newsreaders: 'It seems unnatural to
a lot of people to see a woman behave in that way. During
the war, could you imagine any other than a male voice like
John Snagge saying "This is London"? There is always bad
news about and it is much easier for a man to deal with
that kind of material.' He also gave advice to women wishing to succeed in television. 'They will have to say that they
will devote themselves totally to a career and that they
won't be away every two or three years to have a child and
that it won't matter if their husbands fall ill, they will stick
to it.'

Although the number of women holding high administrative
posts in the BBC or represented at board level in ITV is
minimal, there is one job for which there is certainly no
male competition; that of secretary. All kinds of excuses
are given as to why most women are secretaries, but basically it suits the male power structure to keep them unambitious so that the machine is kept running. WITHOUT THEM

TELEVISION WOULD COLLAPSE. Current affairs series which send reporters all over the world at short notice could virtually come to a standstill if the girl who books air tickets, finds hotels and changes foreign currency decided to walk out. A BBC producer of children's programmes said in the 'Sunday Times': 'One sloppy secretary could shake us to the foundations'.

Many production secretaries know more about television than the men they work for, who even now can come straight from university to a directing post. Paid the same rates as a woman working nine to five in an office, she is exploited more than any other television worker. Here is an advertisement for a producer's assistant, viz. secretary:
'BBC WALES requires Producer's Assistant (women only) for television in Cardiff. Works to a Producer responsible for radio and television programmes, and in addition to secretarial duties runs the production office and assists in studio gallery and on location, involving travel away from base. Thorough knowledge of Welsh essential. An interest in agricultural programmes desirable. Training salary £971 p.a. rising when fully trained to £1,130 p.a. and then by annual increments to £1,470 p.a. (plus continuing irregular hour working allowance 15%). '

A man holding similar responsibility and qualifications would be paid at least twice that amount. There's no need for the BBC to put 'women only'.

The precise duties of a production secretary will vary from company to company, but on the whole she will: take letters from dictation (rarely is she allowed to compose the simplest letter herself); type scripts; act as continuity girl on location; make and be responsible for complex arrangements; have a thorough knowledge of the technical and administrative workings of television. She will work all hours when necessary and will at all times consider her private life secondary to her work. As a special concession she will be allowed time off to go to the hairdresser and that is considered one of the perks of the job. She will be expected to show a passionate interest in the programme without actually having any opinions of her own, or at least no strong ones. Her prime role is to 'make the crew and director happy', which means being constantly equable, cheerful, motherly, efficient and above all liked by staff and people in the outside world with whom she comes into contact. In order to convince her that she is not just a secretary, she will be called a production assistant, or some other name. In the BBC women are notoriously exploited by the use of a name. A production assistant or P.A. will often direct programmes, write scripts and do research as a special privilege, thus enabling her to be paid a full grade below the rate for the job, making a saving to the employer of £500-£1000 p.a.

The possibilities for a change in attitude towards women might, on the face of it, seem easier in the BBC with its more liberal humanist tradition than in the tougher, more commercially orientated ITV. ITV's dependence on advertising revenue to make programmes leaves little room for hope. After all, however enlightened or provocative a programme may be, if it is put out by a commercial company it will always be followed by an advertisement contributing to the indoctrination and continued involvement of women in the consumer society. The view of women put over in the commercials is bound to affect not only the viewer, but those in power within the programming companies. If their female directors, researchers or production assistants look as though they were the blonde in the advert, so much the better. The ad mentality dies hard in television, and it's often difficult to tell a leather-jacketed copy writer from a leather-jacketed TV director.

The root of all evil in television as far as women are concerned extends far beyond the commercial, the natural first target for women's lib, and far beyond chauvinistic attitudes to women within the various companies. It lies in the close similarity of structure and attitude within both BBC and ITV. Strictly to the letter, no, the BBC doesn't have commercials and it doesn't tell you that X is good for you, but advertising is as much about the promotion of a way of life as about the promotion of a named product and it is quite possible to maintain the right climate for the advertiser without showing advertisements. You don't have to have soap commercials to promote the consumer society, and the similarity of programmes on BBC and ITV points to this. Over recent years, the BBC has arrived at a position of openly competing with ITV in audience ratings figures and parallel programming. ('How can I get the audience to switch over from ITV to BBC?' Answer: 'Give them the same thing'.)

The changeover of the BBC into an industry like any other came out in the open when the Director General called in the all-powerful management consultants, McKinsey, who usually hack their way through the dead wood of business firms top-heavy with inefficient male management to ensure greater productivity. The BBC had realised that the days when the code of men from the Army and Civil Service ruled their managerial heirarchy were over. It had to be replaced by the structure of private industry. The Director General said of McKinsey's men: 'They helped us to see how a corporate public body without shareholders and without uniform standard products could make better use of management techniques derived from the world of private industry.' Since he'd spent public money on employing the notoriously expensive consultants, McKinsey had to be right. It has not yet been proved that better management techniques conspicuously change the male power structure, either in the BBC or anywhere else.

As there's sometimes confusion about the two systems of broadcasting we have in this country, particularly as most women are at the bottom of the pyramid and often unaware of what happens at the top, I'll give a brief description. Firstly, the British Broadcasting Corporation: this is a body set up by royal charter and operating under licence, which means it is meant to act as 'trustees for the national interest' and provide a service for listeners and viewers paid for by them through the broadcasting receiving licence. The structure of the BBC is aimed at ensuring the independence of broadcasting and 'it is the duty of the Corporation to keep in touch with public opinion and to weigh such representations as may be made to them'.

Like the BBC, Independent Television shares certain broadcasting principles, mainly that programmes should disseminate 'information, education and entertainment'; but as the main reason for its existence is to make money for private companies through advertising, which the BBC is not allowed to do, it has stricter controls in the form of the Independent Television Authority (now the Independent Broadcasting Authority) which was set up after the Television Act of 1954, and a government levy on advertising. Each individual ITV company pays rent to the ITA for the use of their transmitters and finances its programmes from the revenue obtained from advertisers paying for the showing of commercials in their area. The IBA is supposed to act as a caretaker of public taste and morality, constantly taking into account public pressure groups, as well as having a large say in the allocation of programme 'slots' to each company, the balance of subject matter and the agreed technical standard. Each of the five major independent companies produce both local programmes and ones seen all over the country, network programmes. The main aim is to shape the day's schedule so that the audience rating figures are as high as possible - the larger the audience viewing figure, the more enticing to the potential advertiser.

In 1969-1970 the net revenue for all the ITV companies from advertising was £93,375,563. From August 1970 to September 1971 that figure had increased to £102,397,458. Gross profits of the individual companies for the year ending December 1970, that is before the deduction of programme costs, the advertising levy, salaries, rent, etc, were as follows:

Thames	£23,148,000	Westward	£2,438,000
London Weekend	£18,534,000	Southern	£10,528,000
ATV	£21,166,000	Anglia	£6,441,000
Granada	£19,080,000	Ulster	£2,042,000
Yorkshire	£13,333,000	Scottish	£3,758,000
Tyne Tees	£6,110,000	Grampian	£8,881,000
Harlech	£9,934,000	Border	£1,240,000

These figures do not include revenue brought in from overseas sales of programmes or from subsidiary companies.

Within the regional areas they inhabit, ITV companies have great power. As they have on their boards the strongest representatives of local interests such as newspaper owners, owners of breweries, cinemas, chain stores, etc, they keep a very careful watch on programmes which go against their interests. These men are in the end much more influential than those who advertise on their station, although the two are sometimes identical. Even if they don't operate the restrictions of the American sponsors of programmes, and keep well away from the production offices, you soon feel their weight when they sniff as much as a breath of serious controversy or are suspicious that radical ideas are getting heard too much. If you take the trouble to unearth the interrelating interests of the men on an ITV company board, you will find they're involved in millions of pounds worth of investment with various interconnecting non-programme companies. The major shareholders in these companies are the ones who benefit most, and none of them make programmes. If you think earning £4000 a year as a director is high, the executives above him are on a scale rising as high as £30,000-£40,000 a year for a managing director, plus liberal expenses. (The Free Communications Group magazine, 'Open Secret', has published a brilliant breakdown of the mammoth empire of Sir Lew Grade, managing director of ATV. Their address is 30 Craven Street, London WC2.)

I've emphasised the money side of commercial television because this partially explains why women have no say whatsoever in its running. (At a meeting to decide the future of the fourth television channel, there was not one woman present.) Once again as a woman you're up against the image pushed by the ads that deep down you're a big spender and can't be trusted with other people's money. In an industry dealing with programmes costing thousands of pounds, you can keep women from controlling areas of finance because all men know that they're scatterbrained and don't have a head for figures. This masquerades under the excuse that women are not equipped to deal with the tough male world of television, a sexual inferiority, apparently, but few men are honest enough to say that their fears are more rooted in losing money than in women not being able to cope. (Children's programmes and education programmes, two areas women are safely allowed to inhabit, are notoriously under-budgeted.) Only actresses and pop-singers are allowed to be expensive, provided their names are big enough to be thought worth the investment.

The subordination and exploitation of women within television is not unique and it is bound to reflect their situation within marriage and work in general. But now that there is a growing awareness amongst women that there is a possibility for change, and that they are a force for change, this can give confidence to those working in television to break through their isolation and challenge what they have been

taking for granted for too long. Even if the secretaries at
Yorkshire Television came together only to insist on their
right to wear trousers in the office, this action alone in an
unmilitant profession was enough to make nationwide news.
There's a long way to go, but often change can happen in a
lunch hour.

The first thing for all women working in television to do is
MEET and TALK, as the greatest enemy is the dividing
office wall. By talking about their experiences, and realising that a secretary has many of the same problems as a
production assistant, researcher or director, women can
start finding out exactly where they stand - and there's a
lot of finding out to do. How much do they earn? How much
do they earn compared with men in the same jobs? How
many women's jobs are graded lower than men's under the
cover of a different description? What is the difference between a secretary and an assistant? What allowances are
made for women with children, for maternity leave; what
nurseries are available? How long is it taking for women to
get promoted as compared with men? What qualifications
are required for different jobs and how do these compare
with men's? What questions are asked at interviews and
what is written on references and annual reports? How much
encouragement is given to women to try different jobs, or
more responsible ones, should they be interested?

Another way of being effective is to see that as many women
as possible join unions and press for women's views to be
heard at branch meetings. Pressure groups can be formed
by women both inside and outside television to see that
programmes are made with women as well as men in mind,
and to protest against sex-role brainwashing in commercials.
(Correspondence to: (1) The Independent Broadcasting Authority, 70 Brompton Road, London SW3. (2) The Director
General, BBC, Broadcasting House, London W1.)

An action group, 'Women in Media', has been formed which
is affiliated to the Women's Liberation Workshop and meets
monthly. Its three basic demands are: (1) all jobs should be
open to women, whether technical, administrative or creative; (2) women should be fully represented at all decision-
making levels; (3) working hours and leave should be flexible
in order not to penalise people with children. The group
consists of women who work at every level in journalism,
television, radio, publishing, theatre, cinema and publicity,
and welcomes women in these fields to come together in
acting against the exploitation of and discrimination against
women generally as well as in the work situation. Contact:
Sandra Brown, Flat 10, 59 Drayton Gardens, London SW10.

Whatever views women in the movement might hold about
the relevance of television to women's liberation, surely
nobody can afford to be indifferent to what millions of women
are viewing in their homes every evening? Now that we are

growing fast as a movement and have the attention of the media, it's up to us to show that we <u>want</u> to relate to every woman in the country, and that we <u>take</u> the means of doing so seriously.

Mis-fit	refuses to conform.
Mis-conception	demands free abortions for all women.
Mis-fortune	demands equal pay for all women.
Mis-judged	demands an end to beauty contests.
Mis-directed	demands equal opportunity.
Mis-laid	demands free contraception.
Mis-governed	demands liberation.
Mis-used	demands 24 hour child care centres.
Mis-placed	demands a chance to get out of the house.
Mis-treated	demands shared housework.
Mis-nomer	demands a name of her own.
Mis-quoted	demands an unbiased press.

'Shrew', November-December 1969

WOMEN ON THE BUSES

'Women's Newspaper' issue no. 2

(The 'Women's Newspaper' came out for three issues in
1971. It was produced by a women's collective, and distrib-
uted through women's groups)

Long awkward hours, aching feet, dirty hands - why do
women choose to work on the buses? Women work on the
buses because it is one of the few jobs in which they have
equal pay. Bus conductresses take home an average of £20
a week. For the majority of women this wage is a small
fortune.

Earning a decent wage is a necessity for women who have
to support themselves and their children. Many of London's
bus conductresses are either divorced or separated from
their husbands. Others are just tired of bringing home tiny
pay packets for long hours in shops, offices, factories.

On the buses the shift system operates, and for all of the
women this presents problems: this week, 8am-4pm; next
week, 5am-2pm; then, 4pm-12pm. Some weeks they may
hardly see their children at all. They are always having to
think about where and how they are going to leave their
children and how they are going to be able to pick them up
when they finish work. When both man and wife are working
they sometimes try and solve the problem by working opposite shifts. What sort of life is it when just to make sure
your kids are being looked after you never see your husb-
and? 'A quick hello in the morning, a quick kiss at night.
When I'm going in the door, he's going out.' Single women
find it difficult too. They often have to work when other
people are enjoying themselves.

Now it's officially the policy of the London Transport branch
of the TGWU (Transport and General Workers Union) to
provide nurseries at the local garages. Resolution, 1968:
'that free nurseries be provided at all garages'. Reality,
1971: there are no nurseries, free or otherwise, in the
garages. But why should it be the union that provides the
nurseries? Why not the employers? In this society, because
women are not paid for their labour in looking after their
children, it is assumed that a woman bringing up children
is not working. In fact she is doing an absolutely vital job,
without which society could not go on, and the employers,
London Transport, should pay for the full cost of a woman's
labour and provide free 24-hour nurseries as long as shift-
work is necessary.

Redundancy and one-manned buses

But the problems facing women on the buses go beyond 24-
hour nurseries. For now there is a real possibility that

many of the 'clippies' will be made redundant. The situation is complex, but it shows very clearly the way the women's struggle is connected with the struggle of all workers against the bosses and for control over their own lives. Women bus workers have equal pay but they do not have equal rights.

No woman in London can become a bus driver or an inspector. 'So much for equal pay - the men drivers get a couple of quid more a week than the conductors.' With the introduction of one-manned buses this discrimination against women will mean that many women will lose their jobs. ONE-MANNED BUSES WILL BE LITERALLY ONE-MANNED. The introduction of one-manned buses (or o/m/o's as London Transport affectionately refers to them) is part of a whole reorganisation of London Transport, which has now been handed over to the Greater London Council, under the particular care of Horace Cutler. Many Londoners remember Cutler from his period as chairman of the GLC's housing committee. It was he who was responsible for the policy of 'fair rents', by which he meant rents comparable to those in the private market - ie rents most people couldn't afford. Now he's trying to introduce a policy of fair fares - ie fares which will bring in a profit but which most people won't be able to afford. (Already introduced. ed.) He hasn't yet tried to sell off London buses to private owners as he did with council houses, but no doubt he would argue that he is encouraging private ownership of cars by making buses too infrequent and expensive to use. One-manned buses are part of Cutler's plans to cut down labour costs and screw even more out of the remaining workers.

What about the Union?

Faced with this position, the bus conductresses get little support from the union. The TGWU (LT branch) oppose women as bus drivers. They argue that women are too weak to drive buses. In the canteen where one of the men drivers said this, a woman immediately retorted: 'If they're too heavy for women to drive, they're too heavy for men. Driving in a traffic jam uses up enough mental energy without the job being physically exhausting as well'. The drivers agreed and then pointed out that the buses are so heavy because they are so old. Still the most common type of double-decker bus running in London is the RT family which were put into production in 1947, though some entered service as early as 1939. All the men bus drivers, having raised the objection that the buses were too heavy for women to drive, agreed that women could easily drive the newer buses.

However, one-manned buses are no bowl of roses for the men. Under the guise of productivity agreements the union has accepted an extra £4 a week for one-man operators. One driver said: 'A miserable £4 for doing two people's work. We have to drive the bus, collect the fares, call out the stops and deal with any trouble which might arise'. Obviously it takes longer for one man to perform two men's jobs. In Birmingham o/m/o's have been withdrawn because the quality of the service is so poor that people do not use the buses, and far from being the heralds of a new, efficient, profitable bus service, the o/m/o's have in fact produced an inefficient, unprofitable service. One might suspect that this is the deliberate intention of the Horace Cutlers et alia. Make the public services so bad that they have to be withdrawn altogether.

Many of the London branches of the TGWU oppose o/m/o's for these reasons. The new 'londoners', as London Transport cheerily advertise them, are neither for the London public nor in the interests of the workers on the buses. In this situation the women's demand for equal rights - ie to be allowed to drive buses - must not be made in isolation. A situation could arise where, if the men were solid in their opposition to the o/m/o's, London Transport might be quite willing to let women drive buses - employers are always willing to use scab labour, and women and immigrants, the most underprivileged sections of the community, have historically been used in this way.

This does not mean that women on the buses must forget their oppression while the men fight the 'Big Cause'. It means that women must be loud and articulate in their demands, must push the men in their garages to understand their position. Only if the women are together and have a full political understanding of their position will there be the possibility of a united militant struggle for the workers and community control of London Transport. The women will not be sold out by union officialdom. They have seen through the union officials. They know they have done nothing for them except discriminate against them. They are in the best position to know that workers can only rely on themselves and grass-roots militancy. If the women are not united, if the men either laugh or ignore the interests of women workers, the old ruling-class policy of divide and rule may succeed again. Even if the men are together in solidarity the women could easily be used to smash that strength.

COMMENTS BY A NATIONAL HEALTH SERVICE NURSE

Pam Smith

(Written by a member of Radical Women in Medicine)

It is difficult to know what to say about nursing without being too subjective, but many of my own reactions represent those of other nurses. Everyone knows that the nurse's 'lot' is a particularly difficult one, but not everyone knows why.

We have many abuses to contend with (and it is often easier to put up with them than to fight them). Most people would say this is for the sake of the patient, little realising that the nurse is perpetuating a situation that can not only do her harm but can also harm those who are sick. There is too much acceptance; no definitions; little realisation of what one is doing and why.

Nursing becomes a reflex mechanism. Someone is ill, he is hospitalised and looked after. Nobody thinks about the patient's participation in his own treatment. The good patient is passive and at the bottom of a structure that involves authoritarian doctors and nurses all too well aware of their correct rung on the ladder.

However, it is my experience that more than ever before people are beginning to question. Frequently I have had informal discussions with student nurses who, although resenting the way in which they are treated, feel powerless to do anything about it. As a group, nurses are weak politically. Since Florence Nightingale there has been a tradition of gentility, dedication, righteousness, Victorian subservience to men - who are the doctors. The nurse's role is domestic, a calm mother-figure. She has never had a skill in her own right. She has been an appendage of the doctor and his work. He dictates and expects: she accepts, at the risk of her own and her patient's integrity. She never thinks of herself as a health worker, nor of herself in her role as a woman.

Constantly one is up against the lack of communication within nursing and hospitals as a whole. The hierarchy breeds spinsters who retreat into administration nurtured in a medium of sterility and authoritarianism. The old adage goes: 'You are here to DO, not to think'. Hence these women perpatuate the system. Instructions and requests concerning staff and even ward organisation and allocation come from a purely administrative office, often unrealistic and impractical, but the nursing staff themselves are powerless to take constructive democratic action.

The school of nursing itself is almost completely remote and isolated from either the wards or the hospital administration. Hence these areas develop as parallels, rarely communicating and converging. Everyone is mutually suspicious of everyone else. There is no representation for student nurses of any significance. Newly qualified staff are left to flounder without help or support. They are not encouraged to work for changes, for better conditions of work or service. Incentives are nil except for those who are ambitious and accept the rat-race. A friend of mine, a newly qualified States Registered Nurse, said: 'You either sit back, conform and get on - or get out'. The good people with ideas, initiative and concern are driven out, coldly, subtly, clinically.

There is no scope in nursing for any development of personality. At 18 one enters young and enthusiastic; one completes training wilted and institutionalised. Little value is placed on the study of psychology during training, little attention is paid to individual interests and values. Hours are either long or badly organised. One is totally tired - physically and mentally. The pay is scandalously low and there is little time and energy for leisure activities and social and personal relationships. Nurses are faced with a perpetual conflict of demands in their lives; one side has to suffer. Perhaps increasingly it is their working side - an understandable reason for a statement by a patient that nurses today are 'harder' than they used to be.

The solution will be long and complex, in a profession which is traditionally conservative. The women who go into nursing are varied: a large proportion are foreign and coloured who simply need a job and qualifications; those in the teaching hospitals are chosen for their educational background and families. Many women choose nursing because they may as well do something useful in between school and marriage, and in any case are waiting for the day when they can opt out of working full-time. Nursing in any case provides an outlet for traditionally 'feminine' characteristics - care, concern, domesticity. The system is weighty and thorough: those who stay in the profession are often too tired and too fragmented by shift-work to be able to get together to organise meetings and action.

Nurses are among the worst exploited of working women. It is essential for us to work together through women's liberation to realise our situation and to act upon it.

Radical Women in Medicine

This group evolved partly from the Women's Liberation Workshop and partly from the radical medics' group which produces the paper 'Needle'. We are interested in two aspects of women in medicine: women as workers in the NHS and how women are treated as patients in the NHS. The following are some of our ideas.

There are no statistics readily available either from the DHSS or from individual hospital administrations on the percentage of women employed in the health services. The figure in the USA is 70% and it is likely to be comparable in this country. Women work as nurses, orderlies, ward maids, cleaners, laundry workers, cooks, secretaries, lab technicians, radiographers, physiotherapists, social workers, health visitors, doctors, to give just a few examples. There is not equal pay in many of these occupations, although hopefully this will be rectified as the Equal Pay Act comes into force in 1975. Women tend to occupy the lowest grades in the various jobs, with low pay and very little chance of promotion. 84% of laundry workers in all grades are women: 84% are in the three lowest grades, whereas only 15% of managers are women. A similar trend can also be shown in the medical and nursing professions: as you reach the top of the hierarchy there are always more men. The 1970 Salmon report on the reorganisation of the nursing profession creates more administrative posts separate from nursing posts, and this will have the effect of recruiting more men into administration and thus into a position of power over the predominantly female nurses.

The position of women in the NHS reflects the inferior position of women in society as a whole, but it is also a special case as much of health work is considered as an extension of woman's work in the home. This is exemplified by the doctor-nurse relationship. On the one hand the female nurse is treated as a sex-object with whom the doctor can flirt, and on the other as his hospital 'wife' who carries out his demands and keeps the ward in running order. In true Florence Nightingale tradition it is considered ungenteel for nurses to take any action over their conditions of work and pay.

Many women are not in a union, but if they are often don't realise it. The wardmaids, orderlies and cleaners often have their dues subtracted from their pay without getting union cards. Many of these workers are black or come from Spain, Portugal and Yugoslavia and are open to threats of deportation if they become militant about their work.

Women must organise within the hospitals by joining existing unions and also getting together as women to break down the barriers between the hierarchically structured groups in the NHS. In this way women can help to achieve a more democratically run health service for all workers, men and women.

Any effective action must be locally based, in individual hospitals, but as a start perhaps handouts and questionnaires could be sent to all women workers to find out what they need or want. 'Consciousness-raising' groups could be started so that women will gain the confidence to demand their rights, and perhaps take action over a common need, for example creche and nursery facilities to be provided in the hospital.

MANIFESTO ON MOTHERHOOD - or What to do to protect
yourself when having a baby...

(This piece appeared in the September 1970 issue of 'Shrew')

1) Decide whether you want your baby to be born at home or
in hospital. If you want it at home, refuse to make any hospital arrangements.

2) Read up thoroughly on the process of birth beforehand.
Dick Grantly Read, Erna Wright, any book you can get your
hands on. Get all the methods for making it easier firmly
into your head. It's worth it.

3) Ask everyone you know who's ever had a baby for their
experiences. Good or bad they will help you decide what you
will and won't put up with.

4) Try to decide in advance your attitude to the authorities
you are going to meet up with. Are you going to do everything you're told, or do you have strong feelings about anything special? Are you willing to have enemas, total shaving,
etc?

5) Make a firm resolution to stick by your decisions - it is
easy to get scared by autocratic, bossy hospital staff. They
may be well-meaning or they may not, but remember that
they really have no authority over you.

6) Don't hesitate to use emergency methods of protest, if
someone wants to do something to you that you don't want
done. Rage, refuse, demand, if necessary, until someone
really takes notice of you as a person.

7) Don't believe every word you're told, especially before
the birth. It can be standard gobbledegook which is dished
out to everything pregnant. Make sure you are communicating past the glazed look on the face of the person dealing
with you.

8) Delivery position, and position during labour is usually
ordained by hospital system. If you want to take up a different position, kick up a fuss.

9) During labour, if you feel in control, don't be afraid to
show it. Don't let yourself be treated like a piece of meat.

10) If you want something, to see someone, to smoke, etc,
don't plead for it. That won't get you far. Do it or demand
it. Threaten to walk out if necessary. This way gets results.
The same goes if you want to see your baby. Hospitals are
not supposed to be courtrooms or jails, whatever the staff
may think.

11) Pinpoint rudeness immediately. Hospital routine is an
automaton. Don't just be a passive victim. If you feel a nurse
or doctor is being insulting, or treating you like an object,
tell them to stop.

12) Where, and if necessary, criticise conditions loud and clear - while you are still there, not after you have left the hospital. Send a posse to see the matron if it's bad enough.

13) Know your way around, talk to as many people as possible, find out what everyone else thinks is best or worst about the set-up. This knowledge could be useful then or later.

14) Stitches are too often accepted as the inevitable outcome of birth. If anyone can find out why this is so, information would be most welcome. Surely the majority of women can't be incapable of birth without stitches? Or are our doctors a little too keen to 'get the whole thing over with'?

15) If you want someone with you during the birth, be it husband, mother or friend, insist, don't beg. It is our understanding that only relatives are allowed. Why?

16) Your child is your own. If you don't feel the way you're told you should, don't pretend. Let hospitals begin to face up to the reality of mothers instead of always the other way round.

17) Finally, if good conditions and treatment prevail, praise everyone and everything to the skies. There aren't nearly enough hospitals where this is true. If you find a really bad hospital, let other women know. It must be possible to publicise the fact more widely, and give the place the reputation it deserves.

'Socialist Woman', no. 1, 1972

INTERVIEW - ON BEING IN PRISON

(An interview with Sandy Grew, 20, who had just completed her second borstal training recall. The interview appeared in '7 Days' on 19 January 1972)

What were you in Holloway for?

Well you'll laugh at this, I was dossing down in St Ives. Somebody gave me three bars of stolen chocolate, so I got done for receiving three bars of stolen chocolate. I got six months borstal recall. Admittedly I've got previous convictions - petty things like stealing a lighter and shoplifting...

You were on a recall, weren't you? How long were you there?

Yes, second recall. I was there seven months - I lost a month - I wasn't particularly liked there because I caused a lot of trouble. Riots, barricades and things like that. I bullied people, but I think my bullying was justified. I tried to tell the girls - look, you're not getting what you're entitled to - and they wouldn't have it. And I had to bully them into it, you know.

Take the remand centre for instance. There's about a hundred-odd girls in the remand centre. They're locked up most of the time. If you want something, you ring the bell. They can't get the barest necessities, like sanitary towels. People are ringing their bells for hours and nobody comes. You don't even get the exercise you're entitled to. There are a certain number of rules - and yet they are twisted the way the authorities want them. In my case, I was sent to borstal training, and by law you're not supposed to mix with prisoners, and yet because they couldn't cope with me on the wing they moved me over into the remand centre with prisoners to do 14 days lock-up. And I couldn't say, I'm not supposed to be here, because they just wouldn't have it. There's no way of getting what you're entitled to. You can put it through as many channels as you want, it's almost impossible.

What sort of training did you get?

Training? It was to get up at about seven in the morning, have your breakfast, which was always toast with either marmalade or sausage-ball. After that you got about half an hour's exercise - by the rule book it should be an hour. And then work.

This is divided into several groups - the garden party, the workroom - where you put pencils into plastic cases - huh, some kind of therapy work. The yards - where you used to empty the bins and clean up the pig-swill, and the kitchen girls who cooked all the meals. As I'm talking about it, it sounds OK, but all the time there's such a bad, apathetic atmosphere, you just sit there. Beyond boredom.

Dinner time you could have your records out. Every single
day of the week was completely the same without any variation at all. The only way it varied was with people's temp-
ers. If somebody got their hair on, that made a change,
people used to look on, because it was something different.

*You said you caused a lot of trouble. Did you try and organise
the girls to get their rights according to the rule book?*

If I didn't think things were right, I'd say so. God, the times
I used to get reported on what they call 'white sheets'. This
was a major report, you know, in front of the governor.
They'd take you down in the morning and say: 'You've been
reported under rule 43, section etc etc for doing such and
such'. And they'd put you down in this cell where there's a
mattress on the floor and nothing else, and there you'd be
left until about 11.30 - they took you down about 7. Then the
governor would come down to see you and say you'd got
such and such a punishment.

If you did anything wrong they couldn't cope with you, they'd
throw you off the wing. If you look at society now, if they
can't cope with someone, they bung you in prison. In prison,
if they can't cope with someone, they bung them in lock-up.
So where does it end?

What were you doing before you got caught up in all this?

I was living at home. There were a lot of pressures and
hang-ups at home - my mother's an alcoholic. So I left. I
first got into trouble when I was 11 - for breaking and entering. I broke into a school with a gang of kids. So it's
something that's been with me, you know, all these petty,
really stupid things.

When I first went to borstal I had the shock of my life.
Lesbianism really shocked me. It doesn't now. I don't think
it is really sexual, it's just a lack of security. Girls used to
hold hands and cuddle one another, but it wasn't really lesbianism, it was a sort of motherly, sisterly love. Though
they used to say 'I'm going with her', because they couldn't
relate it to anything else. It's sad really, because most of
them are from broken homes or in for really petty things
like pinching a bottle of milk and a bag of potatoes.

This is my second recall, so now I've done a borstal and...
I got out in February and I thought, 'This is it, I know all
the answers', you know. And I really genuinely thought that
I'd never get in trouble again. When the police said they
were going to charge me with receiving stolen goods, I said,
'you can't, it doesn't make sense'. It took them something
like 15 hours to get a statement out of me. The solicitors
you get when you apply for legal aid think 'it doesn't really
matter, it's the working class'. You know what I mean... I
get so aeriated about it.

You know, you're trodden on so much that you even begin to believe that you are a troublemaker, that the things you are fighting for don't exist.

When I cut my wrists, they put me in the observation room - it's a type of padded room, the walls have a kind of thin formica over foam padding. They put you into a kind of straight-jacket, which is a canvas thing with stiff padding down the sides, so you can't move or get out of it.

It's degrading, embarrassing, humiliating. It shouldn't happen. When they put you down the Obs, you're fighting with your back against the wall, there's no outlet at all. I'm not usually a violent person, but that was all there was left. I was there with my back against the wall and I'd pick up anything that was in front of me and fight, rather than be manhandled. They really did used to beat you if you put up a struggle.

When you did that, cut your wrists, were you really serious about it?

Yes, really serious. Everything got so bad that I didn't think anything was worth it. They say, 'Why didn't you go to an officer?' You just couldn't, because they weren't interested. One or two were, like the assistant governor, she cared. She used to fight for the girls but she'd never admit that the staff were wrong.

Do many girls get to the point where they are cutting their wrists?

Yes, it happens several times a week. But a lot of it, I think possibly even in myself, is just for attention. But you can't bring yourself to say to a member of staff, well look I'm depressed, I can't take any more. So you do something to draw attention to yourself - either smash the furniture, hit someone, do something along that line, or cut yourself up. A favourite thing was sticking needles in your arms.

You must have had group therapy sessions during your time in Holloway - what did you think of them?

Didn't work at all. I personally don't think you can combine discipline with therapy. They stood you there in uniform, and they analyse you. They don't talk about themselves. You just can't bring yourself to talk about your family and things like that. Everything was too tense, everyone was sitting around with butterflies in their stomachs. The old head-shrinker and the officers sat round and shot questions at you. 'Why did you do that last night?' And you'd freak. The way they put it over was really bad and they'd be sussing you and making all sorts of excuses for your actions and this sort of thing. Everything you do they put down to a certain thing in your background and I don't like that. Because I've

got a mind of my own, though I don't deny that my home
surroundings had some effect on me, they must have done.

**What sort of medicines do you get there? Is it true that if
you throw a tantrum you get doped?**

Yes that's right. If you make a scene or anything, you're
automatically transferred to the Obs. You see the doctor
the following morning and he asks you what the matter is.
And you say I just couldn't handle it, I freaked out. He asks
you if you're on any medicine, or if you want to go on any. I
always refused to take any stuff like Largactyl and Librium -
it depresses you. It's just a way of avoiding the situation - it
just puts you in a state of apathy.

**Did your riots and barricades you talked of ever achieve
anything?**

Yes, I came back from hospital to find that there was no
heating, no windows, no hot water on the wing, and thought
what a bloody cheek. So we started up a little fantasy of es-
caping and digging tunnels - it was a bit of excitement. And
I said I think we ought to do something about this hot water
and heating lark. So the girls went and got a candle and set
light to the curtain. I had enough influence to stop it, and I
said, 'Carry on. Let it go up. If we can't have heating we'll
make our own heat'. The whole room was going up and we
cleared out. The governor came down and said, 'You'll
never get anything if you go on like this'. So I said, 'If we
don't get it, we'll just keep on doing it'. More fires, screa-
ming and shouting and running riot on the wing.

What I think needs to be started is something like a trade
union among the prisoners. If everybody had cooperated,
they wouldn't have been able to do a thing about it. It would
have been possible to do it with a bit of thought.

**Do you think there's any likelihood of anything like Attica
happening in Britain?**

I'm sure something will happen. I know that if I ever went
back in, it wouldn't be for anything silly. If it was, I wouldn't
get out so quick, because I would go to town, I really would.
I don't want to go back, but I want to keep the ball rolling,
you know.

THE BLACK WOMAN

(Written by members of the Black Women's Action Committee, Black Unity and Freedom Party, in August 1971)

'White females are the tokens among women in this society,
in that they have the titles but not the power, while black
women have neither...' (Kay Lindsay)

Historically, from slavery to the present time, the black
woman in capitalist society has been a producer of labour
power in the form of slaves for massa's plantation. In addition, she was the occasional consort of her master and his
sons. The most famous consort recorded by history is
Josephine, the 'Empress' of Napoleon Bonaparte.

Calvin Hernton, a black sociologist, writes: 'As slaves, negro
women were brought to the New World, specifically to North
America, for only one reason - to serve as breeding animals
for more slaves. Simultaneously they served as body toys
for their white masters. True, negro women performed many
other tasks during slavery. They worked in the fields, cooked,
ironed, served as servants and nurses. But these roles were
secondary... Negro women were forced to give up their
bodies like animals to white men at random'.

It is interesting to note that recently in South Africa, Dr
van Nierkerk had sent a questionnaire to all advocates in
South Africa about the racial aspect of death sentences. One
advocate, replying in Afrikaans, added the following note: 'I
have in mind rape. I do not regard discrimination as unfair.
For a white woman, rape, particularly rape by a non-white,
is a terrible experience. For the majority of African women,
rape even by a white is something which can be compensated
for by the payment of cattle'.

Thus, under the barbarous system of slavery coupled with
the 'sexual atrocities' inflicted upon black people in general,
and upon black women in particular, the seed was sown for
the disorganisation and instability of the black family. The
well-known maxim amongst poor black families that 'my
children are my wealth' had its beginning in a real fact, that
the black woman produced children, ie labour power, which
in turn produced wealth, not for herself and her family, but
wealth which was expropriated by the slavemaster. The
black woman in reality became the breeder, with no control
over her body. On the other hand, the black man was seen
not as a father of children, but as a sire; this in turn relieved him of any responsibility towards the woman and the
children, which under normal circumstances he would have
had.

Under colonialism, and in present-day Western society, the
black woman has been ascribed the role of maid, child-
minder and cook. And as in slavery, part of the arrangement

84

includes the black woman allowing her body to be used. These practices are still very common in South Africa, the USA and Canada; in Britain it takes the form of hospital domestics, cooks and canteen assistants in the transport industry. At the same time, the black man has been ascribed the role of valet, butler, gardener and stud.

In this given situation, vis-a-vis the black woman and the black man, the black man has no control over his own destiny. First slavery, then capitalism and imperialism reduced him to a hewer of wood and a drawer of water, an expert in trivial and degrading work. Secondly, he was forced to witness the systematic degradation of the black woman. These were the primary factors in the development of the mentality (consciousness) particular to the black man in capitalist society.

The inevitable outcome of this is the matriarchal, one parent family. This in turn creates problems of identification for the boy. The mother is the breadwinner and above all provides emotional support. She is the main frame of reference in how he sees the world and, in particular, how he sees other black women. Under this situation, the mother usually reacts in one of two ways. She can be revengeful towards the child and treats him badly or abandons him entirely. Or she tries to compensate for the absence of the father by lavishing all her attention on the boy. If there is a girl in the family, this type of relationship affects her considerably, in that she has to carry out the policies of her mother towards the son. She is therefore being socialised into her 'role', the mother serving as her frame of reference.

At some stage the boy discovers that the role of women, and especially of black women in capitalist society, is not as important and at times negative. The symbols, gods and heroes in capitalist society are all white and male. This creates a love/hate relationship with his mother, which is later projected on to all black women. In addition, the problems created by racism demand that the black man constantly prove his manhood by acting as a stud and generally misusing black women.

The white woman, though viewed in the general context as woman, is, being white, upgraded in the eyes of the black man. To 'acquire' her is considered to be more of an achievement, as racism enforces the myth of sacred white womanhood, 'the zenith of status symbols', and at the same time renders her unobtainable to the black man. 'Where the negro is the underdog and the white woman is the great symbol of sexual purity and pride, the black man is often driven to pursue her in lieu of aggrandising his lack of self-esteem'. (Calvin C. Hernton)

Consumerism and black women

All women are subjected to the continuous brainwashing of

85

what 'our' role should be in capitalist society, and in particular in our role as consumers. Cosmetics, up-to-the-minute styles in clothes and hair, matching household goods and numerous useless gadgets all go to make up the ideal capitalist wife, who looks pretty all the time and keeps a house that's sparkling and clean. This stereotyped model oppresses white women most, as 'most black women have to work to help house, feed and clothe their families...and were never afforded such phoney luxuries. Though we have been browbeaten with this white image, the reality of the degrading and dehumanising jobs that were relegated to us quickly dissipated this mirage of womanhood'. (Francis Beale, in 'The black woman: an anthology')

The most destructive form of consumer goods that are manufactured especially for the black woman are the various bleaching creams that promise 'a clearer, lovelier complexion'; the straightening comb, creams and vaselines to turn 'frizzy hair straight'; and European wigs for 'a new you'. These 'beauty aids' which approximate to the white standard of beauty have been imposed on the black woman to make her hate herself. They dehumanise and physically maim; they create a feeling of inferiority which, at times, results in the absurdity of a black woman with a pink face and a blonde wig.

Contraception

It is very important that the black woman understands the forms and uses of contraceptives. Not an inch of progress will be made towards the liberation of the black people as a whole if the black woman perpetuates the role of breeder, a throwback from slavery which is now under the mis-guidance of the black man. The cry of genocide from black men is correct only in its application to the imperialists who use peoples of the third world as their testing ground. (This is also relevant to the blacks and poor whites in America who are being denied their welfare rights under the threat of sterilisation or of being struck off welfare after so many children.) This action of genocide we deplore. But this fact must not be confused or paralleled with the genuine need for the black woman to reserve the right to control her body, to determine when and under what conditions she will bear children.

The black woman since slavery and at this present time is left to be mother and father to her children. The matriarchal one-parent family is the story of her life. This is a heavy burden and, being at the lowest rung of the socio-economic scale and due to remain so forever under capitalism, the black woman must ensure a minimal standard of living to cope with the many needs of a child. Under this condition, black children have a slim chance of growing up fit and normal on a 'woman's wage', with poor housing, slum schools, deprived parental care resulting from the absentee father, and in general growing up in racist, inhuman conditions.

Furthermore, the black woman, the other half of the black race, must contribute her mind and energies to the very important task of the freedom of black people and of black women in particular. And therefore to begin, she must first take control of her own body: this right is hers and noone else's.

The pill is progress of a kind; but it also allows women to be sexually exploited more than before. Sex for the sake of sex, or 'sexual equality', isn't liberation, 'it is bourgeois and is a phenomenon of decay'. But if only for the choice the pill gives - the choice of controlling our body functions so as to free us to get ahead with the real task of liberation - it is useful.

Class liberation versus sex liberation

In capitalist society, the black woman generally finds herself a member of the working class. But within this class, because of racism, she does not find solidarity with the working class woman as such, but with another social group, ie the black national minority.

The pre-condition for the black woman generally fighting on a general women's platform is a commitment by white women, both in word and deed, to struggle for the freedom of the black woman from racism. This is why the black woman's liberation is first and foremost concerned with getting rid of this oppressive system, capitalism/imperialism, which breeds both forms of oppression and exploitation, namely racism and male chauvinism. For the black woman, therefore, class liberation comes before sex liberation. (See section on women in organisations.) This does not preclude women from making democratic demands in capitalist society for free nurseries, free contraceptives, equal pay etc.

Women in organisations

Revolutionary women and men in organisations must speak to and organise around the special problems facing the mass of women, thus uniting the struggle of all sections of the oppressed and exploited in the proletarian class struggle. Many so-called revolutionary organisations in this country pay lip service to this vital work, but are often guilty of using their women cadres to disrupt, sabotage and take over organisations of women in the same manner as these 'revolutionary' groups perennially behave towards each other. But on this question we will allow one of the most forward theoreticians of scientific socialism, V.I. Lenin, to speak: '...we must not close our eyes to the fact that the party must have bodies, working groups, commissions, committees, bureaus, or whatever you like, whose particular duty it is to arouse the masses of women workers, to bring them under its influence. That, of course, involves systematic work among them. We must train those whom we arouse and win, and equip them for the proletarian class struggle... I am thinking not only of proletarian women whether they work in the factory or at home. The poor peasant women, the petty bourgeois - they too are the prey of capitalism... The unpolitical, unsocial, backward psychology of these women, their isolated sphere of activity, the entire manner of their life - these are the facts. It would be absurd to overlook them, absolutely absurd. We need appropriate bodies to carry on work amongst them, special methods of agitation and forms of organisation. That is not feminism, that is practical, revolutionary expediency...

'That is why it is right for us to put forward demands favourable to women. This is not a minimum, a reform programme in the sense of the social democrats, of the Second International. It is not a recognition that we believe in the eternal character, or even in the long duration of the rule of the bourgeoisie and their state. It is not an attempt to appease women by reform and to divert them from the path of revolutionary struggle. It is not that or any other reformist swindle. Our demands are practical conclusions which we have drawn from the burning needs, the shameful humiliation of women in bourgeois society, defenceless and without rights. We demonstrate thereby that we are aware of the humiliation of the woman, the privileges of the man that we hate: yes, we hate everything and will abolish everything which tortures and oppresses the woman worker, the housewife, the peasant woman, the wife of the small trader, yes, and in many cases the women of the possessing classes. The rights and social regulations which we demand for women from bourgeois society show that we understand the position and interests of women, and will have consideration for them under the proletarian dictatorship. Not, of course, as the reformists do, lulling them into inaction and keeping them on leading strings. No, of course not; but as revolutionaries who call upon the women to work as equals transforming the old economy and ideology'.

What is to be done

Since there is no political party in Britain today which is the party of the oppressed and exploited, women have an even greater responsibility to organise themselves. It must however be understood that 'genuine equality between the sexes can only be realised in the socialist transformation of society as a whole'. (Mao Tse Tung) However, this raises a dilemma. Superficially, it appears that the movement can only hope to achieve elementary reforms to long-standing ills. This view, all the same, is rather short-sighted. The success or failure of the Women's Movement in Britain will be determined by its ability to win democratic demands,

88

and simultaneously to raise political consciousness in general to a higher level. It means, therefore, that the women's movement will have to concern itself with politics. In concrete terms this means taking part in class struggle and production at every level. On another level, it means having a firm grasp of revolutionary theory, ie Marxism-Leninism-Mao-Tse-Tung thoughts. In this era in which imperialism is heading for collapse, it also means taking a firm stand against racism, an imperialist yoke which so many black women are forced to carry.

This is an extremely arduous task for any group of white women. The task is doubly difficult for the black woman who has the added burden of racism. But a start must be made. A start can be made by the black woman who has to go out to work to supplement her husband's income, and also the mother who is the breadwinner of the one-parent family, to struggle for nursery facilities. In these conditions, the black mother, owing to racism, is super-exploited and finds herself paying out to unscrupulous 'childminders' up to one-third of her hard-earned wage for each child. This is a democratic demand and one where the black woman must take the initiative.

The black woman has to create new institutions that will temporarily relieve some of her most pressing problems. These institutions will bring black women together as an organised body, and through these common struggles they will arrive at a new and higher consciousness. Such consciousness must inevitably give the black woman a new 'self image'. But of even greater importance is the contribution which this process must make to the black movement in particular and the revolutionary movement in general.

Bibliography

Calvin C. Hernton, 'Sex and racism', London 1969

E. Franklin Frazier, 'The negro family in the United States', Chicago and London 1960

Toni Cade (editor), 'The black woman: an anthology', New York 1970

Clara Zetkin, 'Lenin on the woman question'

'Shrew', vol. 3, no. 7

SECTION 2 : THE MOVEMENT

THE BEGINNINGS OF WOMEN'S LIBERATION IN BRITAIN
Sheila Rowbotham

(Sheila Rowbotham is a member of the London Women's
Liberation Workshop)

It is almost impossible to write about the very recent past.
If I have distorted anybody's experience, I apologise in advance. This account only covers the period from the formation of the first groups in 1969 to just after March 1971. A
lot has happened since then, but you can read about some
of this in the rest of the book.

In the Autumn of 1968 vague rumours of the women's movement in America and Germany reached Britain. We had only
a hazy idea of what was going on. No-one I knew then had
actually read anything which had been produced by the
women's groups. All we knew was that women had met together and had encountered opposition within the left. Some
of the ideas discussed in Germany and America had already
percolated through. In the diary I kept during 1967 there are
persistent references to incidents I'd seen and books I'd
read from a women's liberation point of view. I can remember odd conversations with women who were friends of mine,
and particular very intense moments when I was hurt and
made angry by the attitudes of men on the left. But it was
still at an intellectual level. We didn't think of meeting consciously as a group, far less of forming a movement. We
were floundering around. The organisational initiative came
from elsewhere.

A women's rights group formed in Hull in the spring of 1968
around the campaign led by Lil Bilocca and the fishermen's
wives to improve the safety of trawlers after two ships had
been lost in bad weather in January 1968. Mrs Bilocca had
fantastic courage and resolution. She was ready to take anyone one. She said if the ships sailed without proper safety
precautions 'I shall be aboard and they will have to move me
by force'. It was unusual to see a woman fighting publicly
and speaking, and men on the left listening with respect,
tinged admittedly with a touch of patronage. The response
from the trawler owners was predictable, a combination of
class insolence and sexual contempt. Said the secretary of
the Hull Trawler Officers Guild, 'Mrs Bilocca has not en-
hanced the image the public may have of fishermen's wives.
... The idea of forming a women's committee to fight battles
for the men is to my mind completely ludicrous'.

The wives of the fishermen and particularly Lil Bilocca
encountered hostility also from some of the other women
and men in the fishing community. Mrs Bilocca received

threatening letters and couldn't get a job. Out of this opposition and the connections it had also for left middle class women came the Equal Rights Group in Hull. Though the working class women drifted off, it continued as a group and later organised a meeting for all the sixth-formers in the town on women's liberation.

When the sewing machinists at Dagenham led by Rose Boland brought Fords to a halt, it acted in a similar way to make women on the left feel they could do something. The women wanted the right to work on machines in C grade because although they had to pass a test on these machines they could only work on the lower-paid grades. This developed into a demand for equal pay. It lasted for three weeks and received the full glare of publicity; the papers called it the 'Petticoat Strike' and the women received the usual sexual banter which any action taken by women provokes. It imposed a great strain on their personal lives; Rose Boland said she hardly ever saw her husband and son in the whole three weeks, 'they never knew whether I was in or out'. The strike came out of the particular conditions in Dagenham; in Halewood the women weren't so interested. Rose Boland believed that this was because 'they've got a different way of life up there really, up there the man is the boss. Not so much now with the younger generation but more with people of my age. The youngsters of today won't have it, they want it on an equal basis'.

The Fords strike sent a tremour of hope through the trade union movement. Women who had fought hopelessly at TUC meetings for equal pay took heart again. There followed a period of industrial militancy among women workers which has only been sporadically chronicled in the socialist press, and has never been seriously studied. Rose Boland was undoubtedly right when she said, 'I think the Ford women have definitely shaken the women of the country'.

Out of the Fords strike came a trade union organisation for women's equal pay and equal rights called the National Joint Action Committee for Women's Equal Rights, which organised a demonstration of trade union women for equal pay in May 1969. NJACWER's membership was mainly older trade union men and women in the Labour Party and Communist Party, who were often heavily involved in committee work. It remained rather an official body which had an impressive existence on paper but only tentatively got off the ground in practice after the demonstration.

A small group of women in a Trotskyist organisation, the International Marxist Group, went to the early NJACWER meetings and helped to set up the first NJACWER groups. Interest in the position of women had appeared earlier when IMG was called the Nottingham Group. After Juliet Mitchell's article appeared in 'New Left Review' they held a joint meeting with NLR. But it was the initiative of the trade union women which meant the IMG women could raise the topic in their organisation without being dismissed. Although they had some connections with the American movement, their approach to the position of women was a traditional marxist one. They were terrified of being called feminists at first. In Nottingham and London Socialist Woman Groups were formed and produced a journal, 'Socialist Woman'. Not all the women in Socialist Woman groups were in IMG, but the journal had a broad marxist perspective. The first number announced, 'We are not anti-male, a charge often thrown at those concerned with the woman question. We are opposed to private property, the alienation of labour under capitalism, the exploitation of the entire working class, we are opposed to men who do the "gaffer's" job and assist him to do the dirty on women workers - whether in the home or in industry'. (Socialist Woman, February 1969)

The Fords women also helped to make the question of women's specific oppression easier to discuss on the left. At first the men would only admit that working class women had anything to complain about. Very defensively at first and with no theoretical justification, only our own feelings, women on and around the student left began to try and connect these feelings to the marxism they had accepted only intellectually before. Out of the first faltering attempts at these connections came an edition of the revolutionary paper 'Black Dwarf' in January 1969. There were articles about being an unsupported mother, how to get contraceptive advice, women in trade unions, and marxism and psychology (by a man) and a thing by me trying to relate how you encountered sexual humiliation to marxism. They all appear very obvious now, but at the time it was very hard to make the connections, and just having something down on paper meant you didn't feel either a hopeless bitter rage or as if you were a completely neurotic freak. I remember one left man coming up to me and with a pitying air saying he supposed it had helped me to express my personal problems but it was nothing to do with socialism.

Completely separately another group had formed in London. They were predominantly American and in their mid-20s. Some of them had been active in Camden Vietnam Solidarity Campaign, most of them had husbands who were very deeply involved in revolutionary politics. Many of them too had small children and felt very isolated both as housewives and as foreigners. They started to meet in Tufnell Park and were later to have an extremely important influence, particularly on the London Workshop.

'It was tremendously exciting. We felt like we were breaking through our conditioning and learning new things each week. Maybe small groups have this same experience now, but I think there was probably more tension and emotion because of the newness of it all - no one else seemed to have heard of Women's Liberation - we were freaks. I used to be exhausted and exhilarated after meetings and used to lie awake thinking - couldn't stop. We argued a lot with each other. We were mostly political, mostly not marxists because our experience and identification was American new left of the first half of the 60s type, ie before Marx and Lenin. I'm glad it was that way. We all felt Women's Liberation at a gut level and for me at least it led to reading (starting to anyway) Marx and Lenin... because we were confused and unclear in some aspects of our politics the way was clear for us to admit the truth and feelings of Women's Liberation into ourselves and then try to work it all out... We were really concerned with whether we could change our lives at all in view of our involvement in Women's Liberation. We wanted to be able to break down the barriers between private personal life and public political life. We admired and discussed Helke Sanders' statement to the German SDS conference. That piece also influenced our attempts to organise something for our own children and we met a number of times as adults and as adults with children with German SDS people in Golders Green'. (Letter from member of the original Tufnell Park group, June 1971)

Shortly after the issue of 'Black Dwarf' came out, the women at Essex University arranged a discussion of women's liberation as part of a revolutionary festival there. The atmosphere of Essex at the time was fraught with impotent isolated revolt. The festival was broken up continually by a group of students who regarded any structured discussion as a violation of their 'freedom'. The meeting on women's liberation was in a lecture hall. There was a very tense feeling around. A man carried a girl in on his back. Someone messed about with the lights. Branka Hoare, who was connected with the 'New Left Review', started to read a paper in a very quiet, nervous-sounding voice. There were occasional interruptions and then a curious silent coalescing of the women in the room. We felt a most profound collective urgency. But we couldn't communicate it very well in the discussion that followed.

At various times it seemed as if the meeting would go over the edge and end in acrimony and ridicule. A very clear intervention by a man from the German SDS describing what had happened in Frankfurt and warning the men not to make the same mistakes was important because it prevented it from being just a women's case against the men. For a moment the women's resentment focussed on a man who made a speech about political priorities. He said very self-importantly that in a revolutionary movement you couldn't waste time on trivia, and the fact was that women simply weren't capable of writing leaflets. In the smaller meeting we held later a girl hissed venemously through her teeth, 'I always change his fucking leaflets when I type them anyway'. When we held the little meeting we didn't have any definite

commitment to being an all-woman group. A few men came
and could be said to have played a historic role. One was a
ponderous and patriarchal maoist who lectured us endlessly
on marxism-leninism, another was a twitchy young man who
said we were like a mothers' tea-party because we kept on
giggling.

The next meeting we held we decided not to have men because we wanted to work things out amongst ourselves. One
man came in fact to this meeting and kept saying we must
have a theoretical reason to exclude him. We said we didn't
have one but we were fed up with being told by men what we
ought to think about ourselves and them. This meeting was
very long and rambling. People were going on about shopping
hours and nurseries and Mao on consciousness. There was
a girl from the SDS there who told us about the Kinderladen,
and people from the Tufnell Park group. It didn't occur to us
to form discussion groups just to talk. We were very grandiose about doing things immediately. I don't think any of us
realised we were starting a movement.

Three permanent groups started, one in Essex and two in
London, including the Tufnell Park group. The first news-
letter came out in May. The next issue was called 'Harpies
Bizarre' and reported response from leafletting the equal
pay demonstration and the formation of a group in Peckham.
'Meeting of a group of housewives and students from Morley
College. The group grew out of Juliet Mitchell's classes at
the Anti-University'. (Harpies Bizarre, no.2, June 1969)

The third newsletter was called 'Shrew' and the name stuck,
with the principle established that the editing should pass
from group to group. This issue reflected the disparate influences which went into the London Workshop. It included
accounts of meetings with older feminists and a vehement
denunciation of the maoists in the Revolutionary Socialist
Students Federation who had criticised feminism. 'I do not
intend to ask permission from Peking before proceeding. I
do not intend to neurotically consult Marxengelslenin before
baring my teeth or my teats. I do not intend to give ladylike
(read suck ass) reassurance to radical chauvinists during
the course of this struggle, even if it means losing their
friendship (ie patronage)'. (Shrew no.3, July 1969)

But in the same issue Irene Fick wrote, 'While fighting for
economic and social equality in general, under the present
capitalist society, women must oppose male chauvinism and
domination in personal life'. Only with the ending of 'class
society' was women's liberation possible. The Workshop had
from the start a cheerful eclecticism. Any woman was welcome, 'communists, along with maoists, trotskyists,syndic-
alists, Seventh Day Adventurists, nuns, anarchists, Labour
Party members, etc, in short feminists'. (Irene Fick)

The women who came in fact tended to be young housewives

who were only mildly left-wing. But there was at least one link with an older feminist tradition. A woman of 78 who was a pensioner wrote in the September 'Shrew', 'It has been pointed out that no exercise of power is ever relinquished voluntarily. It always has to be overcome by overwhelming force - not necessarily physical force, but the force of public opinion. In my view it is futile for women to rely on men to fight their battle for them. They must do it themselves - even at the risk of being dubbed "battle-axes" or any of the traditional moves to discourage revolt.'

When the Tufnell Park group produced 'Shrew' in October 69 they raised questions which have continued to be discussed by many other groups since. They presented them in conversational form. They hinged on the old problem of how explicit the aims of any organisation on the left must be.

'Do we present ourselves as socialists? I think we should work with women in any action which is relevant to them as women, not necessarily as socialists.'
'No, this could lead to manipulating people: it is using a common problem to mobilise people under false pretences. To organise as many people as possible at the expense of hiding half our ideas is dangerous and is ultimately going to backfire.'
'We have to make it explicit from the start that women's common problems can only be solved by means of a radical social change in the framework of the existing system.'
'If we had a mass movement of women who were aware of their common problem, but never got beyond that, I wouldn't be interested in them as a political movement. Women have to understand the causes of their oppression... Women have to believe that revolution is necessary for themselves, not just for some abstract group of people called the working class. They have to feel that they are part of it, and that they can participate.'

The Workshop remained open and theoretically only vaguely defined. There was an instinctive emphasis on politics from below, a trust in personal experience, a suspicion of theory, and a belief in the small group as a basic organising point.

By this time other groups had started in other towns. There was a Socialist Woman group in Nottingham, for example, and a group in Coventry which had originated in the University but spread to include some working class women on a local council estate. In autumn 1969 a few of us held a completely informal meeting at Ruskin College in Oxford during a meeting on working class history, to suggest having a similar meeting on women's history. An American girl from Coventry who was in International Socialism said we shouldn't have an academic history meeting but a general meeting on women's liberation. We planned this for February 1970 and met several times in London to organise, though a small group of women in Oxford bore the main strain.

We thought perhaps a hundred women would come. In fact more than 500 people turned up, 400 women, 60 children and 40 men, and we had to go into the Oxford Union buildings because Ruskin was too small. I'd never seen so many women looking so confident in my life before. The night we arrived, they kept pouring into Ruskin with bags and babies. The few men around looked rather like women look at most large predominantly male meetings - rather out on a limb. The reports on the Friday evening session were the most interesting, because you felt part of a movement for the first time. This was captured again in the Saturday evening workshops but tended to go during the very large open sessions when there were papers on the family, crime, work, and history. The National Co-ordinating Committee was set up with a very loose structure in order to circulate information round the groups. (This was dissolved at the national conference at Skegness in September 1971 and replaced by a more workable structure.)

It was really from the Oxford conference in February 1970 that a movement could be said to exist. The earliest activities had been propagandist and educational, speaking in schools, leafletting the Ideal Home Exhibition, demonstrating outside the Miss World competition in 1969. During 1970 all the new groups faced the problem of sudden growth, combined with rapid turnover of membership. Inevitably this forced the organisation of groups, informally, upon a few women who came regularly. There were very few women with experience in organisational initiative. Even the ones in political groups had tended to take action on the cue of the men. We went off into leafletting-type political work very quickly, often as a result of the enthusiasm of apolitical women to do something, and the guilt impressed on the marxist women about simply talking to other middle class women.

In contrast to America where the movement in some places became very inward-turning because of exhaustive consciousness-raising, in England we rather over-reacted against this and have never built up the independent strength they achieved. We have not solved the problem of translating the personal solidarity of the small group into external action either. We made obvious beginners' mistakes. The Sheffield group, for instance, gave out leaflets on contraception at a factory gate at 6 in the morning. Not surprisingly, the women teased them mercilessly. 'Sex at this time in the morning. You must be joking.' York organised a meeting on equal pay without contacting trade union women thoroughly first. Nobody came.

Although the movement is nationally committed to four demands, equal pay, improved education, 24-hour nurseries, free contraception and abortion on demand, action for these, apart from the demonstration of March 1971, has been very localised and groups have taken up issues as they came up.

The Liverpool group for instance was involved in opposing the Catholic lobby for making abortion illegal. Birmingham worked with the Schools Action Union to support the woman school teacher who was sacked for appearing masturbating in a sex education film for schools. The initiative for the four national campaigns came from the Socialist Woman groups and the Women's Liberation Front (Maoist). They were concerned that the movement would disintegrate into 'psychological' discussions of problems. The difficulty about these campaigns was that they didn't grow out of real organisational developments from below. They floated down from documents prepared by little groups. They are handy as answers for us when we don't know how to reply to the question 'But what do you want?'. But they did not come from any understanding of how our movement had come into being and what our strategy should be. Instead we found ourselves caught between being a new movement which is still essentially for mutual education and propaganda and, at the same time, a movement trying to organise without any explicit theory, of where our strength lies within capitalism and thus of how we can act, how we relate to other left groups, what is distinct about the ideas in women's liberation. It is true, of course, that you learn too through doing. But it takes time to collect and circulate information and experience from which to draw any conclusions. We are only just beginning to establish ways of getting information through.

Although the first groups tended to consist of students, later on they became less important. The women who have joined tend to be still predominantly middle class, in their twenties and thirties, housewives and white collar workers. A few groups include men - Liverpool and Leeds for example. The real growth came after the demonstration in March 1971. Groups have formed more slowly in Scotland and Wales. Many of the women who join have no previous political experience and only very vague political ideas.

All the revolutionary left organisations have had an awkward relationship to women's liberation. The personal and emotional emphasis and its middle class membership put them off. But its growth and its appeal directly to the women in left organisations, often almost despite themselves and against all their training, makes it difficult to ignore. From the start a small group of maoists, almost exclusively based in the London area (Women's Liberation Front, later Union of Women for Liberation), and the IMG women in Socialist Woman groups, of which there are several throughout the country, have each worked as an organised political tendency in Women's Liberation. The Maoists have been the least successful. Their somewhat talmudic approach to marxist texts and their intense conservatism about any new idea for fear of dogmatic heresy have meant that they consistently fail to communicate. Their initial strength lay in their zeal for attending committee meetings, and their prolific duplication of unintelligible documents which terrified people into believing they must be very high-powered because they were so difficult to understand. The IMG women have worked more flexibly and have consequently gained more support. They have had a strong activist emphasis which has attracted people, and they stressed the importance of working with women in industry: their meetings are relatively formal. It is evident, however, that there are certain tensions between being members of an international trotskyist organisation and being members of the unaffiliated Socialist Women groups, whose members are united simply by accepting the name 'Socialist'. This has already produced a split in the Socialist Women groups, and it raises the whole question of an organisation with its politics clearly formulated working as a tendency in an ill-defined movement.

International Socialism, a semi-trotskyist group, and the Communist Party haven't encountered this problem as explicit tendencies because their members entered women's liberation as individuals without official backing. The official attitude in IS has shifted from joking incredulity to grudging support. The change has been a result of pressure from IS women, at first only a handful, mainly in Coventry and London, who argued for women's liberation from the start. The initial response was to OK political activity with working class women and an admission that women weren't playing their full role in the organisation of IS. But as more women got involved they have started to push the implications of women's liberation home. At the first IS women's conference in summer 1971 the question of how revolutionary organisations should relate to movements like Women's Liberation, of the connection between sexuality and personal attitudes to political consciousness, and of the lack of any marxist analysis to explain the position of women who work as housewives were raised.

Within the Communist Party there was more attention to women's issues, and more of a tradition of a limited kind of emancipation, than in the more recently formed marxist groups. There is a women's organisation and a women's organiser in the Party. But the official line tended to favour safe questions - equal pay, nurseries - and avoid any discussion of the family or sexuality. When a small group of young women in the Communist Party raised these issues they provoked uproar but also gained quite a lot of support, and controversy trickled into the 'Morning Star'.

Unfortunately, most working class and trade union women know about women's liberation mainly from the media, except in particular cases where people from Women's Liberation have supported them, as in the Night Cleaners' Campaign which started in autumn 1970. The only way their suspicion can be broken down is by us explaining ourselves and giving them practical support. At present women's liberation

as a movement is very mysterious to them. They have noticed it seems to grow, but it rarely enters their lives in the
shape of people they know. Many of them have been campaigning for equal pay and nurseries for years and feel understandably suspicious of publicity suddenly given to young,
middle class women. At the same time, women's liberation
has communicated itself rather as a symbolic slogan of def-
iance, particularly to young working class girls.

Sandra Peers who is in IS describes a discussion at a TUC
school in Newcastle on equal pay when women's liberation
was raised. 'All the women had doubts about it, and some
were very hostile. By the end most were won over, though I
doubt if any of them will ever join women's liberation organisations for reasons of time as much as anything... Their
chief objections were the glorification of outside work as a
means of liberation, the anti-men image and the bra-burning
image - most of which derive from TV interviews rather
than from actual positions taken within Women's Liberation.
The chief argument that won them over was that it is largely
the attitudes of women (and, to a lesser extent, men) to
women's role in society that holds back militancy, and most
of them eventually agreed that Women's Liberation had at
least got a useful propagandist role to play in getting at
these attitudes. One thing that rather surprised me was the
extent to which the women accepted without any show of
concern that monogamous marriage and the present family
structure are on the way out, and supported abortion on dem-
and. About half of them agreed with it.' (Report on a TUC
weekend school on equal pay, 'IS Women's Newsletter')

It has been easier in America for women's liberation to relate and develop in practical activity with other movements.
In Britain the student movement was collapsing as women's
liberation started, and the Vietnam Solidarity Campaign was
already dead. The real political initiative has come from the
labour movement, in the struggle against the Industrial Relations Act, and opposition to unemployment and wage cuts,
in which the Communist Party had the most influence but
where even the small revolutionary groups were better
equipped to intervene than Women's Liberation. The structure of Women's Liberation serves an educational propagandist function but is difficult to mobilise. Also it is almost
impossible to act in a concerted way without any clear agreement of what your aims are. The fact that working class
opposition to the Tories' economic policies is predominantly
male makes it more removed from the experience of women
who are not left-wing in women's liberation. Accordingly the
response has been limited to supporting demonstrations,
organising meetings to discuss the Industrial Relations Act,
or trying to communicate to working class housewives about
trade union rights and rising prices. Particularly the Northern
groups though are aware of the way in which the economic situation is going to affect women's militancy, especially at work.

Gay Liberation started in England in the autumn of 1970. It was started by two men and influenced strongly by the American movement. The men took the initiative and tended to dominate the movement in the early meetings. As it grew, some of the women decided to meet on their own as well, although other gay women opposed this, identifying with the men. Unconsciously the men manoeuvred the women, just as the straight gay world in prison reproduced 'masculine' and 'feminine' characteristics in relationships between people of the same sex. Gay women are in a complex and intricate dilemma.

'We share the experience of our gay brothers but as women we have endured them differently. Whereas the men in GLF (Gay Liberation Front) partake of the privileges of the male - you have been allowed to learn to organise, talk and dominate - we have been taught not to believe in ourselves, in our judgement, but to act dumb and wait for a man to make the decisions. As lesbians, "women without men", we have always been the lowest of the low. Only through acting collectively can we overcome our own passivity and your male chauvinism so that together we - the whole of GLF - can smash the sexist society which perverts and imprisons us all. WE'RE WOMEN. WE'RE LESBIANS. WE'RE OPPRESSED. WE'RE ANGRY.' ('Come Together', Gay Liberation Front, Women's Issue)

At the same time women in GLF feel uncomfortable often in women's liberation because straight women are suspicious and afraid with them. They have also noticed a 'liberal silence' which opens up whenever a gay woman starts to speak.

'One of the great aims of women's liberation has been sisterhood. All women are oppressed so all women must join together. Given this view lesbianism can be seen as particularly important or attractive because it can be viewed as the epitome of sisterhood - women completely together. It is important for women to learn to love and trust each other because like other oppressed people we have been divided against ourselves, taught to denigrate each other and so ourselves. However, sisterhood cannot be an end in itself. So more and more women come together, so there are more and more sisters - so what?

'There is also the temptation for straight and gay women to think that by being or by becoming gay they achieve a more revolutionary position. But abandoning the privilege of the oppressors, in this case the straight world (in all senses) is of itself no more revolutionary than going into holy poverty, dyeing one's skin black, or putting on a donkey jacket and spitting on the floor to kid yourself you're a worker...

'I think one's relationships with other people, and the sexual responses must be an integral part of all other responses, must spring out of one's relationship to society. And basically the question here is whether the relationship is one of attack or passive surrender. One is not attacking the system by hopping from one oppressed category to another'.

(See end of book for full list of groups and more information about the Movement.)

'Shrew', vol. 3, no. 2

ORGANISING OURSELVES

(This piece appeared in the March 1971 issue of 'Shrew', written, edited and produced by the Tufnell Park group of the London Women's Liberation Workshop)

The Women's Liberation Workshop, in common with some other women's liberation organisations, is broken up into small groups. These groups have between 10 and 15 members, are locally based and meet weekly. There are about 12 groups in the London area. (Since this was written the number has increased to over 60 - and may well be even more by the time this book is published. ed.)

In recent issues of the Workshop newsletters there has been some discussion of the value of small local groups. We are a small group that has been running for nearly a year and we feel increasingly convinced that the small, local group is a basic and necessary part of the movement. We wrote this article in an attempt to say why.

For a woman, awareness of one's own life is the first step in the realisation of general oppression. It makes real what could be merely rhetoric. The group process encourages this awareness and initiates the understanding of the predicament of women.

What is 'the small group process'?

It is a truth universally acknowledged that women in large political meetings do not, on the whole, participate. Inarticulacy, shyness, the habit of depending on a man to say better than one can oneself what one thinks work against women taking an active part. The small group provides initially for women new to the Women's Liberation Movement a secure, accepting, positive place where they can feel safe enough to reveal themselves both to themselves and to other women. They can open up without feeling either threatened or liable to scorn.

Sharing oppressive experiences with other women gives them the understanding that many of the situations described are not personal but social. The awareness that revealed problems are common to all the women in the group consequently shifts the attention away from one's own inadequacies towards finding the real causes of these problems and gives a perspective that can lead to action. It also gives strength to go back to those inadequacies and start to change them.

It becomes apparent too that the only way to work towards the liberation of women is by joining with other women; the warmth and comradeship of the small group reinforces this conviction.

The third stage in the group process is the experience of analysing the reasons for and causes of the oppression of

103

women. This analysis comes out of the questions posed by
the first stages of opening up and sharing experiences. This
analysis, therefore, is rooted in the reality of the women's
lives - in what they have discovered together - rather than
being simply one handed down to them as correct. They can
begin to look now with some objectivity at the predicament
of all women.

The small group gives to women, sometimes for the first
time in their lives, an identity independent of a man's. They
shed the roles of wife, mother and sex object and establish
both their social worth and their worth as independent thin-
kers. The assumption that takes hold in the group that women
can think provides the initial step towards actually discussing and developing the political theory of women's liberation.
They begin to be able to build a vision of their human potential and a strategy for the action necessary to achieve it.

Practicalities of the small group

In order to avoid repeating the unpleasant experiences of
most women in male-dominated groups, we suggest some
practical steps:

1) The number of members should be limited. There should
not be so many members that it becomes impossible for
each member to have enough time to contribute to the meetings. Sitting for hours with something one burningly wishes
to say and not being able to get it in through lack of time is
a frustrating and destructive experience.

2) Members should not merely have a commitment to participate, but a commitment to participate in the right way.
They must be sensitive to the needs of other members of
the group. Obsessive talkers, for example, should become
aware that they may be taking time away from less confident and articulate members. And particularly in the early
stages of the group it is better to be overcareful and over-
sensitive about not interrupting, not getting angry, not putting one another down. The freedom to react absolutely
spontaneously in anger or sharply in criticism in the initial
stages is secondary to the freedom of the group to sustain
the trust of its members.

3) Since the small group does not have a chairwoman, the
responsibility for the serious, logical development of the
meeting rests with each member. Each member should feel
responsible for re-ordering the discussion should it stray
to no useful purpose from the main topic.

A word of warning

None of this is to suggest that the process of understanding
one's oppression in a group situation is a soft or necessarily
painless experience. There are difficulties.

One has to deal, for example, with the uneasiness that comes with a shift in loyalties from one's husband or lover, maybe, to the group. The safety and reflected power that makes it comfortable to identify with one's oppressor has to be given up and strength found to identify with one's own oppressed group and other oppressed groups. The group itself should provide this strength.

The group also has to keep its own closeness in balance. It shouldn't become, as it were, an extended privacy shut up against both new members and outside action in a kind of protected elite. It has to see itself finally as a tool for the liberation of all women, its meetings being to refine and strengthen that tool.

Additional notes on the group as a political force

We see the small group as a model for political work and a microcosm of a future good society. It makes possible the working out of an organisation which reflects the aims of its members.

The small group is autonomous - it makes its own decisions which arise directly from the experience of its members. A federation of small groups extends this principle and provides a political structure which incorporates many members but avoids a gap between members and society.

The group works against the isolation of its members. It establishes a community which is protective of them in a society hostile to its aims. It provides support for women participating in extra-group activities. It builds a community where women themselves are more important than the services they provide. It enables women to participate in all aspects of the running of the group, from typing and other secretarial activities to the writing of papers, talking to schools, etc. It teaches them skills they do not already know. This reinforces for women the knowledge that women are capable of undertaking activities at all levels.

It makes the assumption of leadership meaningful by having it grow out of specific necessities of the group. Initiative is taken by different members according to their interests, enthusiasms and capabilities.

Because of the personal nature of the commitment to the group, work which has to be done is seen not as a chore but as a contribution.

Why local groups?

The group based and functioning in one locality has advantages both personal and political.

1) It is convenient for members: it cuts down time and money lost through travel to and from meetings. It makes extra-group contact accessible, therefore cutting down the schizo-

phrenia of most political action.

2) The group is based in a community which affects its members, in which therefore it has a stake and can work in a real way. It can respond and react immediately to the needs of the community. It gives continuity and connection to group actions and provides for more concentrated work.

3) The national campaigns have more hope of success if they are locally based: one is neither working in a vacuum nor on imagined needs. One does not have to rely on the media to perceive results and reactions. One gets a real sense of which action should develop from which.

Why the small groups for old members?

Hopefully, the small group, in which relationships and solidarity have been built, can continue to be the place where criticism and synthesis takes place. Things done outside the group, be they local projects or larger movement work, can be discussed and evaluated not only in terms of themselves but in terms of the whole fabric of Women's Liberation.

It is possible to bring back to the small group experiences of working with others outside, to share them with the group and so build an overall picture of what is happening and what should be happening in Women's Liberation.

We can also continue to change ourselves and the time this takes obviously has no limit. The small group integrates all these processes - we aren't trying to change the lives of other women and our own lives in a vacuum or in isolation but in constant struggle with and support of one another.

(Other articles on small groups which were very helpful in writing this one are: 'Small group: big job' by Arleen Sunshine and Judy Gerard, and 'The small group process' by Pamela Allen of Sudsofloppen. Other helpful ideas on the small group came from 'On strategy' by Geoff Richman. For details of where to get these and other pamphlets, contact Agitprop - address at end of book.)

THE SMALL GROUP

Michelene Wandor

(Written as an impressionistic account of the process of the small group by a member of the London Women's Liberation Workshop)

'I do not claim that females have no organisations; obviously they join and are active in a great number of social and service clubs. But female organisations affect political activity far less than male ones... women do not form bonds. Dependent as most women are on the earnings and genes of men, they break ranks very soon'. (Lionel Tiger, 'Men in groups')

Week 1

I am nervous. There are about eight women in the room. I go and sit down at the edge of the group. People smile. I don't think I've been in an all-female group since I left school. The only person I know is Lynn. Our kids started playing in the street and then we met. We talked about our children a lot, and got friendly. Then she suggested I should come to the meeting.

Lynn introduces me and everyone else says their names. There's a long silence. No-one looks particularly authoritative. Finally Jenny explains that they started talking about jealousy last week, and she thinks we should continue the discussion. Susan says she'd like to start, because it's something that's bothering her at the moment. She has had rows with her boyfriend Joe, because he flirts all the time and then denies that he's doing it. Angela says why does she mind if he does flirt with other women? Susan says it's got worse since she moved in with Joe and gave up her job. Also she wants to have a baby and he's not very keen. Judy asks if she's afraid he might leave her. Susan says she's not sure. Jenny says she thinks jealousy is a capitalist emotion. Lynn says that's a meaningless statement.

Jenny: What I mean is that in a society which measures people's worth and their right to survive in terms of money, we start seeing people as things, as possessions.
Susan: I don't see Joe as a thing.
Jenny: But if he pays the rent and buys the food, that means that you depend on him for money, for survival, as well as for an affectionate relationship.
Susan: Well, I suppose I never used to be so obsessed by his flirting when I was working. I still don't think of him as a thing, though.
Jenny: Why don't you get another job?
Susan: Because I can't stand the humiliation of being mentally stripped every time I go for an interview. I'd rather depend on Joe. Anyway, he's earning enough for two.

We talked a bit more about possible jobs that Susan could do. I didn't say anything. Then we arranged for someone to go to Manchester from our group to help arrange the next national conference in June. Ann said she'd like to go.

Week 4

This is my fourth meeting and the group's eighth. In the last two weeks we've talked very generally about our childhood and families. Ann, who is rather quiet, said her father was very dominating and never let anyone else have an opinion. She said she finds it hard to talk in groups or more than two or three people. Judy said that maybe some people were naturally quiet and some people naturally talked a lot. Angela said she'd felt more able to talk and think since coming to the group; she'd always thought of herself as quiet and shy. So it wasn't necessarily a natural thing.

We got on to talking about the ways in which we had become conscious of the fact that we were female; how our parents treated us differently from brothers (if we had any); the way we were told (or found out) about periods and sex. Then Lynn said she'd been thinking quite a lot about bringing up children and teaching them, because she was having to counteract the sort of unconscious sex-role slotting her children were being fed at school.

Lynn: At the school's Easter concert all the boys sang a song about a dragon and a sword, and all the girls sang a song about pretty dresses and lovely smiles. How can you attack that sort of thing?
Angela: It's part of the whole system which says that mothers must look after their children completely till they're five, and then hand them over to a system of education over which parents and children themselves have no control.
Judy: I think it would be better if parents themselves weren't quite so fierce about their children. I don't particularly want kids, but I'd like to get to know other kids better. Mothers always put up brick walls round their children.
Lynn: Well, it's hard not to. If you've been told having babies is a natural urge, it's hard not to be fierce about your kids, especially if you know there's no-one else to look after them and love them.
Judy: I think babies are boring.
Lynn: I still get a sort of 'broody' feeling every time I see a small baby. How can you account for that?
Jenny: Takes all sorts to make a world.

We moved on to talking about the relationship of sex to reproduction; and on to sex in general. Whether monogamy followed the pattern of relationships in general, or whether it was simply a structure imposed on the system because of the nuclear family, and its perpetuation for the sake of ensuring legal paternity, so that any property remains in the hands of the individual family. At least that's a digest of something which Angela quoted from Engels, 'Origin of the family'. We're going to study that more thoroughly later. We ended up talking about men, everybody throwing around vast generalisations and experiences. It all got very heated. Ann kept trying to say something but everyone else was too loud.

Week 6

We've continued our discussions on men and sexuality. We spent a bit of time on sexual competition.

Susan: I really used to hate women. Well, I distrusted them really.
Ann: So why did you come to a Women's Liberation group?
Susan: I only realised I was disliking other women after I started coming to the group. Up till then I thought simply that men were more exciting than women. I suppose I came because I found it easier to talk to women on their own, without men around. As soon as men came in the entire atmosphere changed. It was as though the serious business only started when they were around.
Ann: I really resent the feeling that I'm not complete unless I'm with a man. You're a valid unit if you're a couple; if you're alone you're only half a person. You don't see many women going into pubs alone.
Susan: Make-up is another thing. I can't go out without make-up. It's a mask to hide behind.
Jenny: You're all talking like a lot of gossips; all those things are about how we've accepted men's view of us. How are we going to change this? That's much more important.
Susan: If you're aware of the ways in which you've been conditioned to feel inferior, you have a basis for realising that there is no need to feel that way, and that in order to change the situation you have to go into it in a different way. If men stare at you in a pub, they're expressing an attitude. By confronting them, perhaps by simply not looking frightened and being on your own confidently, you're affecting a change; it's slight, but still a change.
Jenny: I think that's trivial and irrelevant. I'd rather create places where people could feel free to go, whatever their sex or colour or age. You'll never change pub mentality.

Week 10

After a few weeks of very general discussions, everything seemed to lead to ideas about the family. Everything seemed either to go back to what had happened to us as children in our families with our parents or to what was happening now to those of us who were with men and/or children. We began to think about alternative ways of living, and to discuss whether it was possible to adapt to a more collective way of life.

Jean, who came for the first time last week, was very quiet

109

till Judy said she didn't see how anyone could be politically effective as long as they were still living in a nuclear family structure. Angela had just moved into a commune and agreed.

Angela: The only thing is that at the moment we find it takes all our time to run the commune; getting adjusted to taking collective responsibility for the kids, arranging who's going to shop, etc.

Jean suddenly got very angry. She said why were we talking about personal salvation? Moving into a commune wasn't working for the revolution.

Ann: What do you mean by 'revolution'? It's meaningless to talk about 'ologies' and 'isms' unless you understand the way in which they permeate your everyday life.

Jean: It's narrow and self-indulgent to think that starting a commune with a few privileged people is going towards a revolutionary situation.

Ann: But if one of the things you believe in is a revolutionary society in which private property has been abolished and no-one is discriminated against for any irrational reason, if you believe such a society will bring about different relationships between the sexes, between adults and children, you have to start now. We all have a lifetime of conditioning to unlearn. You've got to start now otherwise you won't be ready in time for any revolution.

Jean: But you're all privileged people. What about women who haven't got enough money to live on?

Ann: Well, I'd think it was patronising to suggest changes other people should make in their own lives. Those are decisions we should all make ourselves. But in the office where I work some of us secretaries have had our tea breaks cut because the boss thinks we spend too much time doing make-up and chatting. We've decided to go on strike next week. We've also started talking about a lot of other things. I don't think changing your own life means you can't take part in bigger changes. Also I don't want to talk about 'theory' until I know who I am and how I got here. Then I'll discuss revolutionary theory.

Jean: You've got to have a theoretical framework to fit discussions into; just going on strike for ten minutes or whatever it is doesn't give any grounds for thinking that secretaries will go on to think about other things.

Ann: They'd be far more put off if I produced an immaculate theoretical analysis which didn't mention us, and which we didn't understand. We all understand what cutting down on tea breaks means.

Susan said we were trying to get away from working in other people's theoretical structures, and this meant working from what we knew best - our own lives and experiences. And for women who, whether they did paid work or were housewives, were subject to similar oppressions, it was important to start from base; nobody could do it for us.

We had to do it ourselves. And anyway, said Ann, how many male revolutionaries had any experience of the children for whom they were supposed to be changing the world? A commune was the only way adults and children could work out new ways of interacting and working together. But political theory, on which to base change, said Jean. Okay, said Ann, we'll get to that. This is our way of doing it.

Week 15

Judy and her husband have separated. She says that a lot of things which she was dimly aware were wrong with their marriage fitted into a pattern since coming to our meetings. She said she was beginning to see marriage as a social institution which had certain consequences, rather than just something nice which two people wanted to do together. From being taxed together, to the way in which their friends treated them as a unit, instead of two distinct people; she said that they'd never discussed their marriage outside their own kitchen. It was a private thing. Now she realised it was a social structure, and as such imposed the same pressures on everyone. She said she'd valued the discussions we'd had about marriage, and felt they'd helped her understand. Jean said a therapy group could have the same effect. Judy said she didn't know of any therapy groups which read and talked about Engels', 'Origin of the family'.

Week 20

The last three or four weeks have been the most theoretical. We worked out a very short reading list, in order to discuss the question of women in relation to class. In the course of trying to define the new feminism, to work out whether women, simply by virtue of the biological fact that they bore the children, were inevitably going to be oppressed because of it, Jean suddenly said that she was now certain that this was what had held women back, and would go on holding them back. Susan said, did that mean we were all going to have test-tube babies? Jean said possibly it might, and so what? Most people exploded at that. We went on arguing for quite a while; I have a clearer idea of the arguments for both sides, but I still find it confusing. Jean finally said she felt we had a long way to go before we as women could work politically with men. Ann said that since she'd moved into the commune she was sure it was vital for men and women to begin working out both the theory and the life together. The rest of us were more undecided. Jenny thought there was still a real need for women to get together to understand their position as an oppressed group; we were still a minority as a movement and until many more women were involved we couldn't decide for them what was the best thing to do.

Jean: Well, it seems that I've decided on the best way for me. At the moment, that is.

As a group we seemed to have reached a point where some
of us wanted to get involved in more specific activities;
Jean has got involved with a group of women in a local factory who are fighting to be accepted and heard by their union, and intends to spend more time on that and the Equal
Pay campaign. Jenny's interested in more immediate practical work, and with another group is campaigning for the
local council to provide free contraceptive services run by
women themselves. Angela is moving out of London, and
will probably start another group where she is going. The
rest of us have decided to form a more systematic study
group. We're going to concentrate on the history of the family, and try and formulate some sort of theory about the
way in which at the moment it reflects and reproduces all
that is most pernicious in our society.

Week 24

This is our last meeting in this form. We're going to try
and assess what we've gained from the 'small-group' experience, and where we can go from here. Obviously it isn't
ended for all of us; most will continue to meet as a study
group. Other small groups in the country have split up completely, yet others are continuing while their members also
get involved in activities elsewhere; the base group acting
as support and solidarity, where they can discuss and assess their activities elsewhere.

We decided to go round the group and each of us say what
she had found most important or useful.
Judy: I think the phrase 'consciousness-raising' is misleading. It doesn't refer to some magical point at which you
can say someone's consciousness is raised to a level of
political security. What it seems to me is that it raises to
the surface discontents and reactions which are there within us - more clearly defined and more politically conscious
in some women than others. The most important thing I've
learned is the process of connecting what has happened in
my own life to abstract thought, and to a way of seeing society as a series of large and complex structures. I've got
much more of an understanding of the meaning of the word
'political', and also of the direction I think we can go to
change things most effectively. I think that some form of
socialism is the only answer; and that's what I'm interested in trying to define now. I think though, that it must always
be done with reference to people's personal experience.
Susan: The most difficult thing for me to accept was the
business of identifying myself as part of a group of women,
but that's also been the most important. I'd always thought
of myself as isolated, as on my own. It's been good to learn
that other women thought of themselves as defensively;
ironically enough, it's only since I've felt more confident
as part of a group that I've been able to act more independ-
ently in other things I do. Perhaps they're both different

aspects of the same thing.

Ann: Well, I've found that I can think. I mean that I've got a mind as well as a body. I always thought that people who were educated and could quote things were intimidating. It seems now quite clear that there's a lot we have to do: not only to work for more women to participate at every level in society, but also to work on things that other groups (radical, or revolutionary, or whatever they call themselves) don't: people's total relationships to each other, as well as to the structures in which we live. At the moment only women talk about, and do things about, children, sexuality, who does the washing up.

Jean: I suppose I came with the strongest history of previous political activity, and a very tough training in Marxist theory and method. Being in the group, which is very different from other groups I've been in, has forced me to be a bit more patient than I used to be. On the one hand it's very important so that so many women with a very wide range of political awareness are getting involved in the movement, on the other hand it could be a dangerous thing and just drift. I'm more convinced than I was about the importance of the personal experience, but I think people should be aware that there is a danger that the euphoria will give you the strength to change just a bit of your life, to make you more confident as an individual and possibly not necessarily more likely to want to continue to work for more massive changes with larger groups of people.

Jenny: I agree with bits in what everyone's said; I also think that the small group structure - self-responsible, encouraging each person to contribute freely and work out her own responsible relationship to the group - is important not only in terms of political organisation. Not just so that decisions can be taken as democratically as possible; but also because it shows the possibility of a real, widespread interaction between autonomous individuals who want and need to work together in a non-authoritarian way. I mean if most families were based on the sort of honesty and exploration we've tried to achieve, we wouldn't be where we are.

Angela: I think you're idealising the group a bit. I think there was a lot we didn't cope with. But I don't think that's all that crucial. I've been thinking about what we're doing now, and thinking back to when the group started. We came together in a fairly random way; because we all live in the area, and because it's where women live, in the home and the family that many of the conflicting pressures of capitalism meet. Then we had a historic commitment to each other; we were aware in different ways that our history and experience as women in a society that treats women as inferior, was cause for complaint and analysis. Having worked out what some of those common factors are - marriage, sexuality, motherhood, attitudes to work - I think we're now facing a much more complicated question. That's our

113

political commitment to each other. Whether or not we agree about the origins of our situation and about the ways to change it.

This is a schematic description of our group. I've selected incidents which seemed to me to make certain points. No two groups are alike; each creates its programme according to the needs and interests of its members. The people in the description are not 'real' people, but they say real things which have been said at different meetings and places.

The pattern of development within the small group is that the more you discuss and analyse, the more appears to be discussed. Gradually a complex and comprehensive picture of social and political structures builds up, in which, as you constantly refer back to your own life and experiences, a basic tension and interaction appear: that between the individual life and the collective life of the society. Because women have been caught between the two - expected to embody as individuals collective political and psychological images (in paid work to support industry as a collectively underpaid and exploited group, and in the family to contain and transmit youth, love, comfort and sex), we have a basic comprehension of the way our lives are fragmented and isolated. But perhaps because women rather than men have become symbols of emotional qualities, we have lost touch with our internal selves.

We are involved in a movement which is exploring the internal experience - inside the home, inside the head, inside the bed - as well as the external, verifiable experience. We know about oppression and isolation in both these areas. The small group structure, in its openness and range at the moment is the only area in which all the so-called specialist areas of study meet: we discuss consciously and unconsciously theories in psychology, sociology, philosophy and politics and the forms in which they appear at life-level. One example of sneaky ideology struck me after I had been in Women's Liberation for a few months. I noticed the name of a chain of shops that sells things for maternity and babies. They're called 'Mothercare'. We had been talking about the influence of the ideas of Dr Spock and Bowlby, who had assumed and insisted that children could survive only if their biological mothers brought them up. This has been a particularly confining, emotionally blackmailing theory; and its entry into everyday consciousness in the form of a word on a shop front is the kind of manifestation we must fight. By buying something in that shop, you're not only probably over-paying, you are also buying another drop or two of brain-washing powder. The attention to details possible in the informal, intimate small-group discussion is vital for an intricate political understanding of an intricate political situation.

114

I am hesitant about crystallising the small group into an absolute definition; there are many different groups which function over a wide range of subjects and thoroughness. The political direction of the movement has not yet settled; but perhaps a tentative defintion could be offered. The small group can be seen as a psycho-political group, which both in its intentions and structure (content and form) seeks to connect the inner and outer experience, to analyse it and come to far ranging political and practical conclusions. At the moment these focus on the way in which we can work best to make contact with and change the situation of women, and the theory of the situation we want to create. The pattern created by the 'small group' moves from the individual to the group; from group to other small groups, and thus to the collective of groups which constitutes the movement. It is a constantly moving pattern of different atomic structures; its prevailing political tendency is not yet very clear, perhaps its sense of itself shifts, but because of this structure, it is potentially a movement in which each individual contributes concretely to the total development and theory.

WHAT IS FEMINISM?

Rosalind Delmar

(This piece appeared in the 15 March 1972 issue of '7 Days'.
The author is a member of the London Women's Liberation
Workshop)

Feminism raises the spectre of the old sex war. The feminist becomes the figure of the castrating woman. Feminism
creates divisions where none were before. It is, after all,
disturbing to think that perhaps we might not be living happ-
ily ever after. The feminist, in the descriptions of anti-
feminists, often suffers from psycho-sexual problems; she
is misguided, unhappy and wrong and takes out her own personal inadequacies on the male sex.

Feminism is the political movement of women produced by
the contradiction between men and women. It is women's
response to their own oppression. The real power and privilege which men have over women produces the political
movement of feminism. Women's politics in the past 150
years have taken various forms and had a diverse history.
There was feminist agitation at the time of the French Revolution. Olympe de Gouges produced a 'Declaration of the
rights of women'. She was shortly to perish on the scaffold.
Women were prominent in the Paris Commune, and demanded there the right to organise themselves separately. German women in the nineteenth century, faced by a law which
made it illegal for any woman to join a political organisation,
formed friendly societies to subvert the law. In England,
working women formed political clubs and their own trades
unions. They were often banned from male trades unions,
and if allowed to join were excluded from the right to be
elected to office.

The women's movement here, like the American movement,
united on the demand for the vote - the basic democratic
right of any citizen in a liberal democracy. They compared
their struggle to previous suffrage movements, and when
they faced the violence of the State, being forcibly fed in
prisons, felt themselves the inheritors of the struggle at
Peterloo. The American movement was founded when female delegates were excluded from the World Anti-Slavery
Convention held in London in 1840. They fought for the emancipation of the slaves, certain that when this came they
themselves, slaves too, would also win new rights. When
these were denied them, they turned bitterly to their own
struggle for the vote. But the American movement is now
as politically distant from the American suffrage movement
as the black American movements are from the anti-slavery
movement.

Feminism has historically been heterogeneous. Different
analyses, different tactics, different strategies have been

put into practice and debated. The Anglo-American movement produced what can be called 'Liberal feminism': it was a feminism which tried to manipulate the possibilities of the political system of the ruling class in order to gain new rights for women and to ameliorate women's conditions. Betty Friedan's 'National Organisation of Women' is a modern example. There were two main strands in liberal feminism. One was 'equal rights feminism', which understood the women's movement as essentially a struggle for the recognition of equality of opportunity with men, for equal rights irrespective of sex - the problem for them was one of a discrimination backed up by the weight of habit and custom, which legal equality could overcome. The second was 'social feminism'. The social feminists dedicated themselves to educational reform, philanthropic activity like the temperance movement, and religious work. They established nursing and teaching as female professions, and believed that women had unique qualities, usually connected to their maternal vocation, which if socially mobilised would make the world a better place to live in.

Where the liberal feminists in England took their inspiration from J. S. Mill's 'On the subjugation of women', socialist feminists have followed the analysis of Frederick Engels' 'The Origins of the family, private property and the state'. Engels set himself the task of analysing the cause of women's oppression in the light of the scientific method discovered by himself and Marx. His fundamental argument was that women's oppression coincided with the development of private property, and that once the structure of private property was abolished, the pre-conditions for women's liberation would be established. He tried to establish that the fundamental cause of women's oppression was in the 'division of labour' between men and women. At a specific point in time, he thought, there was a development in the means of production outside the home (where the man worked) which gave men the economic power which would allow them to subjugate the woman, and the world of the home.

Recently, within America, a new analysis of the structures of women's oppression has been developed by the radical feminists. They argue that the subjugation of women involves not just an economic oppression which has to be overcome, but also a psychological and biological oppression which must be overcome. Therefore to concentrate narrowly on the question of economic oppression is inadequate. The development of radical feminist analysis has made a profound impression on the politics of modern feminist movements.

It seems clear that in countries where the two demands for women which arose out of Engels' analysis, and have been since adopted by almost every socialist movement - woman's entry into social production, and the socialisation of child-care - women are still oppressed. Indeed, these devices have not even led to the abolition of that sexual division of labour which was, for Engels, the root of the matter. The concrete meaning of those demands is that women now do socially what they previously did privately. Where child-care facilities have been set up, women run them; where canteen facilities have been initiated, women work in them. The sexual division of labour within the family has been complemented and strengthened by a sexual division of labour on a social scale.

Engels' view is an anthropologist's view. He reached his conclusions after studying anthropological texts, and much of his work is based on the researches of Lewis Morgan. Claude Levi-Strauss, the French anthropologist in 'The family', which is a critique of aspects of Morgan's work (in 'Man, culture and society', ed. H. Shapiro, London) describes the sexual division of labour as, 'nothing else than a device to institute a reciprocal state of dependence between the sexes'. The only 'solid ground' for this division of labour is, he writes, 'the woman's biological specialisation in the reproduction of children'. The radical feminist analysis explores this 'solid ground'.

The unity of the contradiction which holds men and women together is not, they argue, the division of labour, but the system of reproduction. Men seized control not just of the means of production, but also of the means of reproduction - women. Women can therefore only be liberated when they overcome the biological determinants of their oppression. It is now possible to see the first glimpses of the technical pre-conditions for this. Developments in hygiene and nutrition have meant that it is no longer necessary for women to produce six to eight children in the hope that two will survive to adulthood. Developments in birth control have made it possible for women consciously to limit their number of pregnancies. And progress has at last been made towards the reproduction of the human species in extrauterine devices. For the first time there is the possibility that maternity will become an option for all women, rather than a vocation they are trained for. The demand that maternity be an option rather than a social duty for women was a part of the free love debate which accompanied the early feminist movement. Today, the right to free contraception and abortion on demand is inscribed on the banners of every women's movement. What was denounced fifty years ago as a 'bourgeois demand', has at present been shown to have a genuine mass appeal. However, there is no reason why, within present institutions, genetic technology should not be used as a further instrument of women's oppression.

The institution of the family has been built up around the system of reproduction. Analysis of the family has been the pivot of the analysis of women's oppression.

Women and men are prepared for their different biological and social functions by the very process of 'humanisation' in the family. Differential development provides the psychological basis for women's oppression in all forms of social life, by programming the female to passivity, submission and emotional dependence, and the male to self-assertion, dominance and independence. This personality difference between men and women assures the male a privileged position in all forms of social life, quite apart from the privileges that result from particular forms of property.

The importance of this process of the formation of the individual human being has drawn the attention of the women's movement to Freud. As with Engels, the new feminists have enjoyed a polemical relationship to Freud, and their work is sometimes rejected outright. But a study of the structures of the unconscious and of the work of psychoanalysis is as important to the development of a scientific theory of women's oppression as is the study of the economy and the works of Engels and Marx. Another new feature of modern feminism is its analysis of ideology. American feminist groups started to discuss the visible manifestation of women's day-to-day oppression. This led to a critique of 'male chauvinism': the ideology of male domination. The way in which male chauvinism was discussed and expanded was in terms of individual personal experience. The possibility of using personal experience as the raw material for a re-analysis of women's condition was put into practice in what are usually called 'consciousness-raising' groups. Within these groups women explore their own oppression, and discuss male chauvinist practice, outside the groups they combat male chauvinism where they find it - in the home, in the streets, at work. But, of course, if the analysis of women's oppression remained at that level it would be as ideological as its enemy. What has even more recently emerged is the concept of 'sexism'.

What 'sexism' fundamentally involves is the complex unity of the four distinct levels of women's oppression - biology, the unconscious, the economy and ideology. It is a structure which exists in most known forms of society, although its form can vary between one society and another. The basic institutions of sexism are the family and the system of sexual differentiation which is produced by the socialisation process. This system of sexual differentiation confines women to a social position determined by their 'natural' biological function, by economic, ideological, and psychic means. The family reproduces this system from generation to generation and will continue to do so until women organise to abolish it.

Modern feminism insists, as did historic feminism, on the need for separate women's movements in order to combat women's specific oppression. This does not mean that these movements should not enter into alliance with other movements in order to achieve common goals. It is clear that the abolition of all forms of private property is a pre-condition for women's liberation, since women themselves are a form of private property.

Women therefore have an interest in uniting with revolutionary working class movements in order to abolish private property. But the abolition of private property does not automatically entail the abolition of male privilege and male domination which is the ultimate political aim of women's liberation. To achieve this a united women's movement is needed which mobilises women on the basis of their own oppression, and which is held together by the political solidarity of women - 'sisterhood' - capable of unlocking and overthrowing all the structures which imprison women.

TEACHING A GIRL ABOUT HERTZ IS TEACHING HER TO SAY YES

Before every new Hertz girl meets
her public, she has to learn to always
say Yes to a customer.
It's easy when you work for Hertz
because there's no limit to what
Hertz has to offer. In fact, it takes
us six weeks to fill her pretty head
with all the facts and figures.
We start off with the easy ones. .....

What we don't spell out in the book,
we know a Hertz girl can handle
naturally. We choose her because
she's the kind of girl who enjoys
solving all the little things that
don't seem so little at the time.

Yes, I'll phone your wife to tell her
you'll be late.
Yes, I'll find the briefcase you left
in the car.
Yes, I'll sew the button on your coat.

The next time you want to rent a car,
ask a Hertz girl. You'll see how well
she's learned her lessons.

(Advertisement in 'The Times', 12th
October 1972)

SECTION 3 : SOCIETY - STEPS IN ANALYSIS

A. The family

WHEN IS A HOUSE NOT A HOME?

Sue Crockford and Nan Fromer

(This piece appeared in 'Shrew', May 1971, an issue about the family, written, edited and produced by the Belsize Lane group of the London Women's Liberation Workshop)

Ask a small kid to draw a house. Not his or her house - a house. It'll be two storeys detached, with a smoking chimney and, if you're lucky, a garden, a very wide path and large flowers. How many smiling detached houses exist? are planned? are possible? How is it that our universal house is a dream impossible for the majority ever to realise.

Housing in Western society is designed and built for nuclear families, usually in the most economically viable way... for the builder that is, and for those who make profits, not for the family. It should be possible to share a lawn mower, a large freezer, bulk buy, between households. Few do. Your home may be the thickness of a thin wall away from your neighbour but you have to go through two front doors and a state of mind to get to each other. We live in the houses that are available. We adapt to their inflexibility. (When did you last remove a wall for a party or a meeting and put it back the next morning? - It's possible. It's even cheap, but it's not allowed: the building trade blocks any new housing scheme that involves too few basic units). These houses, rigid and barren in conception and design, condition the way we live, and then condition us to believe that the way we live is the basically desirable norm.

Think about adapting existing residential architecture for purposes other than housing nuclear families. How do you house an extended family without serious overcrowding? The largest housing units in the projected Highgate New Town, North London, have only four bedrooms, though the area to be rehoused is a working class district where 6 or 7 children to a family aren't uncommon. How about a commune? Well, things aren't desperate...yet. We still have the fag-end of Victorian and Edwardian terraces left in most towns; houses large enough originally for middle class family and servants and so sufficient today, given the money to adapt, for fairly large groups of people. But how much longer will such houses exist? Look around at what's taking place. How do you knock rooms together in high-rise flats? When did you last hear of a council house commune?

Our education is geared to answering other people's questions, not asking our own; to apply the detail to a tacitly-held concept of society. It teaches us to paint our world picture by predetermined numbers: to sew cushions or make bookshelves for a house, but not to study whether the existing housing is a Good Thing.

If the inhabitants of houses are woefully ill-equipped to ask larger questions about the way they live, the designers of those houses are equally limited. Who are they really building for?

Tom Woolley, a former President of the British Architectural Students' Association has written: 'Architecture has been recognised by some as a social science, but it still remains a professional activity...a respectable occupation for a privileged middle class. Its laborious indoctrinal rites (called education), lasting five years, usually make little attempt to give students an understanding of how society works... Architecture is practiced by people who become willing slaves of anyone or any organisation in a position to commission a building... (the architect) rarely understands the danger of his being in a position of making assumptions and decisions about other people's lives instead of allowing others to find their own self-expression'.

But the self-expression Woolley speaks about is difficult to find and encourage in a society so thoroughly conditioned to want what is best or most convenient for the maintenance of the system. He writes: 'It is pointless for architects to design buildings with partitions that can be moved, to permit freedom of expression, when our whole educational development is one that teaches us that we cannot control our environment. Most people would never dream of affecting the built environment, or of planting trees themselves on the barren piece of "keep off" grass outside their house. Not till kids in school can tear their building to bits every term and re-erect it to their own design can we see people really expressing themselves in their building'.

It's so easy to be conned. Along with the 1971 Census forms came a two-tone reassuring splurge on 'why this Census is so vital'. Well it's so that your friendly government can plan the future. (Of course it's planned.) 'How many new homes are needed?' the sheet asks. 'How many bedrooms? Where should they be built? How many existing homes can be improved? Needs vary from place to place - where there are mostly young families or more retired people. And we have to know what the picture will be in some years time'. Comforting, isn't it, to know that they care? However, the actual questions on the census form do not in any way give scope for people to express their particular needs or desires: they simply force the 'heads of households' who fill in the questionnaire to define the relationship between their housing and the assumed optimum: private sink, cooker, hot water supply, loo... If you leave it all to Them - the big boys, the government, the councils, the businessmen - when

122

will your needs ever be the priority? Of course the system needs changing, but who's going to do it? Houses are made up of small units: bricks, window frames, rafters. The 'housing problem' comprises smaller problems which are easier to grasp. Dissatisfaction with the details is a good starting point for dissatisfaction with the whole. It's easier to find the energy to deal with one specific Rachman landlord or yet another new block of flats with no play-space for the kids, than to find one's motivation for change in contemplation of Shelter's statistics of homeless families.

Who knows most about what it's like to live in the houses we've got? Women and children. Who better to define alternatives? To work effectively we should use our own experiences, and if we think about them our experiences can be pretty bad. Give me the child till the age of seven and I'll give you the man. If that child was reared by a lonely mother in a flat on the fourteenth floor and played in the gales among the stilts of the concrete giant he lived in, what kind of man will he be? Nobody's going to change things for us.

CHILD-REARING AND WOMEN'S LIBERATION

Rochelle P. Wortis

(This paper was read at the 1970 Women's Conference in
Oxford. The writer was at the time a member of the London
Women's Liberation Workshop. The paper is also available
as a pamphlet from Agitprop: see end of book for address)

A principal contradiction in society today is that women are
encouraged to have more socially useful and productive
roles while the restrictions which are imposed by the home
and family are maintained. 'Of course, we shall never be
wholly equal', writes Mrs Joyce Butler, member of Parliament for Wood Green, London. 'Whatever job we do outside
the home means we lead a double life, because whatever the
labour-saving devices or help we might be able to get, the
organisation of the home always comes back to us'. (Women's
Own Encyclopaedia, pull-out supplement, no. 8)

Modern psychology, with its emphasis on individual development, individual achievement and individual advancement,
has encouraged the isolation of the adult woman, particularly
the mother, and the domestication and subordination of females in society.

All observations and experiments made in the field of human
behaviour are designed to define, or suggest, causal mechanisms. But since final explanations often depend on many
factors - biological, biochemical, psychological, sociological
and historical processes - some of which are not fully understood or analysed, a lot of so-called explanation remains
on the assumptive, theoretical level.

John Bowlby, whose theories on child development have had
a major impact on the ideas popularly held about child-
rearing in society today, believes that 'for no other behavioural consequences, perhaps, are standards of appraisal in
man more clear-cut from the start, or more environmentally
stable. So stable indeed are they as a rule that for babies to
love mothers and mothers to love babies is taken for granted
as intrinsic to human nature'. (J. Bowlby, 'Attachment and
loss', London 1969) Bowlby's theories about the importance
of the biological mother have been sharply criticised by several workers in the fields of psychology, anthropology and
sociology. It is worthwhile, therefore, to examine some of
the assumptions popularly held today and to illustrate the
contradictory points of view.

Biology or cultural conditioning?

Margaret Mead has pointed out over and over again that the
conscious care of the infant is a cultural, not a biological
invention. Whether or not the mother is the principal figure
in the child's environment is a socio-cultural question, not

a biological one. In our society, the vast majority of women are conditioned to expect that the child-rearing function will be their individual responsibility.

Owing, to a large extent, to the influence of the psychoanalytic schools on the kinds of investigations which have been made in the field of child development, the 'biology is destiny' argument has been perpetuated. Doctors and psychologists actively encourage the belief that the biological mother must necessarily provide the major stimulation conditioning and emotional satisfaction which are considered essential for the child's development. Their logic goes something like this:

Observation 1: Mothers and infants, because of their biological tie during pregnancy and at birth, spend a large amount of time together.
Observation 2: This affects the subsequent development of the child.
Theory: The mother's consistent attention to the infant is vital for the child's healthy development.
Conclusion: Mothers must spend the vast proportion of their time with their babies.

An important step missing from such an argument is the observation of alternative patterns of child-rearing and the study of their consequences. In fact, alternative patterns have been studies, but what has been emphasised most in the popular literature are the experiences which seem to have led to gross deleterious effects. Furthermore, in a society in which 'mothering' is the principal mode of rearing children up to the age of at least three, any variant pattern which occurs (such as infants being raised by their fathers, or mothers allowing their infants to be placed in day-care centres while they work) is considered unusual. People who do these things are constantly reminded of the fact that it is just a poor substitute for the 'normal' pattern. This implies that they haven't a chance of equalling, let alone improving upon, the norm. As Barbara Wootton, the sociologist, wrote: 'so long as the study of the role of the father continues to be so much neglected as compared with that of the mother, no opinion on the subject can be regarded as more than purely speculative'. (B. Wootton, 'Social science and social pathology', London 1959)

Separation versus deprivation

The suggested harmful effects of mother-child separation (the Bowlby hypothesis) is a principal argument used to encourage women to stay at home with their babies for the first three years of life, at least. However, most of the studies of mother-child separation have been based on children in institutions who often suffer from inadequate environmental and human stimulation. Barbara Wootton, evaluating the work in this area, wrote: 'Nor has adequate information been produced about the reasons which led to the children studied being uprooted from their homes or about the conditions in which they lived before this happened. One can hardly assume that the boys and girls found in a children's home constitute a fair sample of the child population generally: something unusual either in themselves or their environment must have happened to account for their being deprived of ordinary family life'. The kinds of separation which seem to have produced dramatic effects in normal infants have been those which caused a break in the continuity of the child's physical and emotional experience. Positive alternatives to traumatic separation have not been sufficiently discussed or evaluated in the literature. Margaret Mead, however, has been an outspoken critic of Bowlby's maternal deprivation theory:

'At present the specific biological situation of the continuing relationship of the child to its biological mother and its need for care by human beings are being hopelessly confused in the growing insistance that child and biological mother, or mother surrogate, must never be separated, that all separation even for a few days is inevitably damaging, and that if long enough it does irreversible damage. This... is a new and subtle form of antifeminism in which men - under the guise of exalting the importance of maternity - are tying women more tightly to their children than has been thought necessary since the invention of bottle feeding and baby carriages. Actually, anthropological evidence gives no support at present to the value of such an accentuation of the tie between mother and child... On the contrary, cross-cultural studies suggest that adjustment is most facilitated if the child is cared for by many warm friendly people'. ('Some theoretical considerations on the problem of mother-child separation', American Journal of Orthopsychiatry, 1954, no. 24)

The evidence today suggests that the following factors are important for child development: consistent care, sensitivity of the adult in responding to the infant's needs, a stable environment, the characteristics of which the infant can learn to identify, continuity of experience within the infant's environment, and physical and intellectual stimulation, love and affection. We now know that the human infant acts on its social environment in a way which helps the adults who care for it to develop appropriate responses which will bring about the satisfaction of its needs. The infant, therefore, not only responds to social contact, it actively initiates social interaction and is capable of modifying the behaviour of the adult who cares for it.

Attachment to whom?

A study of the social attachment patterns of children in the first year of life by Schaffer and Emerson revealed that children form strong attachments to their fathers as well as their mothers, and to other individuals as well. ('The development of social attachments in infancy', 1964) They concluded that there was no evidence for the assumption that attachments must be confined to only one object, the mother, nor that all other attachments are subsidiary to the mother-infant bond. In fact, Schaffer and Emerson point out that while the mother tends to be present in the child's environment for most of the time, this does not guarantee that she will provide the quantity and quality of stimulation which is necessary for optimal child development. They concluded: 'Whom an infant chooses as his attachment object and how many objects he selects depends, we believe, primarily on the nature of the social setting in which he is reared and not on some intrinsic characteristic of the attachment function itself... To focus one's enquiry on the child's relationship with the mother alone would therefore give a misleading impression of the attachment function... In certain societies multiple object attachments are the norm from the first year on: the relevant stimuli which evoke attachment behaviour are offered by a number of individuals and not exclusively one person, and a much more diversified system of attachments is thus fostered in the infant'.

Particularly absent from the psychological literature is an analysis of infants' responses to their fathers, or to men in general. We do not know the effects of masculine attention and male child-rearing. Nobody seems to want to know, either. How can one assume the natural superiority of women as socialisers of children when we do not know the effects - and think how positive they might be - of more male interaction with the infant at all levels of the socialisation process?

The home

We are taught today that the best environment for the growth and development of a healthy child is provided within the individual home. The home environment, however, is socially sterile because mobility, outside stimulation, exchange of ideas and socially productive relationships are severely limited there. The home, therefore, is physically restrictive and, for many women, is felt to be socially restrictive as well. In the home one's personal and economic tensions and problems are most pronounced. These factors and experiences have a profound effect on the mother and child confined to the home, and are a principal influence on the physical, intellectual and social development of children coming from different social class backgrounds. Recognising this, some investigators have begun to encourage entry into day nurseries at much earlier ages than is customary. While these efforts were, at first, strongly criticised by workers in the field, the findings were very encouraging: children from lower-class families who were enrolled in a day-care centre from about the age of one did not differ from home-reared children in the strength of attachment to their mothers. Likewise, mothers of day-care infants did not show any differences from home-mothers in intensity of attachment to their infants. The study showed that while the home-reared group showed a decline in IQ at 30 months, the day-care infants showed an increase in developmental level. (Caldwell, Wright, Honig & Tannebaum, 'Infant day care & attachment', American Journal of Orthopsychiatry, 1970, no. 30)

While, for many women, caring for a young baby is a rewarding and happy experience, it is also a monotonous and isolating one. There is the overwhelming feeling of being cut off from the outside world. In Hannah Gavron's study of young mothers in London ('The captive wife', London 1966) both middle-class and working-class wives expressed very ambivalent feelings: 'They want to work, feel curiously functionless when not working, but at the same time they sense their great responsibilities toward the children. In both groups those who were at home have the children as their main reason for being there'.

Working mothers

Many women still feel that it would be wrong to go out to work because they have been led to believe that it would be harmful to the infant, even under circumstances in which adequate child-care facilities, such as day-nurseries, were being provided. However, studies of the children of working mothers have not demonstrated systematic differences in behavioural, physical and mental development from children who are at home all the time. (S. Yudkin and A. Holme, 'Working mothers and their children', London 1963)

The real problem for the working mother, that which affects her own personal well-being, and therefore her relationship to her family and friends, is whether the work experience is a worthwhile one, measured in terms of economic gain, socially productive work, personal fulfilment, social contact or numerous other factors. Another problem is that of bearing the responsibility for the organisation of the home and arrangements for the children, when she also has a job.

Robert and Rhona Rapoport, a social anthropologist and a sociologist-psychoanalyst respectively, have been surveying the problems of professional, middle-class couples who both work - the 'dual-career families', as they call them. They have found that 'for the woman in particular there is "emotional overload"! Apart from the fact that her life is terribly involved in arrangements and making everything work, there is the constant anxiety of being seen as different, of open or implied criticism of her stepping out of the traditional "feminine role", even hostility... ' A good deal has been talked about 'role identification' and sexual identity (ie of the boy with the father and the girl with the mother) and, the

Rapoports say, a good deal of it has been nonsense. They believe that children 'identify with bits of parents and internalise the relationship'. If a child knows his father does not consider it undignified to do the washing-up, he is unlikely to worry about it or feel confused... The Rapoports take the argument one step further. Male and female activities are not 'constants', they say, and have varied from society to society and age to age. 'We reject the argument that women have always performed the household activities and men the work activities as "expressive" of nature.' ('The Guardian', 11 December 1969)

It seems significant to me, looking back on the history of women's struggles for emancipation, that women demand of themselves that they should be able to fill traditionally masculine roles but never demand of men that they should begin to share with women the traditional feminine roles. What an underestimation this is of the importance of children: to deprive them of the opportunity of interacting equally with men as with women; what an underestimation of the importance of children's early experiences, of early socialisation and education!

If the undervaluation of women in society is to end, we must begin at the beginning, by a more equitable distribution of labour around the child-rearing function and the home. Women will continue to bear children and many women will continue to breast-feed their infants. Both of these processes biologically exclude men from participating. However, both take up a relatively small percentage of the total amount of time that is actually spent in interaction with the infant, both on a day to day basis and in terms of the whole period of the infant's development. Men can and should begin to take a more active part in the affective and cognitive interaction with infants than they have done until now. This could be encouraged through educational networks and the social services. First, as in Sweden, boys and girls should be educated equally, by preparing them equally for their sexual and parental functions and by providing equal educational training, from babycare to mechanics and mathematics. Books which differentiate women's roles from men's should be removed from the educational institutions. The competitive market for consumer products which reinforce sex-differentiated buying (eg construction toys for boys and dolls for girls) must be abolished. Paid parental leave for men, and greater opportunities for fathers to participate in the care of newborns is essential. Full-time nurseries at work places, with extra time off for parents to be with their children, and with parents participating in the decisions affecting the organisation and running of the nurseries, are essential. However, unless such nurseries are established at men's work-places and unless they are staffed by men as well as women, the responsibility for the socialisation of children will continue to fall upon women and they will continue to feel that other social responsibilities are not within their domain. This was apparently the experience of women in the kibbutzim in Israel in which, at the beginning, women were encouraged to share the heavy physical work with men, but men were not similarly encouraged to share in the care of children. As a result, many women became overburdened with the strain of both responsibilities and gradually dropped out of productive branches.

How can some of these alternatives be instituted? Are any alternative programmes possible within the present society? Individual cases already exist. Some men do share home responsibilities with their wives. We know of the occasional communal living experiment in several countries. But how can these 'unique' experiments be broadened so that more people can benefit from the results? We cannot wait for the revolution before we change our lives, for surely changing our lives now is part of the revolutionary process.

The creation of alternative patterns of child-rearing, when it involves major changes from what has gone before, is as much a political problem as an educational or psycho-social one. For people to attempt alternatives within this society, they must feel the necessity for change and feel that they are not alone in their efforts to create it. People do not attempt to create even small changes in their lives if they lack the confidence or the ability or the power to make them work. Single individuals or couples cannot do this.

It seems to me that people who share common experiences - eg people living in the same community or housing estate, students at university, men and women in factories, secretaries and clerks in offices, employees in hospitals - must get together and work out ways of sharing the responsibility of caring for their infants and pre-school children by establishing communal nurseries for them and by participating directly in organising and running these nurseries.

We are socially interdependent beings. If existing society does not meet our needs, we must act together to change it. To do so we have to set long-term goals and short-term or transitional goals. A long-term goal, such as the establishment of a socialist society which fully meets people's needs, cannot come about without full participation by large numbers of people in short-term programmes through which we learn the importance of working together for a common aim. Given that one transitional goal is the establishment of non-profit, people-controlled, group child-care, we must begin by challenging existing inadequate practices such as the separation of work from community and home life. Some workers will want their employers to provide free space for nurseries and time off work to discuss ways of organising them. Others will want landlords, universities and companies to provide free space for community programmes, including child-care. These demands are not only legitimate but essential as a first step towards the liberation of all women and all people.

130

NURSERIES

Jane Cullen

(Written by a member of Socialist Women's group, West
London, and presented at a Socialist Woman conference,
1971. For a full analysis of the arrangements mothers
make for their children, see 'Working mothers and their
children', by Simon Yudkin and Anthea Holme)

51% of adult women are working: two-thirds of these, including part-timers, are married. More than half are mothers of children under sixteen; 20% of these mothers have
children under five.

There are two categories of care for the under-fives of
working mothers, individual and group care. Grandmother
is the most popular 'mother substitute'. This arrangement
is unsatisfactory both for the child and the grand-parent.
The grandmother who has probably spent much of her life
bringing up her own children, has to continue this 'child-
orientation', when she could be using her retirement to
broaden her own interests via further education or taking a
job. Being cooped up with an elderly person all day is no
substitute for the social contact and intellectual stimulation
a child would get at nursery school.

The father cares for the children when the mother has a
job which does not coincide with his working hours. Because
the family cannot afford to pay for child-care facilities or
they are just not available, the mother is forced to take evening or night work: the parents get no time together and
the mother has to find time to sleep when she can during
the day.

A neighbour or friend is usually used by mothers who work
full-time and there is mostly a definite monetary arrangement. Very few mothers use paid help to care for the child,
the majority of working mothers being unable to afford it.

There are less than 500 state nursery schools in Britain,
having places for 24, 000 children aged between two and
four. The total of children in this age-group is $2\frac{1}{2}$ million.
A child is capable of reaching at least half its intellectual
capacity before the age of five - only 10% are being given a
chance to develop that potential. The provision of nursery
facilities would also release the mother from the isolation
of the home to develop her full human potential, to take a
job or further education. Capitalism was able to provide
these facilities in the second world war, when the labour of
women was needed, but it was provided purely to release
women for use as production units. The women had no control over it and it was withdrawn as quickly as it had been
provided.

Factory nurseries

There is no doubt that if factories were to provide nursery facilities, they would be used to keep wages low and to induce women to accept bad conditions. Women would be reluctant to exchange jobs, as this would mean either losing the nursery facilities or changing the child's nursery, which could prove harmful to its development. Nurseries would only be provided in factories where women workers were predominantly employed, thus continuing the child-orientation of women. Also, a factory would not be a suitable environment for a child to spend the first few years of its life in.

Nurseries must be small, local units, so that there is one within reach of every family: they must be run by trained staff (men and women) but controlled by the community. There must be a place available at any time (ie open 24 hours a day) for every child.

(Val Charlton, 'Red Rag')

MORE THAN MINDING

'Shrew'

(This piece appeared in the March 1971 issue of 'Shrew', written, edited and produced by the Tufnell Park group of the London Women's Liberation Workshop)

The Women's Liberation Movement in Britain, as in the United States, is demanding 24 hour day care for children. Is it enough simply to make this demand? Shouldn't we also be making explicit and constructive statements about the kind of care we want and about the quality of relationships between adults and children. Our group has spent several months trying to set up a pre-school play group in our locality. We have not yet succeeded in our aims. Nevertheless, work on this project so far has raised many questions about child-care facilities which we hope can contribute to what should be an ongoing process of discussion and action to find alternatives to our present situation.

Why a play group?

Our community, Tufnell Park, is a densely populated residential area of North London. It is largely working class and there are a number of council estates within the area. The existing facilities for children under five are inadequate. More likely than not, a child of three will have to wait at least a year for a place. Given this situation, we chose to try to set up a play group because it would be an immediate and concrete way to break down some of the isolation experienced by mothers and young children alike: to provide children with stimulating play and to relieve at least some mothers of some of the strain imposed by coping with young children on their own in their own homes. We felt too that a play group was a constructive way to reach women who would otherwise remain strangers to us, and that a play group had the potential for forging meaningful relationships among women in the community.

We committed ourselves to the idea that the play group must directly involve the mothers and fathers of the children who attended the group. Parent participation is the accepted practice in all pre-school play groups organised along the lines suggested by the Pre-school Play Groups Association. Initially we were planning to affiliate ourselves to this organisation, largely to facilitate recognition for a local grant.

How then does our identity as members of Women's Lib. relate to the setting up and running of this kind of play group? We wanted to involve local women, whom we assume are not familiar with the ideas of the Movement, in an activity over which they would have some real control. We felt that it should be made clear to mothers - and fathers -

who wished their children to come to the play group, that it was <u>their</u> play group - a collective effort; that it was not being organised and run for them but by them and that without their involvement it could not exist. Involvement would mean making policy decisions, taking on administrative responsibilities and helping out on a rota system in the day to day running of the group. A local play group could provide an opportunity for a community facility to be created, maintained and used by the same people.

We hoped that the relationships we established with other women through the play group would enable us to communicate the ideas of women's liberation. For us, women's liberation provided the group solidarity and confidence necessary to initiate the project. For other women we wanted the play group experience to give them the confidence and desire to consider some of the ideas we have as members of Women's Liberation.

Changing accepted attitudes and relationships

We wanted to work towards breaking down the total identification of women with child-care. Toward this end we agreed to make a concerted effort to involve fathers, other relatives and any other men and women to participate in the running of the play group.

In all ways possible, we wanted to discourage the development of a hierarchical pattern of relationships. For example, among the adults we were against forming any committees as such or having positions of president, secretary, etc. Realistically though, to avoid total chaos, certain duties would have to be the responsibility of a few individuals rather than all, especially perhaps with regard to financial matters.

The children's freedom to express themselves was of course among our major concerns. Any adult figures present should function primarily to provide opportunities to preserve the freedom of each child to explore things and relationships. Adults is a play group are there to provide a stimulus, to care for children's physical needs, to respond to and help children to carry through ideas.

Adults then must help to preserve a very special kind of order, but in this play group we did not want adults to be seen as authority figures. We wanted this play group to break down not to reinforce the power relationships that exist in our society. In trying to implement these ideas, we felt it would be necessary to experiment with the ratio of adults to children at any given session. Too many adults could be overbearing and too few might provide excuses for restricting and controlling children in order to cope with them.

Given these views and the desirability of developing a truly

134

communal spirit of child care, we thought a great deal about the whole question of having a paid supervisor, who would be a constant adult figure in the playgroup, in addition to other adults who would be in the playgroup on a rota system. Ideally the playgroup would be run cooperatively so that the role of supervisor would be redundant.

Some of us felt strongly committed to the idea that a const- and adult figure would be both unnecessary and undesirable because among other things it would reinforce dependency on a parent substitute when we should be giving children a chance to relate equally to a number of adults. Others of us feared that children would be too insecure without a constant adult figure. We could never unanimously agree on this highly complex issue.

What we did agree on in the end was that our ideal structure of relationships required feelings of mutual commitment, solidarity and trust among the adults concerned. Such feelings could of course be an outcome of participation in running the play-group. Initially we would be far from having this situation. We agreed to have a supervisor.

At another level entirely, we needed a supervisor to reassure those who might provide us with premises that we were responsible' and to qualify for recognition which is the passport to getting money. If we were successful in getting the kind of supervisor we wanted, someone who shared our views, we would have found a reasonable compromise.

Clearly, the more links one has with the established system the more formal the structure of the activity has to be. Unless it is possible to find space and equipment and money without appealing to the 'authorities' and at the same time to satisfy the laws about the care of children, any efforts at really radical change are bound to be diluted. But a start has to be made somewhere and we feel that the efforts of locally based women's liberation groups like ours can be a beginning.

Action

The following is a resume of the actions we took.

May	Visited other playgroups and were much encouraged
June	Wrote letters to GLC and Islington Council requesting use of empty property. They refused. Approached GLC councillors for help and received in return more refusals from GLC. Islington Council told us we would be eligible for a grant if we got a playgroup going
July	Continued to solicit Council for space. Investigated local halls and approached local vicar for church hall. He was enthusiastic
August	Church hall was approved by local authorities. Vicar began to have doubts about parent

	participation and low fees proposed ($37\frac{1}{2}$p per week). Meeting arranged between PPA, us and vicar in attempt to gain his support
September/ October	Vicar finally refused us and decided to run his own playgroup with fees of £1.00 per week
November	Continued to search for premises, including an appeal through articles and letter in local press, with no success

We started by approaching the council because we felt, and still do, that properties acquired with public funds, even if earmarked for ultimate demolition or development, should be used to house community activities. We opted for the church hall as a last resort.

In the beginning we considered that our first priority was finding a place where the playgroup could be held. We wanted to go out into the community and talk to people about setting up a playgroup with something in hand. This was because of the distance we felt existed between us and the community.

Our plans for a playgroup in our immediate area now seem difficult to implement. Through trying to evaluate our experience we have changed our minds about what steps to take first. If we had talked with local people first they too would have experienced the frustrations of working through the establishment. Active involvement of the community from the start, we now realise, is essential for real understanding and participation in any project. Had we committed more local people before looking for space we would now be in a position of greater strength politically.

The question of alternatives

The playgroup we hoped to set up would not meet the needs of working mothers, nor could it function to free non-working mothers for very long periods of time. We would like to have been able to do both these things, but initially at least we had to accept the limitations imposed on us by lack of space and time and energy in our group. We did however think that starting on a relatively small scale we might eventually set up some facilities for working mothers.

Many women's liberationists would question our approach to the problem of child care: why not push for more state-supported and run nurseries instead of using valuable time and energy to set up a playgroup which continues to commit women to the concern about child care? But will our problems be solved merely by more money being spent on day care for children, and what attitudes will the staff of these institutions have? Money alone will not ensure anything but space and equipment. If we can concentrate our efforts on showing that child care is genuinely everybody's responsibility and that play centres and playgroups are provided because children need and enjoy the company of both children and adults, we shall be approaching the problem from the right side.

We come face to face here with what women's liberation is about and what kinds of solutions we should be seeking. Women's liberation is not only about getting away from things - in this instance the children whose need for care confines us to the home and can inhibit our existence and development as people in our own right. Women's liberation is perhaps more importantly about coming together. One does not want to release women as isolated units from the care of children. One wants to bring women and men together to care for children and for each other in new ways. Setting up a local playgroup which does involve parents and which also seeks to encourage others to join in the care of children is one way of bringing together people who otherwise would not meet each other and who might never know at first hand what women's liberation is about. Hopefully, together we might begin to see that there are alternatives to the way in which we live.

THE ROLE OF THE NUCLEAR FAMILY IN THE OPPRESSION OF WOMEN

Sue Sharpe

(This article was written for the 'New Edinburgh Review' issue on women, published in Summer 1972. Sue Sharpe is a member of the London Women's Liberation Workshop)

Constituting our most fundamental social institution, the family has been around for as long as history. While in primitive and less developed societies a more extended form is found, the nuclear unit, generally consisting of husband, wife and children, is a feature seemingly characteristic of modern industrialised countries, whose systems of production are more or less capitalistic. Such coincidence is no accident, since the functioning of any society depends on the successful fulfilment of its needs and demands. These mainly involve production for self-survival and reproduction for species-survival. As Engels found in his study on the family: 'The social institutions under which the people of a definite historical epoch and a definite country live are conditioned by both kinds of production: by the stage of development of labour on the one hand, and of the family on the other'. (F. Engels, preface to 'The origin of the family', 1884)

The nuclear family is the form which has emerged to complement the running of society in its present state. There is no reason why it should not change or be changed if circumstances alter the society's demands upon it. Indeed, the nuclear form still contains some pre-capitalist elements, such as the sometimes feudal-like aspects of the husband-wife relationship, which perform useful functions now, but can accommodate changes. It is my purpose to show how this family form contributes to the oppression of the women within it. To understand this more fully, it is first necessary to examine both its economic and ideological functions, before looking specifically at women's roles in these processes.

With social and economic change, with industrialisation and urbanisation, the originally rural-based extended family became fragmented into the small units familiar to us today. A parallel loss in functions took place, for which the state became responsible. These included education and social welfare, with which the small family could no longer adequately cope, now that a consistent wage determined survival. Two major functions however remained. The first is to maintain and sustain the labour force. This subsumes essential operations such as the provision of a socially approved place for reproduction, the early socialisation and care of children, and a repository for the emotions, feelings and intimacies inappropriate outside the family. By so doing, the family in fact constitutes a subordinate mode of production in society, producing and maintaining the present and future elements of labour essential for economic production.

The second function in present-day society is to provide an economic unit of consumption for the products of capitalism. This depends on the continuing privatisation of the family unit, combined with an ideology of acquisitiveness and competition. Each family wants to equip itself with possessions that are supposed to make life easier and more enjoyable and will show their relative affluence. Aspirations to accumulate such commodities as televisions, washing-machines, stereos, cars, etc are repeated in every single family, providing the immense consumer market necessary for this production. Advertising gives the poor housewife the full works, playing on her desire to prove herself a 'good Mum' and to give her children what they deserve - from whiter-than-whites to the right breakfast cereal. Husbands are also pumped full of ideas on what they ought to be able to give their wives. Families feel the need to put themselves up for social comparison one with another. If they were encouraged to do things more collectively, to reject ideas of isolated autonomy, large holes would appear in company profits and the commodity system would sag at the knees. The preservation of the family in its nuclear form is obviously necessary to preserve this system, geared as it is towards needs of production, rather than being organised in the interests of human beings. Despite outward anxiety about the unity of the family, if the needs of production demand shift-work or mobilisation, disruptive effects on family life are put to one side.

If we look at the family as a subordinate mode of production, then within it women provide the necessary labour. They are also seen generally as subordinate to men, an ideology reinforced and believed by both sexes. With the erosion of family functions, women have suffered losses as well, and now mainly involve themselves in caring for their home, husband and children. Women mean love and the home, while men stand for work and the external world. As Sheila Rowbotham says, 'Separation of production for use and production for exchange, the physical distance between the place of consumption and the place of production, and the social division of labour between men and women mean that the commodity system is as dependent on women's work in the home as on the exploitation of labour outside'. (Sheila Rowbotham, 'Women, resistance and revolution', London 1972)

Women provide the intimate personal relationships which are not sanctioned in the work organisation, although the system itself is dependent on the maintenance of this emotional outlet. Women are made synonymous with softness and tenderness, love and care - something you are glad to come home from work to.

It is now time to look more specifically at women working, both in the family and outside. A woman at home is curiously regarded as one who 'doesn't work', because what she does

is not included in prevailing concepts of 'real work'. Yet, if
there are small children to care for, some women work as
many as 80 hours a week. The relationships between men,
women and work are such that in general a man is forced to
rely on his wife's work at home in order to earn a living
wage. This is especially relevant to the working classes,
who after all make up nearly 70% of the population of this
country. Man is considered as the natural breadwinner, and
has history to support him. Why think any different? However
'the labour of the worker and his wife is appropriated, the
one directly and the other indirectly by capital, whilst only
that portion of their labour power is paid (through the man)
which is required to maintain them and perpetuate their
labouring power at the customary standard of living established in the process of class struggle'. (Jean Gardiner,
'The economic roots of women's liberation', paper given
at I. S. Women's Conference, 1970)

Even the housewife does not regard herself as doing recognised work, although she is asked to become, without choice
and unpaid, cook, laundress, housemaid, lover, psychiatrist
and many other roles. It is no wonder that some women cannot fall naturally and efficiently into these roles, but sad
that society can make them feel so guilty about it. Housewives don't 'go out to work' - home is work and work is
home - no divisions between place of work and leisure.
Housework is mainly done during the day, when the husband
does not see it, but he will notice if it is left undone. It becomes repititious, unceasing and all-devouring. There are no
wages, unions or strike opportunities. How then can so many
women put up with this, when similar conditions outside
would never be tolerated? To find an answer, we must look
to conditioning and ideology. Little girls, even growing up
in the freest home environment learn from family and from
society what constitutes the female ideal stereotype. They
should aspire to be submissive, fragile, non-competitive,
emotional and sentimental; they are naturally incompetent
and incapable of understanding anything mechanical, and
have a capacity for long, boring, monotonous tasks - in fact
the ideal characteristics for housework and mother-care.
The status quo can therefore be fully accepted and an economic function served in stabilising the family unit.

What are the consequences of such sustained work in the
home? A woman frequently sinks her identity into that of her
man, becoming a mirror image of his successes and failures
and a receptacle for his joys, sorrows and angers. Her emphasis is on love: she is dependent on her family loving her,
and on giving her love to them. Without this she is no-one.
The husband goes to work, where he takes on a different
role. At home, his wife may find herself wondering if she
really exists at all outside her family. Her own work is
private and unsupervised and therefore has the illusion of
freedom. This attractive feature is really only her isolation,

140

and it is hard for her to achieve any kind of group values, any kind of collective awareness with others, of the oppression of her position.

There are certain ways to aid coping with the situation, such as developing minor illnesses, nervous complaints and so on, which are remedied with tranquillizers, sleeping pills, or a quick drink to keep going. 'Mother's little helpers' have performed their silent functions only too long. Living conditions also often aggravate the situation and for example tower-block life, day in day out, has been shown to have a deteriorating effect on mental health.

Housework may also serve a function in maintaining the family's self-respect, and this may be reflected in the rituals performed. A tendency to become excessively houseproud may just be a strategy developed in order to cope. The idea of indispensability is also very important, and frequently women give their lives (as individuals) to their families. It is not impossible to see trends such as baking your own bread etc as a reaction to technology's invasion of the kitchen, which threatens to devalue the skills and talents originally involved. Women can thus objectively be seen as occupying a very oppressed position inside the family. More subjective awareness is however much harder to achieve, since it questions the assumptions on which they have based most of their lives.

Moving on to women at work outside, we find that the conditions and ideology which keep them at home also underlie their oppression and exploitation in the productive world. Although conditioned to their 'rightful place', the development of time-saving consumer products such as ready-to-cook food, washing machines etc, plus the combination of earlier marriage and more efficient contraception have meant that women can accommodate some outside work. At the same time, commodity production has expanded and new sorts of jobs have been created. Women have become an increasingly integral part of this production, contributing towards further expansion as well as increasing their family income. There is however a large time-lag between such technological advance and accompanying ideology. The family and housework continue to be the woman's domain, but its non-recognition as a job implies also the non-recognition that working wives are actually coping with a double load. In Britain, a parallel expansion of nursery facilities has not occurred, and although more men now give a hand with chores, it remains assumed that it is still the wife's work that they help to do.

Employers, too, frequently regard women as mere temporary labour, and consider that they should be thought lucky to have the opportunity to earn some money for themselves. They can then be used as a surplus labour force, to be employed or laid off at will. The belief that work is of secondary importance (to a family) for a woman serves to justify giving them the lowest jobs at the lowest pay, and for their acceptance of these conditions. Women will not usually bother to organise collectively at work, since home is their true place. Therefore some trade unionists see them as a threat to the stability of their unions. Consequently women remain completely unprotected against exploitation and may even condone it if they believe strongly enough in their own inferiority.

Just looking at the nature of work normally regarded as 'women's work' shows us that these are often large-scale expansions of household tasks. For example, the major industries involved are textile and clothing, food and catering. Other work includes nursing, teaching, clerical and secretarial. Teaching and the social welfare type of jobs are well thought of but notoriously underpaid, this being quite socially acceptable whilst predominantly women are employed. Secretaries often take on extra duties looking after the boss, running errands and doing his shopping. A job little publicised but well exploited is night-cleaning, in which the women are very dependent on the money from their jobs and the employers know it. (See the last section in this book)

The belief that women are naturally suited to dull and monotonous tasks is also made use of in their employment. This nonsense helps to justify giving them such jobs. However, it is more often the case that routine work has to be taken on not because a woman is particularly stupid, but because she does not want two responsibility loads, work and family. A P.I.B. report (April 1971) showed that 25% of working women (in their sample) were sole providers for their families, 20% earned less than £14 per week, and 3% were at subsistence level. As long as both employers and women themselves believe they are an inferior work-force due to their primary attachment to their families, their labour will be exploited.

While observing the oppression that seems to lie concealed in the enveloping folds of family life, and questioning certain beliefs, we may as well include the question of motherhood. We could look at the assumption that women are not properly fulfilled unless they have children, now that there are no longer any natural threats to human survival. However what I am more concerned with is the bolstering belief in mother-attachment. It comes complete with partner, maternal deprivation, which is itself kitted out with delinquency effects and personality defects. Psychologists, sociologists, doctors and many others have contributed towards belief in the necessity for strong mother-child attachment. Condemned is the mother who shirks her duties while her children are yet young, even if she is just trying to make ends meet. The first major person to study and expound this theory was John Bowlby, who as early as 1947 was saying: 'It appears that there is a very strong case indeed for believing that prolonged separation of a child from his mother (or mother substitute) during the first five years of life stands foremost among the causes of delinquent character development and persistent misbehaviour'. ('44 juvenile thieves', London 1947)

His conclusions have had a widespread effect ever since. Based as they were upon children in residential nurseries, they provided more a study of institutionalisation than of maternal deprivation. Research in the area has continued, producing results both for and against, and ending in controversial uncertainty. Grygier et al, in a review of research, question the whole mode of research. ('Parental deprivation: a study of delinquent children', British Journal of Criminology, 1969, vol. 9, no. 3) It seems that evidence not supporting the theory does not find a willing ear - it would provide too great a threat to the social order. Similarly the parental role is under-researched since it would be too disruptive to discover that fathers could fill an equally demanding role. Women do fulfil an important function by providing the most economically stable way of bringing up a child in its dependent years. It is therefore necessary that they believe wholeheartedly in their role.

Out of such ideology the working mum has been given a bad name, and the burden of responsibility for her child's later development hung like a millstone around her conscience. Despite the lack of any consistent supporting evidence, beliefs in the coincidence of maternal employment and neglect persist. It would seem more relevant to study the subject at a more individual level, instead of making meaningless generalisations. As Siegal and Haas conclude: '... it is our impression that the way a woman relates herself ideologically to the world of work and to the world of motherhood is centrally significant in the woman's identity and in her relations with her family'. ('The working mother: a review of research', Child Development, 1963, no. 34) For example, other research has suggested that effects on child-rearing are more positive if a mother is satisfied rather than dissatisfied, regardless of whether she is working or not. (M. R. Yarrow, 'Maternal employment and childrearing', in 'Children', 1961, no. 8)

Without denying the importance of early life experiences for the child, it is obvious that it is the relative isolation of the family unit which puts the mother-child bond into its primary position. But it is necessary for the running of the present system of production that both men and women believe in it and act on it. The lack of agreement in the evidence for regarding mother only as the critical character leads to at least consideration of the possibilities and implications of alternatives. As Lee Comer concludes in her article, which well covers this subject: 'Mothers are no more essential to their children than are fathers, grandmothers and indeed anyone else who loves them with the right kind of care and understanding'. ('The myth of motherhood', London 1971)

Looking back over women's involvement in the nuclear family, it can be seen like an interlocking jigsaw of conditions covered and perpetuated by a pattern of assumptions and beliefs which keep it in stable equilibrium. This produces the least disruption of social order and provides the most efficient utilisation of the area of reproduction. The apparent optimum conditions for production are realised, but at the expense of the realisation of human beings. The picture produced can be outlined, and I hope that if it has not done so already, the role of the nuclear unit in providing a source of oppression will become clearer.

A society run under a capitalist system of production needs a mass healthy and reasonably educated labour force. This labour force is produced and maintained within the family, where a woman cares for her husband and children, receiving her keep indirectly through her husband's wages. It is convenient and cheap for the state that children be reared and educated (including payment for education) in the confines of the family. Women, on marriage, become in a sense and for some legal aspects the property of their husbands. Children become their responsibility, and are similarly 'possessed'. Women themselves are conditioned from an early age, learning their roles as wives and mothers. Their primary purpose is to marry, bear children, and care for the family. Models are expounded in all available media, especially women's magazines. Work is generally seen as being of secondary importance, only reaching significance if marriage does not occur. Women are prepared for their places in the subordinate mode of production. They accept their oppression at home, and if working outside as well are sustained in the knowledge of their indispensability to their families and their expendability at work. They accept as justified their lower pay scales and less secure job agreements, and therefore provide cheap surplus labour. Women can thereby become their own worst enemies, allowing themselves to be blackmailed by their own images of love, tenderness and sentimentality. The sad thing is that at present the family is conceived as the only place where human emotions can be contained, and so anything appearing to devalue this aspect is seen as a potential threat. Women therefore often can only see their oppression through a veil of protective misconceptions, preferring to stand aside and laugh with the media at women's liberation protagonists, who seem to be trying to attack and demolish the very essence of their lives.

The nuclear family unit, then, by the confines of its structure, the isolation of its position, and its surrounding ideologies, does oppress women, whether or not they are able to recognise it as such. And it is frequently the case that radicals, seeing how efficiently the family bolsters the status quo, immediately recommend its abolition. As alternatives, ideas about communities run on more collective lines are voiced, within which resources are pooled and people have more freedom and control over their own lives. I shall not be attempting to go into further detail about alternatives here, as I do not feel confident enough to be more than vaguely speculative, although others may be more equipped.

Instead, it seems equally relevant to examine more thoroughly the potential for change and the possible implications under the present system. It is reasonable to suppose that conditions within the same system may change in such a way as to require an altered form and ideology of family. Changing demands for labour power could necessitate quite a radical reformulation of structure and beliefs. To illustrate, we could take an increase in demand for educated labour, already indicated in a P.E.P. report (1971). Today, women constitute the largest untapped source of educated labour. In order to draw them into the labour market, however, the picture pattern on the 'jigsaw' described earlier must be changed to include justifications for these women to leave their families for work. Disruption of the nuclear family could happen if production needs demanded it. Ideology can be altered and employers can provide nursery and other facilities if they think that it will indirectly benefit them. The point to be noted here is that changes sought in the family and the work situation to relieve women's oppression could be quite easily instituted within the same oppressive system. It is also very important to examine the effects of such changes on different classes separately. In this case, where educated women are required, changes are sanctioned which will predominantly attract the middle-class woman back to work. The present government is even prepared (according to the same report) to use the more extremist groups, ie Women's Liberation, as their ideology-exploding dynamite. Working-class women however need not be affected at all by this and may even find that increasing labour at higher levels results in a decreasing demand at the unskilled level and therefore further accentuates the role of working-class women as a surplus labour force. This could happen in a subtle enough way to kid liberationists that they have won a victory, while the ruling class, the owners of production, laugh behind their sleeves and watch their profit margins rise. Another example may be drawn for working-class women from another angle. It may be found that successful campaigning for the provision of nursery facilities from employers of mass female labour leads also to a greater dependence on the employers for these services. This could render the women more accessible to manipulation and exploitation, and the children themselves open to conditioning on a grand scale.

Such speculation may seem ridiculous to some people, but these are definite possibilities that should be allowed for. In demonstrating women's oppression in the family and calling for its end, we must ensure that what is demanded really changes the oppressive interlocking structure of our 'jigsaw'. It is not enough just to replace the picture that covers it.

SEX-ROLE LEARNING: A STUDY OF INFANT READERS

(Written for the book by the Northern Women's Groups
Education study group)

We often talk of men's and women's attitudes and roles in
society as having been 'culturally determined', but where
does the process take place? Where does it start?

School is the child's first important experience outside the
home, so it seems possible that the determining of a child's
future sexual role may be greatly influenced there. A large
part of the first two or three years in school will be taken
up with working through one of half a dozen popular reading
schemes. These reading books consist of a series of domestic scenes and incidents, which are supposed to relate to
the child's own environment. The 'Laydbird' scheme, for
example, claims to 'embrace... the natural interests and
activities of happy children'. (Introduction to all 'Ladybird'
books) Now, do these books contain any sexual bias, and if
so, is it presented in such a way that a child's future attitudes could be affected or even determined? To answer this,
we must examine, in some detail, the sort of life reading-
book children lead.

Reading through these graded series, it soon becomes obvious that the reading-book children live in a world untouched by any of the harsher realities of life. For example, in
the 'Ladybird' books it is always summer - except when it
is Christmas. This means that Peter and Jane, a brother
and sister of about the same age, are nearly always free to
play with their huge selection of expensive toys in a garden
where rolling lawns and deep herbaceous borders are surrounded by a mellow brick wall. The garden grows without
the aid of man (or at any rate, not Mummy or Daddy). Down
the crazy paving is Daddy's shed where he stores rosy app-
les and a few bunches of onions; he also has a carpenter's
bench where Peter works, building models and a hutch for
his rabbits. Round the side of the house is the garage where
Daddy keeps his four-door saloon. The house is detached,
and there are little chains slung between concrete pillars
along the edge of the front garden. Inside the house, it is all
very comfortable. Full-length curtains brush the fitted car-
pet, and a carefully arranged bowl of flowers stands on a
polished table. Unlike any other children in the world, Peter
and Jane are never cold, hungry, thirsty, cross, bored or
angry. They never quarrel. Mummy and Daddy never say No.
It is remarkable how in the 'Ladybird' world there are simply no problems at all: the comfort of the home, the expensive toys, the absence of any personal conflict - surely these
things are not essential to the teaching or reading? We must
remember what these books claim to be: a picture of the
'natural interests and activities of happy children'. In fact
the school child who reads these books is not just learning

the 'Ladybird Keywords': he is learning the normal behaviour of a middle-class adult, and he is learning the compelling importance of conformity.

More important for our purposes than the unreal class-based fantasies which make up the life style of the reading-book children are the ways in which the different sexual roles are introduced or reinforced.

When we looked at the 'Ladybird' series (and both text and pictures are important here, since an artist will often, perhaps unconsciously, supply a relevant detail which is missing from the text) we noticed three main ways in which this reinforcing of sexual roles is achieved. First, we noticed the entirely different roles of the parents and the ways in which the children were shown to be imitating them. Secondly, the children themselves lead very different lives: the boy's and girl's toys, clothes and hobbies are sharply differentiated. Thirdly, we noticed the overwhelming degree to which the male characters, boy and father, take the initiative. We will look at each of these three points in turn.

The 'Ladybird' parents portray rigidly defined male/female active/passive roles. Daddy drives the car, goes out all day to some unspecified work, paints the house, washes and looks after the car, plays with the children, especially Peter (helping him to build a boat, a model aeroplane, a tree-house), and leads them in their most interesting activities - for example, he teaches them to use the camera he has bought them. Mummy is very rarely seen outside the kitchen; if she does venture out it is to help the children tidy their toys, feed them, put them to bed and wake them up in the morning, or to send them (and Daddy) shopping. She does not drive the car. She has no other existence than a purely domestic one: her life and personality are consistently dull. Incidentally, there are no books in the house (except the encyclopedia in the sideboard), no pictures on the walls and no television.

As these separate occupations suggest, the parents lead very separate lives. The children rarely see them together: 'Peter and Jane are in the car with Daddy. Mummy is at home'. (3b, p. 16) In the one or two instances where they do appear together, their separateness is even more apparent: '"We all read at home," says Daddy. Daddy reads and Mummy works'. (4b p. 50) 'Mother is not to be with the children on their holiday. She has to be at home to look after Daddy'. (7a p. 4)

Naturally enough, the children imitate their parents, and are even exhorted to do so: 'Peter helps Daddy with the car, and Jane helps Mummy get the tea'. (3b p. 20) '"Yes," says Peter, "you make the tea. I will draw." "Yes, I will be like Mummy and get the tea," says Jane. "I like to get the tea". ' (4a p. 14) 'Peter wants to make a car like Daddy'. (4a p. 4) 'Jane wants to make cakes like Mummy'. (4a p. 6) '"I will be the man in the shop", says Peter. "Then let me be Mummy," says Jane'.

(4a p. 20) 'Peter has to help Daddy work with the car. Jane has to help Mummy work in the house'. (4a p. 22)

The children's different roles are reinforced in a second way: they are shown to have very different toys and interests. In one book the children visit a toyshop; Peter buys a gun, a rope for climbing and a book about trains; Jane buys balloons, a skipping rope and a scrap-book. (9a p. 4) At home, Peter has a punch ball, a toy aeroplane, an electric car set. Jane has fewer toys: she likes drawing, arranging flowers, doing jigsaws. On another visit to the toyshop the text is neutral: 'Peter has a toy and Jane has a toy', (1a p. 40) but the picture shows Peter with a crane and Jane with a doll. At Christmas they open their parcels. Again the text makes no comment but the picture shows Peter with a racing car and Jane with another doll. The children choose very different activities: 'The girls want to get some flowers. The boys want to make boats. Then they want to put them in the water'. (5b p. 22) This holds, even when they are playing the same game: 'Mary and Jane pretend to be nurses in the hospital... In comes Bob. He pretends to be the Doctor of the hospital'.

Time after time, Peter plays the active part, Jane the passive. 'Peter has the red ball. He plays with the boys with the red ball. Jane looks on'. When Peter sails his boat on the pond, the picture shows him knee deep in the water with his boat: Jane is watching from the bank. (3b p. 36) It is made quite clear that Jane prefers, indeed selects, to play the passive role. '"Mary and I won't play if you fight," says Jane. "We can't fight and we don't want to be hurt".' (9a p. 12) Sometimes this preference for the passive is projected into the future: '"They are big men," says Peter. "You must be big to do work like that. I want to be big like that." "Yes, I want to be a big man," says the other boy. "I do not want to be so big," says his sister. "I like to be as I am now".' (5b p. 38)

By now we have an overwhelming impression that, in the 'Ladybird' world, boys and girls lead very separate lives. To quantify this impression we took two books, 3b and 9a, and listed all their activities, dividing them into active/ masculine and passive/feminine; eg painting the house, sailing a boat, driving the car, playing with mechanical toys were put in the first category, and watching other people, asking permission, doing domestic chores, playing with dolls came in the second.

book	characters	active/masculine	passive/feminine
3b	Peter & Daddy	14	2
	Jane & Mummy	1	14
	Mixed sexes	1	0
9a	Peter & Daddy	13	4
	Jane & Mummy	4	14
	Mixed sexes	4	0

148

This dichotomy between boy and girl is not confined to the 'Ladybird' series. 'Through the rainbow', a series which uses photographs of 'real' people for some of its illustrations, tells the same story. 'Here is Mummy. She is working in the house'. 'Mummy is making the dinner, she is making the dinner for Daddy'. (Orange Book, pp. 5-21)

The roles once laid down, the children are directly encouraged to play them. 'Can you help Mummy in the house?' 'Can you be Daddy and go to work?' (Red Book pp. 8-21) In the first 'Janet and John' series, one of the words introduced in the first reader is 'aeroplane'. Naturally the aeroplane belongs to John. '"I like aeroplanes," said John. "One day I will go up in an aeroplane."' And sure enough John and Father go for a ride in a real aeroplane, while Mother and Janet stay safely on the ground. (Book 1, 'Off to play') This incident seems particularly outrageous - would any family, albeit middle-class, give such a treat to only one of the two children? Janet's preferred occupations are playing with her soft brown puppy and shopping for toys in John's toyshop. When the whole family goes out in a motor boat, Janet sits with Mother, John with Father.

In 'The Pinkwell Family' Mrs Pinkwell actually has a job - the only working mother we encountered. She keeps a shop, but 'she gets up early and does the housework', (Book 1 p. 20) and on page 2 she is shown holding a mop and broom and wearing an apron. Meanwhile Father is sitting reading a newspaper. So the children are bound to conform to the same pattern. The girls do the work in the kitchen of the old house and cook for the boys: 'When everything was ready, the girls shouted to the boys and they came running into the kitchen for a feast of hot cakes and jam'. (Book 3 p. 15)

Even in this short survey we have covered enough ground to see that heavy sexual bias is present in a child's first experiences in school. A child may begin to learn his appropriate sexual role from his parents or from the comics he reads at home, but once at school he is subjected to a number of more powerful pressures. There are of course the teacher's expectations and influence as to what is suitable behaviour for boys and girls; but more important, the child's first reading material is written and presented in such a way as to leave no doubt that boys and girls are very different sorts of people and that the differences are not a matter of choice. Peter and Jane are not merely exemplars but the vehicle for a social pressure exerted with all the force of an older generation, as represented by the teaching establishment. These readers teach widely separate sexual roles, and also the social and economic values of a society based on just such a separation; throughout, they stress the importance, the naturalness, the inevitability of strict conformity to the norms of behaviour that they present. All in all, they form an ideological prison from which the child would be lucky to escape.

WOMEN AND UNEMPLOYMENT

(This is the first part of a paper written for the Claimants'
Union conference on unemployment held in London in 1971)

Women are never out of work

We're either working at home, feeding, clothing, cleaning,
looking after kids, supporting our husbands, or we're working outside the home in the same kind of service jobs - as
waitresses and cooks, machinists and textile workers, cleaners, teachers, nurses, secretaries, clerks, telephonists -
always the lowest-paid, most monotonous jobs that qualify
as 'women's work'.

But you'd think we never work the way we're treated

We don't get paid by the hour for the work we do in the home,
we've no wages, no way of demanding wages, because it's not
regarded as 'real' work. What it is is an endless treadmill
of shopping, cooking meals, housework, putting kids to bed,
getting them up - none of it has any future or meaning.

At 'real' work we're paid pig-shit - 50% of working women
(4 million) are paid less than 25p an hour. The majority of
working women aren't in unions and the unions show very
little interest in them, so we've got little chance of upping
our wages. We're threatened with the sack if we try to unionise, like the night cleaners.

Women are cheap. Women are docile. Women are slaves.

The bosses realise this while women still don't. In the last
ten years, women's employment has increased by 12%, men's
employment has decreased by 1.5%. Women are able to go
out to work more and more because:
1) housework is becoming eased by automation - hoovers,
   washing machines, etc;
2) in general women are spending a lesser amount of their
   lives giving birth to kids and bringing them up;
3) nurseries and play centres are making it easier for them
   to get out to work;
4) rising prices are making it urgent and necessary for
   women to supplement the family income.

Industry is quickly mopping up women as a labour force, using us as a cheap labour pool, sometimes wanted, sometimes
not, depending on what the demands of the labour cattle market are. At the moment industry needs us to cope with the
increasing paper and administrative work produced by
creeping control - just look at the amount of complicated
legal hassles and paperwork brought in by the Industrial
Relations Act, the Immigration Act and the Redundancy

Payments Act. Electronic and technological industry is growing - Creeping Control requires computers to handle and store information efficiently and secretly, requires transistorised components for bugs, micro-cameras, mini tape-recorders, all of which (as well as being cheaper to produce, replace and distribute) require 'womanly' skills such as dexterity, concentration, attention to detail, in production. Tourism (controlled leisure activity) is increasing, requiring maids, waitresses, cooks, guides, couriers - wherever it is, women's is always service work.

Women are being used as cheap scab labour

This is to keep wages down and threaten men's jobs so as to divide and weaken workers even more. In Coventry, at Lacey's, they made hundreds of men redundant - a few weeks later, ads started appearing in the local papers offering the very same jobs to women!

The ruling class is increasing its profits by using women to do the same jobs as men for less money, using the irrational, insane argument that because it's 'women's work' it's worth less money. And they're confident that women who are resigned to slavery in the home won't protest at slavery and exploitation in the factory.

When they don't want us any more, like the immigrants, they send us home

Women working part-time are the first to be laid off when the bosses start cutting down on their labour force. Thousands have already been laid off that we don't get to hear about because they're working under 20 hours a week and don't qualify for the unemployment statistics, and because married women don't get unemployment benefit and so don't register as unemployed. 20,000 jobs for women vanished in the manufacturing industry in June 1971; 100,000 altogether since January 1971, which indicates a much larger number if the women who were working part-time were included.

But women aren't seen as unemployed

We get less unemployment and sickness benefit, pensions for women are less than men's. Married women aren't even entitled to unemployment benefit if their husband's working, and if husband and wife are out of work, the man claims for both of them. Women who've been working part-time aren't entitled to redundancy payments because you have to have been working over 21 hours a week to qualify.

So what is work?

This is how some women describe it: 'You know what my first impression was? I must be a raving lunatic! I just stood there with my broom in my hand looking at that whole floor...

151

If you did everything you were supposed to, you'd go in at
seven and come out at seven. At first I used to sit and have
my tea on the floor; I didn't know I could be with the other
girls - nobody tells you anything. And they shove you from
building to building. It's always awkward when you go to a
new building. You have to find out where the equipment is
and the extensions... there's no time to settle in. One girl
said that in two months she was shifted every night to a
different building. I'll tell you another catch with night-
cleaning - they'll put you in a building, leave you there
until 1.00 and then decide to take you to another building.
They expect you to get the other building as clean as you
would if you had started at 10.00. You're really doing a
building and a half.'

'I'm a trained machinist, but I can't work during the day
because of the kids. I can't afford to have them looked after.
I'd rather do day work, but I'd live in poverty if I didn't do
night-cleaning. People don't do night-cleaning for fun.'

'With the man it's awkward - when you're coming in, he's
going out, and when you're going out, he's coming in. You
never really have enough energy for your family. Maybe a
couple of days you can sleep only two or three hours, but
you should sleep four, otherwise you're really whacked in
the night time. When you're sleeping you must confine the
children. I can't go to bed until somewhere near 11.00;
you've got to see to the baby in the morning. Soon the
children are home from school... I think you're very irr-
itable when you do night-cleaning. Some girls work morning jobs too. This one girl worked a day job and night-
cleaning - she collapsed on the job. All the girls have
children and most are either separated or divorced. They
work one year on average. After that they don't have enough
energy'.

WOMEN AND THE TRADE UNIONS

Felicity Trodd

(Felicity Trodd is a member of Socialist Woman, London)

9 million women are in paid employment, out of a working population of about $25\frac{1}{2}$ million - about 38% of the workforce. Well over half of them are married. One third of working women are in semi-skilled manual jobs, one quarter in clerical, and 15% in unskilled. One third are employed in the manufacturing industries, one fifth in distribution, 17% in professional and scientific services, and 15% in miscellaneous services.

Of a total TUC membership of over 10 million, around 21%, 2 million, are women. About one in every four women in paid employment is in a union, compared with about one in every two men.

In 1969, 110 out of 151 unions had women members, but three-fifths of these were in seven unions with over a million members between them. The most recent information (1971) on the unions with the largest women membership (above 50,000) is as follows (total union membership in brackets):

NUMGW	245,685	(853,353)	AEU	140,860	(1,202,218)
NUT	228,855	(310,536)	CPSA	121,629	(184,935)
TGWU	222,866	(1,638,686)	NUTGW	100,123	(117,573)
NUPE	220,768	(372,709)	SOGAT	71,799	(192,920)
USDAW	170,742	(329,890)	CAWU	66,834	(125,541)
NALGO	167,797	(439,887)	UPW	52,369	(209,479)

Women officials are comparatively rare, particularly in the higher reaches of the union bureaucracies. Two of the 35 seats on the TUC's General Council are specifically allocated to representatives of the women workers group; women could in theory hold other seats representing the trade groups, but in practice don't. Unions catering for women workers hold a TUC Women's Conference every Spring and elect 5 members to the TUC Women's Advisory Committee; the other members are taken from the General Council. Over the last couple of years there have been moves - particularly from the non-manual public sector unions, where the status of women is more equal - to do away with the separate conference for women on the grounds that it conflicts with the principle of equality. The Women's Advisory Committee has resisted this on the grounds that it would lead to even less representation of women members.

The unionisation rate of women is however much higher than that of men. Over the 20 years up to 1970 TUC membership increased by 938,000, of which 605,000 were women. This is partly due to growth of the distributive/service sector where women predominate, relative to manufacturing - NUPE's women membership for example has risen 28% in the past year.

WOMEN, WORK AND EQUAL PAY

Leonora Lloyd

(Leonora Lloyd is a member of Socialist Woman, London.
This paper was first presented to the Women's Weekend at
Ruskin College, Oxford, in February/March 1970)

In a period of increasing unemployment, we must be sensitive
to the fears of both male and female workers that moves towards equal pay will increase joblessness. But it is essential
that women's industrial campaign takes as one of its main
tasks the fighting of unemployment, putting the blame for it
squarely where it belongs: not on any group of workers, whether classified by sex or colour, not on wage demands or
strikes; but on the capitalist system that has never been able
to provide full employment, which, in fact, depends on the ex-
istance of unemployed workers to dampen the militancy of
the employed. The presence of a large number of women,
potentially available to fill jobs held by men or employed
women, has always been a threat to organised labour. It is
entirely in the interest of the working class that more women enter the working force - so long as they do so under
entirely equal conditions of pay, opportunity and other conditions; otherwise they will continue to be potential black-
legs, they will continue to undercut male labour, etc. Of
course, it is necessary to recruit women into the unions, to
educate them politically, but then the men also need educa-
ting on these questions.

Women's liberation has a part to play in this educative process, as in the practical aspects. We must recognise that
entering the workforce does mean two things in particular:
it gives the woman some degree of economic independence,
and it paves the way for her to become part of the labour
movement, something that would have been unlikely to have
happened if she had stayed within the four walls of her home.
Also, as long as she remains at home, dependent on her husband to provide the necessities of life, the psychological dependence on men which women's liberation is seeking to
attack will continue and be reinforced. As long as the majority of the working class depend on wage labour for their
existence, as long as capitalism exists, we shall always have
to make the choice: to be exploited by the capitalist class
(something which the vast majority of men have no choice
about) or to be to some extend parasitic, and to a large extent wholly dependent, on a man. In any case, for a significant
number of women, both with and without men to 'support'
them, there is no choice about work either: they must work
or go without.

The choice before women's liberation is not wholly an either/
or one; it is not entirely between campaigning for, say, allowances for stay-at-home mothers or jobs-and-nurseries for

all. We must campaign for a combination of these - for a real alternative for mothers of young children, in particular. It would be wrong, in the context of a capitalist society, to say that all women should work, no matter what the circumstances; but it would be equally wrong to call for wages for housewives, thus <u>continuing</u> the prevailing feminine myths.

Above all, we must recognise the situation as it is now, with millions of women going out to work, in unsatisfactory conditions, for unsatisfactory pay; under-represented and disregarded. It is to these women in the first place that we must turn our attention. Various factors combine to show that, given enough jobs and satisfactory conditions (hours, shopping, child-care, etc) the majority of married women, including mothers, would work. Without discounting campaigns and activities directed towards housewives, those concerning working women raise so many more issues, and are so much more likely to raise the consciousness of the women concerned, male workers and ourselves, that we must regard the industrial campaign as a priority. In order to put this campaign on a proper footing, we in the movement should arm ourselves with the facts and figures, as well as with the theiry. It is to help with this groundwork of facts that the next section is included.

Women in industry

Out of some $17\frac{1}{2}$ million women about 51.4% are workers (full and part-time) and, of these, about 62% are married. Of 11 million workers in industry (including non-manual workers) over 2.9 million are women. In May 1971 over 100 thousand women were registered as unemployed, excluding school-leavers. (DEP Gazette)

Over half the female workforce is employed in semi-skilled and unskilled jobs. (Semi-skilled is usually defined as needing between six and one months experience or training.) Large numbers of women are found in the distributive, clothing, footwear, textile, engineering and service sectors. Within these and other industries, they are to be found concentrated mainly in the clerical, semi-skilled manual and unskilled manual jobs, and in the servicing jobs. Women make up about 38% of the total workforce. 18.5% of all women workers in industry are part-timers.

In the professional field, women are to be found overwhelmingly in two occupations - nursing and teaching. There are very few fields, either professional or non-professional, where absolutely no women at all are found, but whatever the field, women are to be found clustered on the bottom rungs of the ladder, thinning out rapidly as they get to the top. In terms of the total workforce in their area, women are found in greatest concentration in the north-western area of Great Britain, and in the lowest concentration in Wales.

Why women work

Generally, women are classified merely as married or unmarried, and it is difficult to get further details from ordinary job statistics. The most recent figures available are
those compiled in the 1966 partial census (results of the 1971
census are only now beginning to be published). At that time,
women made up 52.5% of the sample over 15 and 35.7% of the
economically active population. Of these, 57.1% were married,
34.3% single, 6.9% widows and 1.6% divorced. 4% were self-
employed or employed others, and 3% were registered as
unemployed.

Surveys into the question of why women work nowadays take
it for granted that the unmarried woman will work and concentrate on the married woman living with her husband, or
on the once-married woman presumed to have some means
of support (pension, etc). In the 'Survey of women's employment' (Hunt, 1968), the following answers were given (a) and
in the PIB report on contract cleaning a similar survey among part-time women cleaners produced answers (b):

table 1 : Reasons for working

(a)			(b)	
Financial	80.8%		*Financial for family	78%
For company	39.5%		Social contact	16%
To dispel boredom	28.4%		(*this included 14% working	
To give independence	11.5%		for their own benefit)	

Of course, part-time workers cannot be compared to full-time
workers, in the sense that they could not earn enough to become financially independent.

Professional women are more likely to give as reasons for
working the need to use and keep up their training, to be socially useful and to dispel boredom. They generally claim that
for the professional married woman, tax demands mean that
it is not financially attractive to work. Women taking up professional training may sometimes take into consideration the
ease or otherwise of continuing to work after having a family
- and certainly the career books encourage them to do so -
but for the majority of women, their choice of work is extremely restricted.

Many factors influence women's choice of work and combine
to limit it. Of course, many women have a poor education, as
do many men, but in addition they are less likely than men to
get training at any level. So a large number of women are
competing for a limited number of unskilled jobs. (Defined as
those requiring less than one month's training or experience.)
In the cleaners survey quoted above, 28% mentioned the kind
of work they had the ability or training to do when questioned
on factors influencing their choice of job. The hours of work
were important too (56% were influenced by this), especially
for married women. Many women must take jobs near home
and 24% of the cleaners were influenced by this factor. Naturally, pay matters too, but not so much as for men. Women

generally see their pay as extra money, which seems to have the magical effect of making any sum seem like a lot. Women consider certain conditions at work important, especially their work-mates, and will often try to get work at a factory where a friend works. Employers use such enticements as cheap goods, hair-does, stamps, etc, to induce women to work for them. Being tax-deductible and easily with-held, they come cheaper than better wages. An insignificant number provide nurseries. Employers wishing to attract men need to offer high wages, good parking facilities and extensive sports facilities, all heavily subsidised. Once women are happy with a job, they will settle in, as the Peak Frean survey (1960) showed, and then have a better record in terms of turnover than men. Women have a higher turnover than men for the first six months, but once over that hurdle, they are more stable employees.

The main reason why employers want women workers is obviously because they need to pay them less. But other reasons are that women are less organised into unions than men, traditionally less militant, work harder, and women workers keep wage rates for all workers down, as we shall see.

Pay, earnings and hours

Pay and earnings are not the same thing. Basic pay makes up 77% of women workers' earnings in industry, and 66% of mens'. Basic rates are already lower for women, but in addition men have far more chance to earn extra money. (See table 4). So the predominant fact about women's earnings is that they are low. Table 2 shows numbers (in millions) whose gross weekly earnings in April 1970 were less than the figures given. (All full-time workers)(National Economic Survey 1970)

table 2	£28	£24	£20	£15
Men aged 21 or over	5. 8	3. 9	1. 9	0. 3
Women aged 18 or over	4. 5	4. 3	2. 8	2. 6

Because women work shorter hours than men hourly rates of pay provide a fairer rate of comparison than weekly earnings, but are nonetheless shocking for all that. (DEP 1971)

table 3	Men (over 21)	Women (over 18)
Average weekly earnings		
Oct. 69	£24.85	£12.10
Oct. 70	£28.05	£14.00
Average hourly earnings		
Oct. 69	54p	34p
Oct. 70	62p	37p

(Hourly earnings are to nearest np)

When we turn to those supposedly earning equal pay, the picture is not so much different. In October 1969, earnings in national and local government, including education (teachers), and NHS workers were £32.03 for men and £20.02 for women, per week.

Some 66% of women workers are full-time*, ie around $6\frac{1}{2}$ million, of whom over $2\frac{1}{2}$ million of those over 18 earn less than £15 a week, so the problem of low pay is a big one. (*This figure is for all women workers: 18.5% of women workers in industry work part-time.) The TUC is now talking in terms of a £20 a week minimum wage. In the TUC publication 'Problems of low-paid workers' they make the observation that a minimum wage would be of far more benefit to women than equal pay.

Although women, in comparison to men, get low earnings for the work they do, two groups in particular do badly. These are women doing 'women's work' - either work in factories etc not done by men, or service work, and manual workers in industry generally.

When we look at the way earnings in manufacturing industry are made up, we see that women earn extra mainly through payment-by-results schemes, and it is no accident that they earn a higher percentage of their total pay by this method than men do. It is very open to abuse, particularly when not supervised by a strong union. As the woman becomes more skilful, the basis on which she earns her payment-by-results bonus may be altered, so that her earnings remain static, or nearly so. This is done by using a sliding scale - 6p for the first thousand, but only 1p for the third thousand, for example.

This method, or piece-work as it is generally known, is also subject to the quality of the materials, the speed of the machine or the other workers on the same bench, and other factors outside the control of the individual worker. Bonus systems, based on the time taken to do jobs, are open to similar abuses.

Nearly 90% of women workers still do not get equal pay and this situation is not really improving, despite the Equal Pay Act. In a few isolated instances, differentials in pay (though not necessarily in earnings) are improving or even disappearing. Thus, retail workers in pharmacy and meat now get equal pay, as a result of their last increase. But in other cases, even though industries have made plans to implement the Equal Pay Act, the differentials - both in terms of percentage and in cash - are increasing. For example, women working in the tobacco industry earn a minimum of £9.90 (February 1971). In 1969 they earned £3.14 less than men on the minimum rate, now the difference is £3.40. Other industries which have not yet made plans show even bigger increases in differentials.

As we have said, even where equal pay applies, lack of opportunity for training, promotion and advancement means that women are found predominantly on the lower rungs. Thus, one third of all full-time civil servants are women, but only 8% are in the administrative class.

Many women are found doing jobs only done by women and - almost by definition - these are low-paid jobs. (About the only exception is secretarial work in London and other large cities). Indeed, when women make up a large proportion of any industry or service, wages for the whole sector will be low. It is interesting to compare male rates in three such industries (group 1) with three industries employing comparatively few women (group 2)(DEP)

table 4 : Average earnings for men, Oct. 1970

group 1	per hour	group 2	per hour
Food, drink, tobacco	59.83	Vehicles	76.49
Textiles	56.58	Coal & Pet. prods.	70.05
Clothing & footwear	58.12	Paper, printing, publishing	74.35

Of course, the claim that the proportion of women workers in these industries is the only, or even the main reason for these differences would be difficult to prove. (Reasons for low pay of women in general are suggested later) In October 1970 the average weekly wage for non-manual workers was £19.59 for women and £36.12 for men. Many non-manual workers are covered by 'equal pay' agreements; in addition, male and female non-manual workers tend to work more or less the same hours, so that the difference is only explainable in terms of the different jobs these workers do, ie the level of work they do.

A very important reason for women doing badly on the industrial front is their poor showing in the trade union movement. We could discuss many shortcomings of the trade union movement; it has failed to secure a larger share of the national cake for its members (see 'Whatever happened to our wages?' Norman Atkinson, M.P.) But those groups who have been under-represented, or have had no union representation have tended to fall back in the race, and women workers are a prime example of this. It is not just that fewer women are in unions - only 21% of union members are women, who you will remember make up 38% of the workforce. They are even less in evidence in any positions of influence within the unions, from shop-stewards to general secretaries. The 2 out of 35 seats on the TUC's General Council held by women are specifically allocated to them.

However, women are joining unions at a much faster rate than men - nearly twice as many women have joined unions in the last 20 years as men. This is mainly due to the fast growth of the distributive and service sector relative to manufacturing (over the last 50 years, the number of office workers has been increasing at six times the rate of manufacturing employment) at a time when the non-manual unions have been carrying out quite aggressive recruitment policies.

But of course, underlying all the reasons for women's low

pay mentioned above is the fact that women's role is still conceived as being in the home, not at work; her wage is still considered subsidiary to the man's. This attitude is held by men and women alike, to the benefit of the employers only. It is the philosophy of the women's liberation movement, which understands the pervasiveness of this attitude, and is seeking ways of fighting it, which is one of the reasons why the movement has a part to play that more traditional groups cannot. The two aspects of a married woman worker's life - home and work - impinge deeply on each other. If real economic equality is reached and husbands and wives realise that the woman is no longer dependent on the man, what effect will this have on their relationship? For millions of men and women, the fact that the man is earning the larger wage has deep and profound effects on their marriage. Men's feelings of 'manhood' are dependent on this fact. Women whose earnings are as much as or more than their men's worry about the effect this will have on this 'manhood'. What will happen when this case is no longer an exception? To imagine that the present Equal Pay Act will bring about this state of affairs is to exercise a good deal of imagination.

The Equal Pay Act: provisions of the Act

The Equal Pay Act 1970 comes into force on 29 December 1975. It seeks to eliminate discrimination between men and women both in regard to pay and to terms and conditions of employment by:
1. establishing the right of the individual woman to equal treatment when she is employed (a) on work of the same or a broadly similar nature to that of men or (b) in a job which, though different in nature from those of men, has been given an equal value to men's jobs under a job evaluation exercise;
2. providing for the Industrial Court to remove discrimination in collective agreements, employers' pay structures and statutory wages orders which contain any provisions applying specifically to men only or to women only and which have been referred to the Court. ('A guide to the Equal Pay Act 1970', DEP)

In addition, the Act allows the Secretary of State for Employment to make an order, subject to the approval of parliament, requiring that women's rates be raised to 90% of the male rates by 31 December 1973 (in those cases where the Act applies). However, this is at the Secretary's discretion.

The Act applies whenever a woman is doing the same or broadly similar work to a man employed in the same or an associated company, where that company has a uniform wages policy for the male employees. Thus, if all charge-hands throughout the various factories in a particular group are paid the same and are subject to the same conditions of employment, and this applies to all grades of workers, then a woman in factory A doing the same work as a man in factory B must get the same wages. But if different wages apply for men doing the same job in the different factories, then the woman's work must be compared to that of a man in her own factory.

What is meant by 'the same or broadly similar work'? First, it means work done by both men and women, as we would expect; second, where work has been the subject of a job evaluation scheme and been given equal rating to men's work; third, where the job evaluation led to different values only because of different weighting or evaluating schemes being used for men's and women's work, but which without such differences would have been equally valued; fourth, where the worker or employer has referred the case to an industrial tribunal and the tribunal judges that the Act applies; fifth, the Secretary of State for Employment may also refer cases to the tribunal. (In both the last two cases, reference to the tribunal may be made up to six months after ceasing the particular employment.) Back pay may be claimed for up to two years (but not before the Act comes into force, ie not in respect of any earnings before 29 December 1975).

When unequal wages are paid, the employer must show that it is 'genuinely due to a material difference (other than the difference of sex) between the two cases'. The criterion is that the system of payment must be just as capable of paying more to the woman as vice-versa.

In addition, no collective agreements may be made after 29 December 1975 which distinguish between male and female rates of pay. However, where no provision is made for a male rate in a particular category, then a specific female rate may still apply, but it must be no lower than the lowest male rate. The example given in the DEP's guide is as follows: 'If a collective agreement laid down a skilled male rate of £20, an unskilled male rate of £15 (but no semi-skilled male rate) and a woman's rate (for all classes of work performed) of £12, the Court would amend such an agreement so that, irrespective of sex, skilled work was paid at the rate of £20 and unskilled work at the rate of £15. In other words, skilled women workers would be entitled to £20 and unskilled women workers to £15. The original women's rate - a rate "applying specifically to women only" - would continue to be required for women employed on semi-skilled work, because there is no category of semi-skilled men provided for in the agreement. In those circumstances, the Court would amend the women's rate, which had to be retained, from £12 to £15, namely the lowest rate in the agreement applicable to men'.

This aspect of the Act - that no women's rate may be lower than the lowest male rate - may prove to be of more significance than the equal pay aspect, because of the greater number of women to whom it will apply.

Discrimination in terms and conditions of employment is also

dealt with by the Act - covering such things as holiday en-
titlement, payment in kind, free meals and bonus schemes.
It does not apply to those cases where women's employment
is affected by other laws, on hours of work for example. It
still allows women to have special terms and conditions in
connection with maternity leave, marriage, retirement and
death. (This latter refers to certain schemes where widows
of workers who have paid into the scheme can claim pensions; widowers of women workers paying into the same
schemes cannot so claim, so that in effect such women are
giving away a portion of their wages.)

How the Act will work

There is no doubt that, from an employer's point of view,
women have certain disadvantages: higher turnover, more
absences, breaks in employment, etc. Against this, we know
that women are found in the least skilled jobs, where these
factors apply to men as well; and above all, women are responsible for the family, so that their more numerous absences may be due to family illnesses, etc. But this is of
little consolation to the employer and, in his view, justifies
the lower wages paid to women. In addition, years of paying
low wages to women have meant that in certain industries
in particular, prices and profits have been scaled accordingly. Equal pay, if applied across the board in these industries,
would result in lower profits and higher prices, the latter
perhaps causing still lower profits if sales fell off. Women
workers have been subsidising both the consumer and the
shareholder, and also bolstering inefficient management.
British industry is notoriously antiquated and in many sectors it is only the cheap labour that enables firms to be
half-way competitive in world markets.

Against this, it is precisely those firms which most rely on
female labour who have the strictest division of labour, so
that electronics firms, for example, will have only women
doing assembly work, with male inspectors and foremen
(trained by the women they are over, very often). Very few
grocery stores employ men as cashiers or ordinary counter
hands. Agreements may not specify that only women are going to be employed on certain jobs, but employers may only
take on women in practice - even supposing that they could
attract men at the wages offered.

In the long breathing space provided before the implementation of the Act, employers are re-arranging work, to make
the divisions into men's and women's work even more stringent; they are introducing more modern machinery, perhaps
some years before they might otherwise have done, thus increasing unemployment and competition for available jobs.
Remember, too, that it is up to the union, individual worker,
industrial tribunal or Secretary of State to initiate proceed-
ings (or the employer, of course, we must not forget him) for

implementation of the Act. In many cases, the women will not be represented by a union - and where they have not been able to organise a union, are the women likely to go to an industrial tribunal? - and in the present industrial climate, especially if the present Conservative government is still in power, who else will proceed on behalf of the women? It will not be illegal to pay unequal wages, unless the Court rules otherwise.

In this connection, it is not amiss to look briefly at the effects of the Industrial Relations Act. The main one for our purpose is that it will be much harder for women to form unions where none yet exist. They will not be able to put pressure on their workmates to join, they will not be able to take the sort of militant action which so many workers do take as a necessary preliminary to building a union in a plant - action which demonstrates the need for a union. The Act is designed not to get rid of unions, but rather to make them ineffective, or even a branch of the state. As such, women will find it much harder to get unions to move officially on equal pay, much less take action to implement the spirit, as well as the letter, of even this mild measure. In every way, in fact, because they start from a weaker level of organisation, women are going to feel the effects of the IRA more than most male workers.

The Equal Pay Act is not going to give more women more opportunity. Those firms that decide as a result of the Act to give women more training and better promotion prospects, on the grounds that they should use their better-paid talents more efficiently, would probably have done so anyway sooner or later. Industries employing many women will continue to have lower rates of pay for all their workers, and other industries will continue to keep women in the lower-paid jobs. Of course, several thousand women will be directly better off, and in some areas, especially those where full employment exists, this will result in somewhat better wages for all women workers.

But the only way forward for women workers is to organise now, to press for real equal pay now, to call for the rate for the job, for socially-provided facilities to ease a woman's family commitments, to demand equal training and job opportunities, to fight prejudice and inequality on every front. We must not let the unions get away with anything: every agreement must be examined to ensure that it advances and does not retard the fight. Every time a group of male workers, with or without the connivance of the employers or trade-union officials, denies a woman the right to work at the job of her choice, all women workers, and all of us in the women's liberation movement, must spring to her defence. The women's liberation movement will stand or fall by the support it gives to women workers. If the movement is to have more effect than the suffragettes - not just in getting

what we are fighting for, but in measuring the importance of
that achievement - then it will be in our commitment or lack
of it to the working class women's fight that we will be judged in the final analysis.

Postscript

Since this article was originally written, a number of developments have taken place, but the overall picture given by
the figures remains. What the interval has done, however, is
to confirm our analysis and show that women are going to
be denied even the little progress promised by the Act. We
see a continuation of the process whereby women are put
into the lowest-paid jobs, even if these are no longer always
designated as 'women's jobs': in reality, they remain wom-
en's jobs.

But on two fronts progress has been made. We have seen a
sharpening of class action, led by the miners, dockers and
builders, and their example has led many groups of workers
to try new forms of struggle. The engineers, for example, in
their series of actions for a national pay claim that included
equal pay, had sit-ins which included women workers. Of
course, as might have been expected, equal pay was one of
the casualties of the compromise solution, and was again
left until 1975. More significantly, independent action by
groups of women workers, such as the Fakenham leather
workers' takeover of their factory, have taken place. Pat
Sturdy has gone on from attempting to form a women's union
to the idea of women's groups in industry, to develop both
the women concerned and their demands. This idea is also
being developed in TASS. The night-cleaners, in their latest
confrontation, this time indirectly with the government, at the
Ministry of Defence building in Fulham, showed that even a
small group of non-industrial workers, given the correct
tactics and the active support of other workers (not to mention women's liberation groups), can win major victories.

So progress is being made by women workers. But within
the women's liberation movement, too, changes can be observed. No longer is the main orientation - towards women
workers, women of the working class - challenged: the debate is around How? A significant number of movement women
are anti-union, even though in practice all major struggles of
women workers in recent (and not so recent) history have
been either for union recognition or by those already in unions. This is not to say that the unions have taken up their
struggles, but it is necessary to distinguish between the rank
and file and the 'leadership' of the unions. It was obvious, to
those involved in the Fulham night-cleaners' picket (July '72)
that much of the support from other workers was seen as
natural - from and for fellow trade-unionists. In any case,
just as the Women's Liberation Movement cannot change the
necessity for many women to sell their labour power in a

capitalist society, whatever idealist notions they may have about work, neither can they change the fact that in the coming period and for some time to come most workers' struggles, whilst continuing to take new and hopefully more militant forms, will still be based on the unions. The most hopeful sign is in fact the extent to which the workers are using their unions for their own methods of struggle, rather than taking the lead from the bureaucracy; but this trend must not be over-exaggerated because the workers still look to their leadership in the first place, and this leadership has had a lot of experience in ways of containment. However, for the Women's Liberation Movement the most welcome sign is that at last a debate is taking place within the Movement on this subject, and many important questions are being thoroughly aired.

For further reading: 'Socialist Woman' carries regular articles on women's struggles (not just in the industrial field) and analysis of both the equal pay/equal work campaign and the Women's Liberation Movement. Past copies, containing details of the various strikes and campaigns mentioned above, are available post free if more than one is ordered at 5p each from 182 Pentonville Road, London N1. As well as my own pamphlet, now available at 20p from the same address, readers should see the various publications around the 'Women, work and trade unions' debate, prepared for the November 1972 Women's Liberation Conference, including one from Socialist Woman (untitled at present).

BLACK WOMEN AND WORK

Hermione Harris

(Hermione Harris is a member of the London Women's Liberation Workshop. This paper was originally written to provide factual information on the location of black women in the labour force to a working convention on 'Racism in the political economy of Britain' held in London in 1971)

'Black women suffer in three ways. 1. We are poor. 2. We are black. 3. We are women. We are poor because the wealth of our countries has been seized by the white western imperialists who exploit us mercilessly. We are poorly paid in the jobs we do more so than the white woman, we are at the very bottom of the economic scale. We are black and are discriminated against in every walk of life. Racism has taken on a life of its own and we have become its victims.' (Black Unity and Freedom Party, 'Black women speak out', 1971)

In this paper I shall briefly outline the situation of black women in the British labour force. Their position as a flexible pool of cheap, largely unskilled labour is a reflection of the three characteristics of their oppression - as working class, as women, and as blacks.

Accurate statistics on black women in Britain are not available. Until the publication of the results of the 1971 census, the chief sources of data are the 1961 and 1966 sample census. The notorious underenumeration of black people in these figures especially affects women. Apart from the difficulty of obtaining accurate returns from a mobile population often living in overcrowded conditions in areas of multiple occupation, there is natural reluctance to provide information - justified by the recent immigration legislation and the use (or misuse) of statistics in political debates over black people in Britain. Further, the nature of much of women's work, being part-time, shift-work or out-work, further renders figures unreliable. However, the main features of black female labour can be determined.

Female immigration

The pattern of entry into Britain by black women has broadly followed the trends of all new Commonwealth immigrants. From the early 1950s, Irish and foreign immigration has declined, while New Commonwealth immigration has risen from 16% to 33% in 1966. In mid-1969 the total number of black people in Britain was some 1,185,000 - 2.1% of the total population. Under half of these are women.

The dual role of a woman as both a wife and mother, and a potential member of the labour force, is a crucial factor in her exploitation as cheap unskilled labour. The entry of black male workers, through the increasingly stringent operation of the voucher system, has been tied firmly to the needs of the British economy, compensating for shortage of skilled or unskilled labour in various pre-selected sections of the economy. (Most 'race relations' literature tends to ignore this fact, and deals with immigration in political or socio-cultural terms. But see S. Allen, 'Race and the economy', in 'Race', October 1971.) Women, on the other hand, enter Britain mainly as dependents. Before 1962, both unskilled men and women from the New Commonwealth could enter without restriction, and from 1962-64 under category C of the voucher system. But it is unlikely that unskilled, unsupported female workers would have entered on this basis in large numbers. Since 1964, on the basis of the voucher system, women could either come in under category A (such as those brought over by large catering firms like Lyons who recruit in the West Indies) or under category B, chiefly in the teaching and medical professions. But, in contrast to men, large numbers of unskilled women have been able to enter Britain through their position as dependents. In 1969 black women from New Commonwealth countries formed only 25% of voucher holders. (Calculated from Home Office statistics, Cmnd. 4327) Without nurses this would have been considerably lower: in 1967 and 1968 the total number of female voucher holders was 1,841. 27% of these were nurses. (C. Hill, 'Immigration and integration', 1970) In contrast, in 1969 94% of adult dependents were women.

Increasingly, therefore, through the restrictions on male entrants through the voucher system, the growing number of immigrants is largely made up of dependents. In 1969 90% of all immigrants were dependents. In 1963 there was a slightly higher proportion of male entrance than female. By 1968 eleven times more dependents entered than male workers. Although the majority of dependents in all groups consist of children, the differing ratios of women entering as proportions of the dependents of various groups reflect different patterns of settlement. For example, in 1962 and 1963 the influx of men from India and Pakistan greatly exceeded the number of dependents. By 1968 96% of the high number of Asian immigrants were dependents. A quarter of these were women, giving a steady increase of Asian female immigrants throughout the 1960s. For West Indians, on the other hand, both male and female adult immigration has declined since 1963, the overall increase being accounted for by children, forming 90% of dependents entering in 1967. (See Rose, 'Colour and citizenship', 1969; C. Hill, op. cit.; Home Office statistics, Cmnd. 4029)

The dual aspect of women as both dependents and a reserve pool of unskilled labour is entrenched in the immigration legislation. Wives of Commonwealth immigrants were allowed in under the 1962 Act, and were not affected by the 1968 legislation when the entry rights of dependents both below and above working age were restricted. But whereas fiancees may join their future husbands in Britain, men from the Commonwealth are not normally admitted to join their prospective wives. This discrimination is even more blatant in the 1971 legislation, where a woman must leave if her husband is deported, but a man's position is unaffected if his wife is expelled from the country.

It is not possible to calculate the average number of dependents to each male worker from the figures of any one year, as there is an average gap of four years before a man is joined by his family. The latest estimate is 2.7 dependents to each male. (Eversley and Sudeko, 'The dependents of the coloured Commonwealth population of England and Wales) Because of the high proportion of children, the sex ratio of black men to women is weighted towards men, the reverse of the total British population where women exceed men. The proportion of women increased during the first half of the 1960s. By 1966 the Caribbean percentage of women to men was 94, but for Pakistanis the ratio was still as low as 24%. (K. Jones and A. D. Smith, 'The economic impact of Commonwealth immigration', 1970)

Black female participation in the labour force

Although the employment of black women must also be seen in terms of the demands of the economy, socio-cultural factors are crucial in explaining the differing participation rates of different groups. In 1966, the proportion of Asian females of working age in employment was 37%, as compared with 65% of West Indian women.

The figure for Asians, because of the inclusion in census data of the children born to Europeans in India, is an overestimate. Asian women are traditionally kept in the home. That this tradition persists is shown in the relative seclusion of Asian teenage girls in Britain today; also by the fact that the vast proportion of children brought over here are boys, the girls being kept at home to be brought up by relatives. Of adult Pakistani women entering Britain in 1969, 42 came as voucher holders, 4,429 came as dependents. Compare this with women from Jamaica: 55 voucher holders and 177 dependents. (Home Office statistics, Cmnd. 4327)

The contrasting West Indian situation reflects the tradition of female labour in the Caribbean. Although this was largely agricultural work, a survey of West Indians in Nottingham found that 16% of West Indian women workers had been employed in factories at home. (Bayliss & Coates, 'West Indians at work in Nottingham', 'Race', October 1965)

Asian women constitute the only black immigrant group, male or female, who fall below the British rates. The number of British women working or seeking work in 1966 was 42%. West Indian women therefore made a considerable contribution to the British labour force between 1961 and 1966, proportionately greater than indigenous female labour, even though this was also rising during this period.

Occupational distribution

In her work situation, the black woman suffers the double oppression of her sex and her colour. Women as a group constitute over a third of the total labour force, but managerial, executive and supervisory posts are largely held by men. The well-known generalisation that black women are concentrated in the worst jobs in terms of pay, conditions and status is amply proved by the statistics. They confirm the use of black women as a pool of unskilled labour. Although the overall pattern conforms largely to the distribution of indigenous female labour, concentrations in certain sectors occur. The significance of these concentrations is only fully revealed if various factors are taken into account: these are (a) regional variations, (b) differences between different ethnic groups, (c) levels of skill within each occupational category.

One of the largest concentrations of black female labour is found in the clothing and footwear industries. In 1966, 4% of British women were employed in clothing, but 11% of women from the Caribbean. Of the total labour force employed in hand and machine sewing alone, 4% was supplied by black women. A further breakdown reveals that black women constituted in 1966 7% of the female labour force in women's outwear and dresses. Characterised by low pay and poor conditions, the shift system broadly adopted by this labour-intensive industry attracts female labour.

The concentration of black women in engineering, ie routine unskilled or semi-skilled factory work, is similarly marked. This accounts for 7% of the black female force, as opposed to 3% of the British. In the West Midlands, a third of West Indian women are employed in engineering, which overall has 4% of its unskilled posts filled by black women.

Although 24% of white women workers are employed in services and 19% of black, it is often the black women who fill the dirtiest and lowest-paid grades, which do not come into direct contact with the public - cleaning, washing-up, work in laundry and dry-cleaning firms etc. 'Colour prejudice' and 'racial discrimination' are generally over-emphasised as factors explaining the distribution of black workers, at the expense of looking at the demand for labour in various sectors of the economy. But discrimination on the grounds of colour seems to be all-important in some spheres. 13% of British women are sales workers; 7% of Asian women and only 1% of West Indian women are employed in sales.

The concentrations in certain white-collar jobs are also deceptive unless analysed further. The third highest concentration for black women is in the clerical sector, which absorbs 18% as opposed to 26% of British women. But this is largely explained by 35% of women born in India or Pakistan (therefore including an unknown proportion of whites) being employed in clerical work. Only 8% of West Indian women have these jobs, and the figure drops to 2.5% in the Midlands. Again, individual surveys have found that black women tend to be predominantly at the bottom end of the scale, and in smaller firms. The proportion of black women in the managerial category is almost negligible.

As with all women workers, these figures underestimate the number of black women working. But their general position as a pool of cheap unskilled labour is quite clear. This is flexible labour in the sense that it can respond to seasonal or shift-work demands within the manufacturing and service sectors. It may also be manipulated against the interests of other women workers, and the working class as a whole. In her book on 'Immigrants in industry', Sheila Patterson found that some engineering firms capitalise on cheap labour by de-skilling - ie breaking down skilled jobs into a number of unskilled processes, bringing in West Indian women to take them over. But their position as women limits their geographical mobility, and therefore increases their risk of unemployment.

Unemployment

Figures on unemployment among women can only be approximations. Firstly, there is the difficulty of deciding when a housewife is technically unemployed and when she is not. Secondly, calculations can only be based on unreliable sources. The criteria usually employed is the number of those out of work signed on at labour exchanges, records being kept by the Department of Employment and Productivity. However, all evidence suggests that the use of employment exchanges by all immigrants is low. The P.E.P. report on racial discrimination (1967) revealed widespread racial prejudice among employers, reflected in the policy of exchanges. Despite official policy during the 1960s to counteract this, little is done to see that it is put into practice. (See B. Hepple, 'The position of coloured workers in British industry', paper for the NCCI conference on racial equality in employment, 1967) Immigrants prefer to look for their own jobs through advertisements, friends and relatives, or through personal applications. The Nottingham survey showed that only 17% of black women found their jobs through labour exchanges.

Another Nottingham survey, conducted in 1962, found that West Indian women formed nearly 40% of registered female unemployed. (J. Lawrence, I.R.R. Newsletter supplement, June 1966) This bears out the argument of Jones and Smith that New Commonwealth unemployment rates tend to be

170

highest where the black population is concentrated. But they do not draw the connection between this fact and the nature of employment where black labour is concentrated as being inherently unstable.

On the basis of registration figures, Rose argues that unemployment among immigrant labour follows the general pattern of indigenous workers, but at a higher rate. So in 1963, at a peak of unemployment, 6% of women out of work were black; following the general decline, in 1966 3%, in 1967 4.5%.

The relation of black female unemployment to labour demands and conditions of economic recession cannot be fully traced until the figures for recent years now being released by the D.E.P. have been analysed. Until then, all that may be said is that of male and female labour, white and black, black women come off worst. This reflects not only discrimination on the part of employers, of which there is ample evidence in the mass of 'attitudinal' race relations research, but also the type of employment they are in, subject to seasonal fluctuations or managerial policies of redundancy. Black workers as a whole are hit by 'last in first out' policies. They are also concentrated in sectors such as the laundry industry - highly labour-intensive, poorly paid, run on a shift basis with a high turnover of labour, and therefore with little opportunity for unionisation and organisation of labour.

The West Indian woman worker

Although Asian women do largely fall into the category of dependents, the reverse is true for West Indian women, many of whom are household heads, solely responsible for their children. This reflects the marriage pattern of the Caribbean where legal marriage is often contracted much later in life. This is a legacy of slavery, when marriage between plantation workers was forbidden. The pattern is now changing among West Indian immigrants, and is likely to do so increasingly among the second generation, but the position of unsupported mothers in Britain is one of personal and economic oppression.

Social security benefits for unsupported mothers are totally inadequate. Besides her rent, she is entitled to £5.80 a week. The additional rates for her children range from £1.70 for under-fives to £3 for 13-16 year-olds. She may be able to claim for clothing, bedding, etc. But if she works, any amount over £2 left from her wage once insurance, tax and fares have been paid is deducted from her benefit. This makes it impossible for her to raise her standard of living. While a man in a similar position is encouraged to live with a woman so as to free him from domestic responsibilities, a woman lives under the fear of being discovered 'cohabiting', and so losing her independent benefit. She may have neither the skill nor the time to obtain a well-paid job, or unskilled employment with overtime opportunities. Child-minding facilities are also completely inadequate; numbers of day nurseries have declined since the war.

But financial necessity forces a woman in this position to work. A recent study in Paddington found that whereas 18% of non West Indian mothers were working, 50% of West Indian mothers were in employment. (C. Hood et al, 'West Indian children and the health services in Paddington', 'Race Today', November 1969) The higher proportion of West Indian women with young children as compared to the indigenous population is a result both of the age-structure of the group and the higher birth rate. This latter factor is again resultant from their age, and a feature of the rural-urban character of their migration. This will therefore be reduced over time.

But at present black mothers are forced along with many of their white counterparts to take such jobs as outwork or night cleaning. The practice of outwork (machining or hand-finishing garments at home) is extremely widespread in all the black ghetto areas in London. There are no fixed rates, and employers benefit not only from this but from their saving of factory space, tax evasions and total lack of responsibility for their employees either personally or in the payment of benefits. (As an example of outwork rates, one firm pays 60p for 100 cushion covers. Each cover requires 3 seams and the insertion of a zip.)

Contrary to most opinion, most night office cleaners do the job not for 'pin money' but as sole supporters of their families. The average take-home pay for this unpleasant job is about £12. A large proportion of night cleaners in London are black women. (See 'The night cleaners campaign', a 'Socialist Woman' special issue, 1971; 'Shrew', December '71)

Added to their own family's demands here may be continuing responsibilities at home. A survey in Nottingham found that 87% of West Indian women were sending money home.

Nurses

The highest concentration of New Commonwealth female labour is found, seemingly paradoxically, among professional workers. In 1966 this accounted for 22% of black female immigrants, as opposed to 10% of the British female labour force. (Sample census 1966) This figure represents one of the chief areas of exploitation of black women, that of British hospitals and medical services. In the West Midlands in 1966 there were four times as many West Indian nurses as other white collar occupations. For the total female population, other white collar employees outnumber nurses 16 to 1. In some hospitals 80% of the staff are black. The most conservative estimate is that 25 to 35% of nurses are foreign born. (O. Gish, 'The training and advancement of non-British nurses', I.I.R. Newsletter, November/December 1968)

The supply of nurses from the New Commonwealth is catered

for by immigration legislation, which restricts skilled category B voucher holders to medical or teaching occupations. Furthermore, the tightening of regulations for students in 1965 enforced return after the completion of the course. That many nurses have not done so is ignored by the Home Office. In 1968 44% of Commonwealth nurses were recruited abroad.

Britain's gain is at the expense of developing countries. Given the inadequate training facilities for nurses and midwives in the third world, British training could be a valuable form of aid. But once admitted to Britain as students, black nurses find themselves excluded from the best training. Only 4% of black Commonwealth nurses are trained in teaching hospitals, compared with 24% of British girls. Black nurses find that they are denied opportunities for taking and passing SRN examinations. Relegated to SEN status, they can be used as exploited labour for the unpleasant routine jobs on wards and in geriatric hospitals. (See 'Black Voice', vol. 1 no. 2 and vol. 2 no. 2) Another result of discrimination in training is that black nurses are not employed in higher grades. In spite of the fact that at least 25% of all nursing staff are born outside Britain, only a fifth of these reach the upper ranks of the profession.

The situation of black nurses also shows up the contradictions in the attitude towards black female labour. As already noted, in 1966 13% of the British female labour force was employed as sales workers. Only 1% of West Indian women were in these jobs. This is usually explained by the British public's reluctance to be served by black employees. In the case of nursing, however, these objections are overlooked. Despite the prejudice encountered by black nurses on the wards, other considerations determine official policy.

Future trends

It is likely that the present high inflow of black female dependents will decline as families of first generation immigrants are reunited. That this should be so is the intention of the 1971 Immigration Act, restricting the entry of women to 'patrials or wives of patrials'. The aim of this is to bring restrictions on dependents into line with the EEC, where the policy is to attract temporary migrant labour and discourage settlers with families. In Western Germany, for example, workers from outside the EEC are not allowed in the first instance to bring in dependents. ('The admission of foreign workers and their dependents; some European comparisons', Runnymede Industrial Unit paper B1, 1971)

The focus will increasingly switch to the second generation. The difficulties of school-leavers in finding employment are already becoming apparent. Young black girls have suffered not only from the educational bias against girls, but also against all black schoolkids. Although a higher proportion of black female school-leavers are going into clerical jobs or occupations such as nursing or hairdressing, the majority may remain in the class position of their parents.

The Donovan Report and employment forecasts predict an increasing need for highly skilled woman power. If present trends in the decline of demand for unskilled labour continue, the insecurity of black female labour will increase.

The aim of this paper has been to provide some basic information on the employment of black women, in relation to the needs of the British labour market for a pool of cheap reserve labour. I have therefore not dealt with the types of racial prejudice and sexism directed towards a black woman and other more individual aspects of her situation. In any fuller analysis of her position, this would be essential. She is not only predominantly a member of the working class, but black and a woman.

C. Crime and the body politic

WOMEN, PRISON AND ECONOMIC INDEPENDENCE

Raya Levin and Judith Brandt

(This piece is based on a paper on women and delinquency presented at the Women's Weekend at Ruskin College, Oxford in February/March 1970)

The notion of 'delinquency' or 'crime' is a socially changing concept. What is perfectly normal practice in one culture may be considered a crime in another. To give just one obvious example, in many Eastern cultures polygamy is the norm; but the Christian ethic in the West has made it a punishable offence under British law.

Committing an act of delinquency, or a crime, implies that some anti-social act is being perpetrated. However, the interpretation of what is anti-social is again a cultural and political question. In fact, not all anti-social acts are punishable. The infliction of bodily harm or damage to property is punishable. But cruelty in the form of psychological humiliation, or that of ill-paid exploited labour, are not punishable by penal law. Nor is the type of manipulation which might involve the manipulation of people's weaknesses, which corners them into accepting a particular role; most familiarly experienced are the games which different members of a family play with each other, and the tangle of emotional blackmail they weave around each other. Another example is the material arbitrariness of the law concerning immoral earnings. It is a punishable offence to live off the earnings of a prostitute (ie to be a pimp), but it is not a punishable offence to live off the surplus made as a result of the labour of large numbers of people: a farmer with the only potato crop which survives a blight who then sells the crop for six times its previous market value is not penalised. This might be considered immoral earnings by some, the progress of society by others.

In general, delinquency and crime could be defined as any act which threatens the existing order of society. Many of the laws which preserve this status quo are more concerned with property than people. A businessman who evicts helpless people in order to tear down their houses and rebuild to make money is praised for his resourcefulness, whereas the gesture of rebelliousness made by a homeless squatter is greeted with punishment.

Every so-called offence is a non-conformist act; a barometer of the degree to which the individual is able to tolerate the pressures of society. In this way it can be paralleled to 'neurotic' or 'psychotic' behaviour, people who go 'mad' and become self-destructive and violent as a response to these same pressures. Social attitudes to mental health have changed a great deal in recent years; we no longer (in theory at any rate) lock up mental patients. They are seen as 'ill' and needing treatment, rather than morally judged 'wicked' and punished.

However, in both crime and mental illness, the gesture of non-conformism, or protest, is personal and individual; and here lies its weakness. As it is an individual rather than a collective rebellion, it lacks the ability to formulate a general challenge, to live within society while fighting it as a whole. Individuals such as these finally only damage themselves; potentially, however, many of them could unite and channel their actions into a collective and more constructive political rebellion. The necessary process is to understand that one's dissatisfaction or frustration stems from a situation in which one is oppressed, and to go on from that to the realisation that there are others in the same state. In America, the Black Panther Party and the Young Lords consist often of people who some years ago would have been 'criminals', rebelling as individuals in the streets.

Women are usually surprised to see how poorly they are represented in penal institutions, in the numbers of those accused of delinquency or crime. The ratio is roughly one woman to every forty men. Apart from offences relating to children, women surpass men in only one area - shoplifting. In 1970, 21,739 women were found guilty of shoplifting, compared with 18,853 men. Both men and women in prison come from almost exclusively working class backgrounds. Why is it, then, that women are apparently so law-abiding?

For men in this society there is only one legally recognised way of getting an income which is not earned in exchange for their own labour: by owning the means of production, by being a capitalist. But for the majority of men this is not a feasible choice, so for them the choice is often between work and crime.

Women have these two choices, but in a far more limited way: however, in addition they also have a third alternative. In our society woman is a commodity as well as a human being, and she can thus use the market value of her person as an alternative to either work or crime. In other words, if a woman can't find a job she likes and doesn't want to steal or commit any other crime, she can always take her third alternative and get married. If a man wants to live off someone else, he has to break the law. A woman doesn't. She can quite legally do it through marriage. Woman's social role is thus also a sexual role; she is wife, mother, supportive companion; the market value of her sexuality transcends class; woman is a commodity, a stateless sexual thing. As a commodity she has real mobility. By virtue of a possible boyfriend or husband she can live on a higher level, and live out the fantasies which advertising and TV project onto her. She can move away from her class origins by virtue of this parasitism. A man, however, to reach the same standard, the same dream, will have to steal the car which his female counterpart rides in. Her act is legal, his illegal. It is no coincidence that the majority of stolen cars are simply taken for joy-rides by men.

Women's third outlet, therefore, is one in which she can stifle any feelings of dissatisfaction she might have by off-loading all the responsibility onto a man. Ironically, the very oppression and exploitation to which she is subject in this role encourage a passivity, a caution which is a major obstacle to women's militancy - historically, at any rate.

A large proportion of women in Holloway prison, London, which draws its inmates from all over south-east England, are in on charges of defrauding Social Security. This involves changing dates and/or details in a social security supplementary benefits book. Most women drawing supplementary benefit do so because their husbands have left them or because they are alone with small children and unable to work. Most of them are simply confused by a complex bureaucratic system which has complicated forms and offers 50p for this and £3 for that. They are alienated by a system which on the one hand tells them they are entitled to benefit, and then apparently arbitrarily takes it away from them. The so-called 'defrauding' is simply the only way in which these women can be relatively sure of at least some money to live on.

Hire purchase offences are almost as common. The pressure on women to buy new and expensive household goods is heavy, and, through advertising and TV, is aimed at women at home. This is all very well when there is enough money and the ability to resist the dreams in washing-machine form. Most offences are not for being behind with payments, but for selling the goods before the final instalment has been paid. This is an offence because until the final instalment the item still belongs to the hire-purchase company. Many women do this in times of crisis, when they haven't got the money for instalments anyway, and often don't have money for basic things like food and rent.

The last group is that of women in prison for child neglect. These women are being punished for failing to live up to society's image of them as good mothers, when the society itself will not give them adequate means and facilities to do so. Again, most women have little money, and are simply and understandably unable to cope with the responsibility for and needs of small children. When they're in prison their children are often taken into council children's 'homes'; a separation such as this is cruel and can only add to any woman's sense of hopelessness and inadequacy.

The most pernicious irony about the prison process is that women in Holloway are often put through a course in management and child care, consisting of training in budgeting and diet. Here she may learn to cope with situations which are totally unrelated to the real situation at home; what is the use of teaching a woman to use a washing machine when all she may have at home is a cold tap on the landing. The wing for child neglect offenders is sprinkled with plastic doilies and ruffled curtains - another reinforcement of the consumer pressures which may have pushed a woman to commit the 'crime' in the first place. The prison wing decorated like a dream home is equated with the home which may have had the feeling of being a prison. In both cases the woman knows a thing or two about isolation.

The offence of shoplifting, in which women outnumber men, illustrates most clearly the secondary, consumer role into which women are slotted by society. She is expected all her life to believe that she wants and needs all the material goods which the advertisers convince her are vital to a full and happy life. It is the woman who uses all the household goods, and since she is rarely the one who is also responsible for earning the money which will pay for these goods, the only way she can get what she wants is through her husband, by urging and manipulating him to earn more money, get a better job. The only other way in which she can get some of the things herself is to take them from the shops which flaunt them in front of her. Many women shoplift out of real need, but many others, often middle class and middle-aged, shoplift out of boredom and frustration, and perhaps as a way of getting back at the stores crammed with goods they can't possibly buy. It was recently reported in one daily newspaper that a large percentage of women now consider shoplifting as trivial an offence as parking on a yellow line is for motorists.

One interesting fact is that women in prison, mainly young women, have a reputation for being remarkably violent and intractable. Many girls in Borstals are known as girls 'you can't do anything with', who won't respond to 'treatment'. They often break up their cells, expressing their violence more directly and destructively than many men. One reason for this might be that since many women do take unconscious advantage of their 'third alternative', those who do end up in Borstal or prison have been subject to the heaviest pressures, and are consequently more violent. Another reason may be that men have more socially accepted outlets for aggression: driving cars, sport, more physically demanding work, the psychological aggression involved in career competitiveness, fights. In the present society we know that men are more violent than women; but this does not mean that they are innately so, merely that women are expected to (and therefore do) repress their feelings of violence and frustration, so that when it does erupt it does so with much more

178

potency.

Prison is not the answer to any kind of so-called 'criminal' activity. In particular, it seems clear that many of the offences by women stem from their secondary economic role - exacerbated when the women also have children. Many women in prison are there for social security offences. By defrauding they are making a stand for financial independence from their husbands, who are probably unreliable about providing cash for the housekeeping, likely to spend it all on drink or to disappear for weeks on end (at which time the woman is entitled to benefits) and then return for a few days only to wander off again. During this time the woman and her children have not only isolation and loneliness to cope with but, with her income abruptly stopped, she has essential material needs. These can be eased slightly by a regular supportive income from social security. Even if her man does return there can be no guarantee that he will give her any money; or indeed that he will have any to give her. Many women in Holloway have often said that they like their husbands as men but loathe them as 'providers'.

Women could be released from the economic dependence on their men by a state allowance provided by the nation's taxes and doled out to those who perform the function of 'mother' for as long as they do, that is, all people who care for children. This could be scaled per child, have no relation to sex or consanguinity and be entirely independent of a blood-father's earnings. It would make the country responsible for its children - as we are supposed to be for its sick and its unfortunate - regardless of whether we have actually parented them. A woman economically independent of her husband might find she can live with him because she wants to and not because she needs to.

Many women in the Women's Movement see this as a dangerous idea that it likely to confirm a woman in her role as 'mother'. Unless there is a sudden rage for test-tube babies, women, not men, must continue to be the bearers of children. They might produce far fewer - which population-wise can only be a good thing - but still they must be the ones that have them. How men and women together as independent beings choose to organise the sharing of responsibility for children would be up to them. If women are to discover their true potential whether as mothers, doctors, labourers or any number of things, they have got to begin by seeing themselves not as slaves but as people with a certain freedom of choice. There could only be a real women's revolution when women have the will and energy to get up and examine their position in society. And they can only do that if they believe in the dignity of womankind, the first step towards which is a release from the degradation of cajoling an individual male for cash.

A WOMAN'S RIGHTS OVER HER BODY

Monica Sjoo

(Monica Sjoo is a member of Bristol Women's Liberation)

Right to birth control and abortion

Local authorities are empowered by the National Health
Service (Family Planning) Act 1967 to give advice on contraception, the medical examination of persons seeking advice
on contraception and the supply of contraceptive substances
and appliances. They also have the power to charge for these
services. All these powers are subject to the direction of the
Minister of Health. Only some local authorities take advantage of these powers, often using the services of the Family
Planning Association. Charges vary from authority to authority, the more progressive ones providing advice free but
charging for the supply of contraceptives. Usually women in
very poor circumstances are exempt from charges if referred by a health visitor or other authority.

There is no law specifying that a husband's consent must be
sought before prescribing any contraceptive appliance or pill
or before sterilisation. It is possible, however, that if a husband's consent was not sought before sterilisation he would
have a remedy at law for his loss of his wife's ability to bear
children. No such action has yet succeeded to our knowledge.
It is a Family Planning Association ruling, adopted by some
doctors as well, that a husband must give his consent before
sterilisation and before fitting an interuterine device.

Women have no legal right to an abortion. Since 1967 doctors
are no longer committing an offence by terminating a pregnancy if certain conditions apply. These conditions are that
two registered medical practitioners must be of the opinion
(a) that the continuance of the pregnancy would involve risk
to the life of the pregnant woman or of injury to the physical
or mental health of the woman or existing children of her
family, greater than if the pregnancy were terminated, or
(b) that there is a substantial risk that if the child were born
it would suffer from such physical or mental abnormalities
as to be seriously handicapped.

A woman's actual or reasonably forseeable environment may
be taken into account when deciding if the pregnancy would
involve a risk to her health. An abortion must be carried out
in a National Health hospital or in a place approved by the
Minister of Health, unless it is carried out as an emergency.

Women need not always keep their mouths shut and their wombs open (Emma Goldman)

One in four, or possibly as many as a half, of all babies born
in England today were unplanned and unwanted. The majority
of women and men are ignorant about contraception and where

180

to get it. The lack of information and education on the subject is scandalous, and contraceptives are expensive. It is women, and particularly working class women, who suffer as a result of this since it is women who become pregnant if contraceptives fail or are unavailable, and it is women who need abortions and who either have to face an inadequate National Health Service or seek expensive private abortions if they are middle class and dangerous backstreet abortions if they are working class. But in our society, and in societies for the last couple of thousand years, it has been men of the ruling classes, priests of patriarchal religions, living in celibacy, and doctors, mainly concerned with their own power and prestige, who have created laws laying down to women what they may or may not do with their bodies.

Even today women and men are deliberately kept uninformed about contraception because this raises the issue of women's right to self-determination. For women to be able themselves to control their fertility questions the functions of the father-centred family and women's part within it as a source of unpaid labour - and so ultimately it questions the entire structure of the society we live in. Women's unpaid work within the family saves society from having to provide communal services such as nurseries, dining-rooms, collective kitchens. The means by which women are made to accept this role is the continuous fear and burden of unwanted pregnancies that forces them into more and more economic, physical and psychological dependence on their husbands. The capitalist society can then give as a reason for women's lack of opportunities in schools, in jobs, in life: 'But you are only going to have children...'

Children should be the social responsibility of the whole society, but in our society the burden of bringing up children falls entirely on lonely and alienated women who are fearful and powerless to protect either themselves or their children. For women it is of the greatest importance to campaign for free contraception and abortion on the woman's own demand, because we cannot even begin to think of fighting for any kind of freedom or change until at the very least we can decide when and if to have children.

It is important to realise that men's control over women's fertility has not always existed and that it is in fact a relatively recent development, since in ancient and primitive societies women were always in charge of the knowledge of contraception, abortion, midwifery. Women have in all ages sought to limit their pregnancies. The first known medical text, an Egyptian papyrus dating back to nearly 2000 BC, contains prescriptions for contraceptive substances to be inserted into the vagina. Women studied alongside men in the medical schools, and both women and men priests helped women in childbirth. The Talmudic Jews invented the vaginal sponge which was used, soaked in oil, until the invention of the Dutch cap in the 1880s. It is even possible that there existed a sterilising herbal draught, to be taken by women, since the hormone progesterone now used in the contraceptive pill exists in various plants.

In so-called 'primitive' societies, fertility rites and contraceptive knowledge existed side by side. Even the menstrual taboo was probably introduced by women themselves as a form of birth-control, since it was believed that this was the most fertile period. Women's menstrual cycle wasn't clearly understood until the 1950s. In fact, contrary to what we are told by many male anthropologists, 'primitive' peoples had a fairly good understanding of human reproduction.

So, what we are told about the primitive woman being continuously pregnant doesn't seem to be true. The Victorian woman was far more ignorant of her sexuality and of contraceptive methods than were her sisters in the past. Perhaps never in history have women been so totally sexually repressed and forced into almost yearly child-bearing as in 'civilised' societies.

It was only with the economic changeover from gift exchange and communal property to private property in men's hands that it became essential to men to introduce the patriarchal father-centred family with all legal, social, economic and sexual rights invested in the father alone. Now women became wives, they were forced under threat of punishment or social ostracism to remain virgins until marriage - all for the sake of establishing legal heirs to the father's property. Philosophies and religions came now to be centred around the idea of the sanctity of Fatherhood, because now it became politically expedient, and theories were elaborated about the 'natural' inferiority of women. The father came to be everything; the foetus was even seen as contained in the man's sperm. Consequently the mother was deprived of any rights, legal or otherwise, over her own body or her children.

Abortion only becomes illegal when church or state define it so. This is the true background to the refusal of various churches to accept contraception and abortion - they are defending the father's absolute right. What is at stake is not the sanctity of human life but power over women. Even today the Catholic church recognises the sanctity of the foetus's life, but not that of the adult woman. In all non-Catholic countries in the West it is now legal to abort a woman if there is a risk to her life if the pregnancy continues - but not to in Catholic countries. In Italy where contraception is also illegal there are as many 'criminal' abortions as there are live births. Many women die as a result of these illegal abortions. These women are being indirectly killed by the church.

The Christian religion is centred around an almighty Father-god, his son and the son's non-sexual virgin-mother. The Christian god was serviced by celibate male priests to whom the woman was the creation of the 'devil'. She alone represented sexuality, her sexual organs were fearsome and unclean, and birth was disgusting and unholy.

During the Dark Ages, the delivery of a pregnant woman was no longer a sacrament but a dirty business, and the women who attended other women in childbirth were frequently the outcasts of society who could get no other work. These midwives belonged to an underground of women who retained women's traditional knowledge of herbs and medicine, who had contraceptive knowledge and who knew how to procure abortions. Dr Margaret Murray says: 'The modern idea of the witch is founded entirely on the records of the 17th and 18th centuries when the Christian church was still engaged in crushing out the remains of paganism, and was reinforced in this by the medical profession, which recognised in the witches their most dangerous rivals in the economic field. Throughout the country, the witch or wise-woman, the sage-femme, was always called in at child-birth; many of these women were highly skilled, and it is on record that some would perform the Caesarian operation with complete success for the mother and child'. The witch-hunts therefore coincided with the rise of a special male profession of medicine, which became more 'scientific' and subject to government and professional control. Even the practice of midwifery, women's particular province since time immemorial, began to require an education from which women were excluded.

Even as late as the middle of the 19th century clerical and medical authorities firmly opposed any methods that would relieve the suffering of women in labour. A painful birth was woman's rightful punishment for being sinful and unclean. Amongst the accusation directed at 'witches' was that relieving women's pain in childbirth was a 'dreadful and impious act against the will of God who in the beginning had cursed Eve and all her female descendants'.

Women doctors didn't appear again until relatively recently and then in spite of great resistance. So that when new methods of contraception became known and available again they were firmly placed in the hands of male doctors where by and large they remain to this day.

Birth control

The modern birth-control movement began in the 1880s. The first person to campaign publicly for birth control was Francis Place, a working class socialist and trade unionist. He had grown up in poverty and knew only too well what effect poverty and unwanted pregnancies had on working class people. He advocated that women use the sponge as a vaginal tampon. Sheaths or condoms for men had been made out of linen or sheep-bladders for some time, but they were expensive and had originally been made to prevent men from catching syphilis from prostitutes and not as contraceptives.

Many of the early campaigners for birth control were appalled at the misery among working class women; women were so downtrodden and fatalistic that they accepted the fact that their next pregnancy might result in death, seeing pain and misery as their lot in life. It was said that if women didn't fear pregnancy as a result of intercourse, they would immediately indulge in all kinds of 'immoral practices'. 'Promiscuity would run rampant if single women could keep from having babies'. The laws concerning sexuality were not only typical class-laws but they wre also sexist laws as they were created by well-off men sitting in parliament and directed against working class women.

The other side of the coin was the fact that there were 80,000 prostitutes in London at the turn of the century. The majority were working-class women who were forced to sell their bodies or starve, and their function was to preserve the virginity of the daughters of the bourgeoisie.

In 1843 the vulcanisation of rubber made it possible to mass-produce condoms. In Holland the rubber diaphragm or cap was invented by Dr Mensinga in 1880. By the 1880s there were also spermicides in mass production, and all that remained was to inform the population that methods of contraception existed and were available. But this didn't happen. In England it was never actually illegal to give birth control advice, but in the USA it was made illegal in 1873 (there are still some states where you can't buy contraceptives). Margaret Sanger was arrested when she opened her birth control clinic in New York in 1910. In France contraception was made illegal in 1920, and only became legal again in 1966.

A Dutch woman doctor opened up the first birth control clinic anywhere, in 1882. She fitted working class women with the Mensinga cap (thus the name 'Dutch cap'). In 1928 Marie Stopes opened the first British clinic in the East End of London. It was free and she too fitted the cap. She assumed that the authorities would soon realise the vast need for contraception, as soon as they saw the improvement in the health of working class women and children. Her clinic was meant to be an experiment and an example which the Ministry of Health would follow in setting up its own clinics. Again, it didn't happen, and now, fifty years later, we still have no freely available contraceptive service under the National Health Service.

The Birth Control Council, which campaigned for contraception early in this century, changed its name to the Family Planning Association in 1939, which was a giving-in to respectability. It was largely a middle class organisation, restricting its services at first to married women. Since 1970, however, all the present thousand clinics in Britain give contraceptive advice to all women over 16, whether married or not. The Association is still a voluntary organisation and a registered charity. However, it does not deal with its contraceptive failures, offering no facilities or abortion service for women who have become pregnant as a result of a failed IUD, a torn sheath or a slipped diaphragm.

The Family Planning Act gave permissive powers to local authorities to provide birth control advice and supplies. So far not many councils have used these powers. The reasons vary, from lack of money and facilities to religious prejudice and puritanism, or lack of concern. Birth control has not so far been integrated into the National Health Service and so it has not been seen as being part of a doctor's responsibilities. Until very recently birth control was excluded from the curriculum of medical students. Many GPs refuse to discuss contraception and see it as none of their business. The fact that a GP is not paid by the Health Service if he/she does give contraceptive advice doesn't make it any easier for doctors who would provide the service if they could. The majority of maternity hospitals don't follow up post-natal care with contraceptive advice; this applies even to women who have had legal abortions in hospitals. The main responsibility thus still falls on the Family Planning Association. The FPA gets no economic support and in order to be able to cover their costs they have to charge women £3 for joining and the cost of contraceptives. They are helped by the fact that many of their workers are volunteers. The FPA will not turn away any woman who cannot afford to pay, but they cannot afford to publicise this fact widely.

In fact the present facilities - FPA, Brook Advisory Centres, health clinics, GPs - would be quite inadequate if women right now demanded contraception as a natural right. The present situation is not caused by people's ignorance - capitalist society relies on people's lack of knowledge about their rights - but on lack of provision and information. A recent survey examined the current pattern of what contraceptives are used. Among couples interviewed a year after their first, second and third child, the most popular form of contraception was the sheath. 30% used the sheath or condom, compared with 20% using the pill and 5% using the cap. An alarming 27% used no method at all or withdrawal. Withdrawal and the condom are male-dominated forms of contraception, and withdrawal particularly is entirely unreliable.

No contraceptives are absolutely safe as yet, and much more research must go into contraceptives that will not upset or change the hormonal balance of the woman's body. Also what about a pill for men? Great numbers of men refuse to use any form of contraception and confuse virility with being able to make 'the wife' pregnant.

For the moment it is largely educated middle class women who use the available clinics, (who know where they are, even) who can afford to pay the fees and are not intimidated by the middle class accents and attitudes of the staff and also of GPs. Most 'ordinary' people are alienated by a hospital-like atmosphere, by being asked personal questions by total strangers in white coats, and many women are fearful of what contraception is all about anyway.

Women must not only be able to control their fertility but also all medicine to do with their sexuality and reproduction. The whole question of medicine, and especially obstetrics, must be looked into by women; it is women who give birth, but women themselves have precious little say about what happens in hospitals. The mystique of obstetrics, and indeed the whole medical myth, must be broken open for all to see.

As far as childbirth is concerned, most women emerge from the experience resentful and shocked. It appears that obstetrical care is becoming increasingly focused on the obstetrician himself who, treating childbirth as a rare disease, places himself stage centre in the delivery-room and relegates the woman to a supporting role. It is not uncommon that a woman asking what is happening to herself is told to shut up or is shouted at. Episiotomies are done for no apparent reason, and the woman feels herself treated as an object, and birth which is great strength and creation as well as blood and pain becomes degraded and clinical. Do we want this - do we want to give birth in a hospital environment at all? Women must decide, women must ask questions about their lives.

It is also of the utmost importance that children are taught about sexuality, about contraception, veneral disease, pregnancy, childbirth and abortion. Whether sex education is allowed in a school or not is now up to the individual head teacher, and they are notoriously reactionary. The only subject that is compulsory in English schools is religious instruction.'

It is the law that says that the legal age of consent for girls is 16 that stands in the way of giving proper sex education to children in schools. Young girls are not supposed to know about sexuality. When this obsolete law was passed girls didn't start to menstruate until the age of 16-17 because of wrong diet, anaemia, lack of physical exercise etc. Today, however, girls start to menstruate much earlier, at 11-12, and are often sexually experienced long before the 'age of consent'. All the law succeeds in doing is to prevent girls from getting contraceptive advice and consequently many girls under 16 get pregnant, and have abortions or are forced into marriages that break up in a few years. An unmarried mother on her own with a child is discriminated against in every way.

We have to get rid of this law and there will have to be clinics where teenagers serve young people. Right now it is only the Brook Advisory Centres that try to make young unmarried women feel comfortable, but they are expensive and they still cannot help a girl under 16 unless she has her parents' permission. In other words, there is nowhere a girl under 16 can legally be given contraceptive advice.

One other form of contraception is sterilisation. Even though vasectomy (male sterilisation) is easy, quick, reversible in many cases, and can be done on an out-patient basis, it is almost impossible for men to get vasectomies performed on the National Health Service. There is still much mystique about male sexuality, and an attitude of not wanting to 'tamper' with it.

Abortion

Abortion was treated as manslaughter until this century, and it was only in 1929 that it became possible for a woman to have an abortion performed if her life was in danger. Before the Abortion Act of 1967 most abortions were illegal, and there are no reliable statistics. However, it is estimated that up to 250,000 abortions were performed every year. Part of the evidence for this was the large number of women admitted to hospital after botched abortions. In 1964 about 35,000 women were admitted to hospitals in Britain after illegal abortions - which goes to show that no-one can force a woman to have a child she doesn't want and that legally preventing her from having a safe abortion simply drives her to seek one elsewhere. In the long run, legal abortions would also be cheaper for the NHS.

The official figure for abortions in 1970 was 80,000, which means that a large number of women are still seeking back-street abortions; and again, as with contraception, it is working class women who will seek a cheap illegal abortionist rather than be intimidated by middle class, condescending doctors and gynaecologists. Until abortion becomes free on the woman's own decision, this situation will not change. Also, until contraception is 100% safe there will be a growing number of women who are more educated in the use of birth control and who will increasingly demand abortions as a result of contraceptive failure.

The Women's Liberation campaign for abortion on demand creates a precedent in medical science, since there are no other situations in which a patient can suggest the treatment he will receive. This is seen as a threat to the powers of the medical profession, whose specialisation makes most people feel that their illnesses exist for the benefit of the doctors, rather than the doctors for them. At present the only area in which women can do this is in private abortion clinics. Many of these are rackets - it is estimated that a doctor can make up to £200,000 a year out of legal private abortions. In fact this would be one of the main reasons why we still do not have abortions on demand - the profits to be had from private abortions on middle-class women. More legal abortions are done privately than on the NHS. There is also much resistance within the NHS itself. The Act states that a woman

187

needs the consent of a doctor and the gynaecologist who is going to perform the operation. There are only 555 consultant gynaecologists in Britain. Given some with religious or 'ethical' reservations, it doesn't leave enough for even the current demand. According to a recent survey of Fellows of the Royal College of Gynaecologists, 192 were opposed to any form of abortion on 'social' grounds. Many hospitals now find that women having abortions are taking up bed-space which otherwise would have been given to urgent gynaecological cases. This creates ill-feeling among nurses and doctors and can only be solved when proper facilities are supplied - best of all would be small units attached to hospitals where the vacuum-suction abortion can be done on an out-patient basis, using staff who are specially trained to do this work.

For the moment, one way is being shown by the Pregnancy Advisory Services in Birmingham and London, which refer women (after consultation) to reputable doctors and clinics. They also run their own nursing home, charging about £60 for an abortion, which is still well above most people's means. The London Pregnancy Advisory Service recently stated that even at £45, abortion is profitable, and from revenue in the past few years they have been able to open another nursing home. We must demand that the NHS takes over the private clinics and appropriates the profits made by the private abortionists for the opening of new free clinics that will really serve women.

It is up to us to demand our rights - nobody else is going to do it. Women must be able to realise themselves, through work, action, creation. For the moment, often the only way a woman is allowed to, or can, fulfil herself is by having children. Women now have children for all the wrong reasons. It is also a child's right to be a wanted child. Children are now supposed to compensate women for all the activities from which they are excluded, and of course children cannot do this. Both women and children end up as nervous wrecks in an impossible situation. Women who feel fulfilled in their lives in the community need not, and will not want to, have many children.

But is must always be a woman's own choice whether she has no children or ten children, and any legislation from above that would force women to have a prescribed number of children, whether large or small, would be unacceptable.

Together with the demand for free contraception and abortion on demand must go the struggle for total change in the economic, work and family structure of society. But this freedom to struggle will not come about until we have control over our own bodies.

FEMALE SEXUALITY: ITS POLITICAL IMPLICATIONS

Pat Whiting

(Pat Whiting is a member of Women's Liberation, and this
piece is based on research for a book she is writing on
female sexuality)

'Deeply embedded in all normal women is the mother-instinct,
and unless this is fulfilled no woman can become what we call
"a complete woman", so strong is it.' (Robert Chartham,
'Mainly for women')

'In the case of female education the main stress should be
laid on bodily training, and after that on development of character; and last of all, on intellect. But the one absolute aim
of female education must be with the view to the future mother.' (Adolf Hitler, 'Mein Kampf')

'I think that it's just sour grapes suggesting that there is
something wrong with a woman devoting herself entirely to
her child. Why shouldn't she if she wants to? I suspect some
of the women's lib people aren't capable of enjoying it.
Many of them may have had poor mothers themselves.'
(John Bowlby of the Tavistock Clinic, 'Times Educational
Supplement', 14 January 1972)

'All this searching after the female orgasm makes women
neurotic. Women must come to accept that it is just not as
important for them as for the male. Lots of women have
lived very happy married lives without ever having experienced an orgasm.' (GP, Islington, 1972)

At this time in history no woman is strong enough to solve
her own problems in the isolation of a heterosexual relationship. Most men are victims of a paternalistic culture
which defines what it is to be a woman and what men should
expect from women. Women, in turn, are victims of male
prejudices and misogyny firmly based on centuries of sup-
erstition, ignorance and fear of the female. Women in the
Women's Liberation Movement are no more free from these
pressures than any other women. We need the support of
women everywhere to 'decondition' men, to rid ourselves of
the double standard and to establish a more realistic image
of female sexuality than that offered us by the male society.

Women are tired of hearing men define what it is to be a
woman - 'a real woman' or 'a complete woman', in their
words. Few if any women would dare to describe what it
feels like to be a man, let alone 'a complete man'. Yet men
have been doing this for us since the dawn of organised society and, what is more serious, the bulk of women, until now,
have accepted the male definition of their own sexuality, or
at least pretended to. The above quotes from men in our own
society reveal their sexist attitudes, their common need to

define and manipulate the female in order to safeguard their own position of dominance.

From our own position of growing awareness and consciousness of ourselves, we have no further need of male definitions of our sexuality; they are obsolete. From now on women want to hear from each other, to construct a body of knowledge which corresponds to reality. Let the male confine his fantasies and imaginings to accounts about his own sex. Brother, you have caused enough confusion already. Keep out!

Part 1

The myth of the female orgasm

In spite of, or perhaps because of the existence of the so-called 'permissive society', many women are still in a state of doubt and confusion about their own sexuality, about their sexual response and how to obtain sexual satisfaction in a relationship. Many use lies and deceit to cover up their own ignorance or anxieties, or to appear to conform to the female image projected by men.

'It is terribly tragic; and many marriages will be shaken when the partners are told that the vaginal orgasm does not exist. It is either a direct or an indirect clitoral orgasm. The clitoris is the spot that arouses the woman's feelings of sensuality.' (Inge and Sten Hegeler)

How can women be confused about their own sexuality? Historically we are only just emerging from a period of formidable sexual repression (see part 2). The conflict about the nature of the female orgasm arose as twentieth-century woman was beginning to enjoy very limited access to contraceptive devices. This conflict between the clitoral and the vaginal orgasm, introduced by Freud, has been the area which has caused most distress in the sex life of the modern woman. The conflict has caused so much damage to the female psyche that no discussion on female sexuality is complete without a study of it. Ignorance on the subject has caused women to play-act, to lie, to deceive and connive or to become completely passive and resigned to the male definition of their make-up.

Whilst our mothers may have accepted the role of resignation and suffered frustration through the partial stimulation of sexual intercourse which did not lead to orgasm, we may have been forced into a play-acting role by a male partner who insists that we have a vaginal orgasm every time and assumes that female orgasm follows automatically from the penis being in the vagina.

Anxious to live up to the image of the sexy young woman, armed with the pill, projected by the admen, we may even have deceived ourselves, either out of ignorance of our own bodies or to flatter the male ego. The admen of the media

show today's swinging woman as always sexy, always eager
to please her man with the right colour lipstick, the latest
fashion, a vaginal deodorant or a vaginal orgasm. Even in the
kitchen she is presented as sexy, perky, always smiling; they
ignore the dirty dishes, the soiled nappies, the howling baby;
the woman appears calm, serene and above all sexy.

The young woman is made to feel that men know what is best
for her and it follows in this pattern that if she does not measure up to male expectations in bed and obtain a vaginal orgasm, she begins to feel a failure, to feel inadequate and develops a response mechanism to stimulate orgasm so that the
male is flattered, convinced that he is a good lover.

At first this kind of play-acting, ie the right kinds of groans,
tossings and turnings, may seem easier than trying to teach
an arrogant male the subtleties of the female response mechanism. The danger of this situation is that it is self-perpetu-
ating. Once the deception has begun, it is more difficult to
reveal to the 'falsely' confident male that you have been
lying. This leaves the modern female, unless she is confident
enough to masturbate, with the same unsatisfied tensions as
her mother lived with. Built up over a long period, these tensions lead to disorders of the pelvis as well as those of the
personality. The situation is not as bad as for our mothers
and grandmothers, however. Women are beginning to develop
confidence in a new way, denied to them historically; they
are beginning to develop group and political consciousness.
That women have been willing to talk about their sexuality to
me for research projects represents some kind of social revolution. From talking to women and counselling girls in two
large schools, I made the following observations on woman's
confusion about her own sexual response, over two years of
research.

Women talking

'I don't know what all the fuss is about. I don't think many
women would get an orgasm without manual or oral stimulation of the clitoris. I think the vaginal orgasm is a myth; it
is for me anyway. I can have any number of clitoral orgasms
given the right mood. How did I learn? My mother used to be
a naturist and left the right kind of books around when we
were about twelve.' (Woman, 35, civil service executive,
Middlesex, married, with a lot of premarital sexual experience)

About 15% of the women interviewed are sure that they only
experience a clitoral orgasm, whether during masturbation,
intercourse or foreplay. These women tend to be mainly under forty, better educated and more sexually experienced than
other women interviewed. I found that educational level is not,
however, a passport to sexual happiness, and university graduates may be just as 'uptight' about sex as women in general.

What these women seemed to have in common, however, was a

high degree of self-confidence in other areas of their lives. They had nearly all achieved recognition in professions which demanded some personal initiative - law, designing, higher civil service grades, medicine or running their own business. This confidence in social achievement seemed to spill over into their personal lives. Most of them described women who could not communicate about their own sexual needs as 'their own enemies'.

As most of these women were married, how did they deal with male prejudices? If these women had encountered male prejudice they had firmly insisted that the male listen to the female point of view; faced with a particularly resistant chauvinist, they quickly abandoned him.

Even these confident women were not entirely free from sexual pressures. A few of them admitted bearing unwanted children for 'social reasons' or because their husbands demanded it. They did not allow this to interfere with their career, however, and soon left the child in the care of an au pair or nanny.

Girls in their married bliss

About 75% of the married women interviewed admitted having serious problems about sexual satisfaction and poor communication with their partners. Most of these women claimed that the 'sexual' or 'intimate' side of marriage had always presented a problem for them. They continued to 'put up' with it for the sake of their husbands, only to abandon the sex act as soon as conveniently possible, ie when the menopause or a few babies intervened. These married women with sexual problems divided roughly into two groups - those who were completely ignorant about their own bodies, and those who had experienced orgasm on occasions but lacked communication with their husbands.

'I think all these young girls who throw themselves at men are disgraceful. Just wait till they get married, then they'll find out what it's all about. But I didn't fail in my duty to my husband, not up until the change anyway, and they should forget about it after that, don't you think?' (Woman, 50, Wales, married with four children)

Women of this first group seem to express a conscious denial of their own sexuality. They quite obviously feel that it is their wifely duty to allow the male to have intercourse, but are convinced that sexual pleasure was the province of the male. They usually feel that marriage is for children and are proud of their role as mothers. These women are either very bitter about men or completely resigned to the myth of female frigidity. Probably the large number of married women who are 'resigned' to their fate prompt the medical profession to make pronouncements on the number of women who lead 'perfectly normal lives' without sexual satisfaction - ie why are the women's liberation groups making such a fuss?

'I can never have orgasm in intercourse, but my husband likes to think that I do, so I just pretend. It flatters him that way.' (Woman, 28, Essex, has two children, works as a nursery assistant)

The women who deceive their husbands on a fairly regular basis seem to be of the younger age group, often 25 to 30. They are of varied educational level and class. They may or may not have had premarital experience. What they seem to have in common is that they all had definite expectations of female sexual pleasure and orgasm at the start of their relationships, but as their marriages progressed they had encountered problems in these areas.

Some of the women claimed that they were able to have an orgasm in foreplay by manual or oral stimulation and sometimes in intercourse if the foreplay was long enough. Usually, however, it was the man who decided how long the foreplay should continue, and this often did not meet the female's needs.

Taboos exist in these marriages which inhibit discussion of female stimulation. Some of them may have tried to communicate with a man in a previous affair and been told that their needs were either wrong, unnatural, perverted or sick. Thus for fear of being thought 'abnormal' these women shun discussion of their own sexuality and begin to pretend that they have obtained a climax. This 'pretence' may only go as far as a meek 'yes' to the habitual question, 'was that alright for you?' or it may become established as a highly sophisticated sexual ritual. The woman may pant, moan, heave her body around the bed, throw her limbs about - all in the name of the eulsive orgasm. Many of us may have played this 'game' at various times. It flatters the chauvinistic male and reinforces his preconceptions about the female response. It doesn't make sense, especially if the female is left pent-up and frustrated, but many women play this game for a good part of their lives.

About half these women said that they masturbated regularly when their husbands were out, but not immediately after intercourse, and were left restless with pains and tensions whilst there husbands slept soundly. The other half said they masturbated on occasions; nearly all the women felt guilty about masturbation, could not discuss it easily and did not really approve of it in their children.

It is interesting to note that some of the women who regularly deceived their husbands started off by trying to deceive me. They wanted to convince me that their husband was a good lover and that they experienced a vaginal orgasm easily. After talking around the problem for some time and realising that other women were also a bit confused, these women would start to explore any difficulties they had with a climax in intercourse. As most of them had experienced an orgasm at some time or another, they were eventually forced to the conclusion that their main problem was one of communication.

'You know how men can relax, don't you? They can get a bit
of "the other". We have to find other means of relaxation,
like dancing or swimming.' (Housewife, 60, Essex)

This woman was bitter, like many interviewed in her age
group, that only men obtained sexual pleasure and release
from intercourse. She thought this had been an unconscious
source of resentment and tension in their marital relationship. They had quarreled about every area of married life,
but always underlying these quarrels, she thought, was the
'intimate' side of their relationship. This woman was convinced that only the male had an orgasm. Their active sex
life had stopped at the menopause but had remained a source
of tension for the husband and still caused quarrels. This
woman has two sons whom she 'uses' to belittle the father at
every opportunity. She tries unsuccessfully to dominate the
family scene. She feels frustrated in all aspects of her life
and had been in and out of mental hospital since the early
years of her marriage.

This woman's story is not unusual for her generation, many
of whom started out with high expectations of personal fulfilment in the post-suffragette era. They had a rational approach to birth control and many of them got fitted with a
diaphragm, but they carried with them a burdensome heritage
of guilt and repression which was impossible to overcome.

These women were heavily conditioned to accept the notion
of wifely duty and consequently accepted intercourse in this
light until the birth of two or three children or the menopause
occurred. Their attitudes to masturbation and foreplay are
heavily guilt-ridden. Many of them suffer from pelvic disorders, pain in the lower back region and nervous tension, all
of which arise from continued sexual frustration (see part 3).
They are often stern moralists; their attitudes to the younger
generation, to promiscuity and abortion are irrationally harsh
- understandably so since the culture gave them such a raw
deal. Some of them said they 'thought' they might have had
an orgasm at one time when they were younger. Some also
admitted that they had masturbated on rare occasions which
were followed by periods of intense guilt which discouraged
subsequent experiments. About a third of the older women
said that they didn't accept that there was an orgasm for
women, denied ever having masturbated, and acted as if the
subject was a closed book to them. It was clear from their
reactions that masturbation was a very emotive area for them.

The homosexual woman

'Well, it's quite natural, isn't it? As you are of the same sex
you are very open to the needs of your partner. There is very
little of the exhausting and annoying conflict which a heterosexual relationship offers. I've tried both kinds, but I would

choose a woman at this stage in history. Relationships with men are much too complicated at present; they tell you what your sexual needs are and don't stop to listen; women are much more sensitive. Vaginal orgasm? I don't know about it; my ex-husband knew about it though, go ask him.' (Woman divorcee, 32, Central London)

The only group of women I have talked to who all seemed consistently satisfied with their sex lives were homosexual women. Only they seem to be able to communicate their needs and desires honestly to each other without playing up to the double standards of the heterosexual relationship.

A few of the women complained that their partners were 'hung up' on male attributes and desired stimulation with an artificial penis. This was quite rare, however, among homosexual women, who seem to rely on manual and oral techniques of clitoral stimulation to bring each other to climax.

The very young woman

'If I'd known it would have brought me all this trouble, I'd never have tried fucking. It was only for a dare anyway. Thing is, I didn't enjoy it. I preferred touching-up like we used to do. Men get all the luck.' (15-year-old pregnant schoolgirl)

Moralists, older women, envious of the new-found freedom of the younger generation, may doubt that the young woman of the seventies has any sexual problems. Those who work with adolescents and are able to talk to them honestly and openly will tell you that the opposite is true.

The adolescent girl is kept in ignorance of her own sexual response; access to contraception is made difficult, so she risks unwanted pregnancy in her associations with the opposite sex. Strong social pressures still make her feel guilt, doubt and anxiety about her sexuality. The double standard holds as true for the vast majority as for their mothers. 'From this section there emerges the impression that there is a group of boys who are keen to lose their own virginity but are critical of girls who provide them with the opportunity. If they wish to marry at all they are intent on marrying girls who are virgins and thus preclude marriage from their premarital sexual relationships. Girls, aware of the dangers, play a defensive role. They wish to protect their own virginity but expect boys to gain sexual experience, and find it acceptable that the boys should be able to do what they rule out for themselves.' ('The sexual behaviour of young people', a wide survey of teenage sex behaviour by Michael Schofield)

64% of the boys would like their wives to be virgins and 85% of the girls who had not experienced sexual intercourse wanted to remain virgins until they married. 42% of girls agree with the statement 'sexual intercourse before marriage is alright for boys but not for girls', 61% of the girls agree that 'sexual intercourse before marriage is wrong'. Only 35% of

boys agree. My own experience with adolescent girls pointed
to the fact that girls who have early sexual experience have
much more to lose than boys, in terms of loss of parental
approval and the warnings of pregnancy which bombard them
constantly. The girls spoke of their parents having 'filthy
minds' and 'always harping on one thing'. As one girl put it,
'My mum, she'll force me to get pregnant one day, every time
I go out or come in at night she goes on about it. My dad, he
said he would kill me if I came back like that, and I'm not
even 'aving it. But my brother, he can do what he likes.' (14-
year-old schoolgirl, South London)

The minority of girls who had experienced sexual intercourse
claimed that they didn't enjoy it very much; they preferred
'necking' and 'touching-up', as they put it. They said some of
their boyfriends felt the same but wouldn't dare admit it to
their mates.

Teenage girls are confused about the double standard. They
wonder why parents and teachers rail against pregnancy and
VD but do nothing to alleviate their problems in these two
areas. At home, they have to play a virginal role, with their
peers they must appear 'sexy'. Why are older women afraid
of discussing sex? Why is petting frowned on and masturbation a taboo subject? Why do adults make so much fuss about
intercourse when it's not nearly as pleasurable as petting for
many girls? Why do grownups think sex is dirty? These are
some of the questions that bother teenage girls. Society has
ill prepared them to deal with their own sexuality. It is not
surprising that they retreat into early marriage and pregnancy, only to discover that the unhappiness bred by sexual
ignorance in the premarital state follows them.

'I am 24 and married with three sons. I have been married
for six years and am now waiting for a divorce. During my
marriage I never once reached a climax during intercourse.
The only way I could have one was for my husband to manipulate my clitoris. We used to end up having rows over this,
with him saying I was frigid and me blaming him for my inability to come. I have now met someone else, and although
things went well at first he is now saying that there must be
something wrong with me. We have tried everything we can
think of to make me climax, but to no avail. I don't want this
relationship to end up like my marriage. Can you please ad-
vise me what to do?' (Letter to Forum Adviser)

Part 2

The roots of female oppression: historical point of view

Woman's confusion about the nature of her sexual response
is nothing new. Historically men have brainwashed women
into believing that the totality of their sexual response lies
in the reproductive act, denying woman's sensuality and eroticism which the male has always both envied and feared.

196

The fantastic stress laid on the reproductive role was originally a necessity to ensure the survival of the species. The
population growth charts of the modern era make it clear
that this stress is at best misguided, if not positively dangerous to human survival. Man's stress on the reproductive
role of women has given him several other psychological and
physical advantages however, so it has been to his advantage
to perpetuate the myth:

a) man has exaggerated the period of pregnancy when women
are more biologically hampered than men, extending the dependency some women feel at this time to the whole female
sex. He thus obtains for himself a free source of supportive
labour and free child care for his offspring;

b) if women are made to appear 'asexual' then they are no
threat to the male ego. They will not desire other men; their
own male partner will not lose his regular supply of labour
or the availability of sexual satisfaction;

c) man has used the 'reproductive machine' argument to keep
women out of the wider society, reinforcing his occupational
superiority and building subtle psychological and physical
barriers to ensure that most women stay at home. Employers
argue that because women menstruate and reproduce they are
not suitable employees; this makes things more difficult for
those women who do not accept their conditioned role and
seek fulfilment outside the home. Because they are the exception rather than the rule, men have seen fit to keep them
as a repressed labour force. At various stages in history man
has twisted the 'reproductive argument' to prove that women
are on the one hand more animal and less intelligent than men
and on the other hand more spiritual, untouchable and asexual
- according to the pressures of his time. Both arguments are
instruments of repression.

Primitive man

This ambivalence towards the female is part of the male's
social heritage and so strong a factor in the male psyche that
no woman can hope to fight it alone. In primitive cultures
men express their ambivalence to female sexuality in rituals
of myth and magic surrounding menstruation and childbirth.
The female mana or menstrual blood is always surrounded by
taboos so that women are separated from men during their
menstrual periods for all aspects of living and eating. They
are regarded as unclean objects. The Australians of Queens-
land bury their girls to the waist to purify their dangerous
condition. The Wogeo of South Australia believe that contact
with a menstruating woman will result in an incurable wasting
disease. Yet men of the same Australian tribes practice subincision - the periodic slitting of the urethra to draw blood
as a magical purification. (See Ashley Montagu, 'The origin
of subincision in Australia) This ritualistic imitation of the
female menstrual period illustrates how man's envy of the
female can exist alongside his fear and vanity.

Some form of menstrual taboos exist in all societies, from the complicated Hindu prohibitions to the Hebrew food taboos and the subtle barriers erected in our own society. The process is still regarded as slightly 'unclean' and the myths which still surround it make puberty a psychologically disturbing period for some girls.

The womb and childbirth have similarly been surrounded by myth and magic which rendered the process 'unclean' and needing purification of the woman. Purification periods of isolation follow birth, varying from 40 days amongst the Swahili to three months in Tahiti. In New Guinea they extend the period for a female birth. Many tribes in addition blame the pregnant woman for any deaths or diseases which occur among the men, reinforcing the mythology of anxiety connected with blood, impurity and contagion. Whilst the birth process is feared and thought to be unclean or degrading, it has also been a source of mystery and envy for the male - if women can create life, they are not going to be allowed social participation as well!

Primitive man expressed the same ambivalence towards the vagina and intercourse. Primitive folk lore indicates that men both desire and fear intercourse, and contains images of the vagina relating it to the castration complex. Folk literature is full of images of the toothed vagina or the snake, ready to tear off the vulnerable phallus. Vivid examples of this are described by the anthropologist H. R. Hays in 'The dangerous sex' and 'The myth of feminine evil', both well worth reading.

A picture emerges of woman as the witch, the animal, the vampire, insatiable in her desires, to be suppressed at all costs. It becomes clear that modern woman has a more difficult task than the suffragettes, with their faith in legal reform, had supposed. We have to break through a whole male cultural heritage of irrational fear and anxiety, and in no area does this operate so strongly as in the sexual area.

Religion and the church

Our culture is impregnated with the mythology of the ancient Hebrews; the original sin of Eve is still with us, as is the sin of Onan. On this foundation of Hebrew mythology, Christianity erected a superstructure of misogyny. As a direct development of the original sin of Eve myth, the early Christians elevated the 'eunuch priest' cult. Heterosexual intercourse was to become regarded as something common or dirty not to be undertaken by holy men. Christ himself was desexualised.

The second cult, the asexual 'Virgin Mary' cult, sustained by the celibate clergy, would seem at first glance to represent another trend. It is however another aspect of how men tend to ritualise that which they fear in women. The Virgin mythology removes woman's dangerous sexual qualities whilst retaining the all-giving 'earth mother' image which men find so convenient to exploit in our own society. Paul's strong influence on the development of Christian practice and theology furthered the cause of misogyny. All accounts show him to be a twisted personality with an obsessional hatred of women.

Throughout the centuries the web of institutions thrown up by Christendom has worked against women's equality and her sexuality. Intercourse has been viewed as an act of marital necessity for procreation. The church has insisted that it is the duty of the wife to submit to her lord and master and makes non-consummation the only grounds for a Catholic divorce. The Catholic church with its adherance to the notoriously unsuccessful rhythm method of birth control has maintained tighter controls over Catholic woman than other parts of the Christian church have managed to do. Catholic women are becoming conscious of their oppression and fighting for the use of the pill. They need our support.

That men have been less affected both psychologically and physically by the sexual controls imposed by the church is to a large extent a measure of their dominant position in our society and of their ability to manipulate institutions to suit their own purposes. Even the repressive Victorians turned a blind eye to 'respectable' gentlemen who used females as prostitutes for extra-marital release. A woman who did the same thing would have been a complete social outcast.

The Victorian era

The 19th century doctor joined hands with the priest and became guardian of public morality, particularly sexual morality. William Acton's 'Treatise on the functions and disorders of the reproductive organs' (1857) is notorious for the view that normal women have no sexual feelings. Women were made 'asexual' to protect the moral athlete, ie the middle class male who must not be sullied with sexual excesses which would interfere with the Protestant work ethic. Women are reproductive necessities, not as intelligent as the male and suited to life in the home.

That woman's 'asexuality' was a bourgeois notion is witnessed by the fact that liaisons with housemaids and prostitutes for the men of the house were tolerated, if not sanctioned, by the middle class society. Unfortunately for the modern working class woman, with the spread of literacy and universal education the bourgeois standard extended to the culture as a whole and became the norm projected on girls by parents.

The repressive Victorian feared female sensuality as much or even more than the primitive, and took drastic steps to eradicate it. All forms of vicious chastity belts were prescribed for young ladies and the operation of clitoridectomy was introduced by Dr Isaac Baker Brown about 1858. A large number of cases, children and adults, were operated on in his London Surgical Home, claiming to cure forms of insanity, epilepsy, catalepsy and hysteria which resulted from masturbation. Masturbation was a disease to be eradicated; the neurosis attached to it haunts our present society.

The practice of clitoridectomy spread to America, where Dr Eyer of Ohio cauterized the clitoris of a little girl. When this failed to stop her masturbating, a surgeon was called to bury the organ with silver wire sutures which the child tore - and resumed the habit. American publications continued to recommend surgery to deal with masturbation up until 1936. (See Alex Comfort, 'The anxiety makers', for a fuller account of this amazing story)

In this country by 1900 there was a well-established link between masturbation and insanity. The fear had been propagated by the medical profession and had become firmly established in popular mythology. The mothercraft manuals until quite recently reinforced the popular fears with warnings about control of the child. 'Untiring zeal on the part of the mother or nurse is the only cure; it may be necessary to put the legs in splints before putting the child to bed.' ('The Mothercraft manual', 1928)

This mythology applied to both men and women, but women had a more difficult psychological situation to resolve; they had to adjust to a schizophrenic cultural notion of their sexuality. On the one hand, they were thought to be asexual, on the other they were thought to be capable of 'self-abuse', of an intensity of sexual activity which warranted surgical eradication of their organ of pleasure.

Freud and his misguided theory of clitoral v vaginal orgasm

Freud did something to break the punitive and repressive attitude of the post-Victorian era. He claimed that women were capable of sexual pleasure and even orgasm, which was revolutionary at the turn of the century. But he confused the whole subject of female sexuality so thoroughly with his notion of the clitoral and vaginal orgasms that the popularisation of his ideas was a disaster for modern woman.

Freud's theories on female sexuality were written towards the end of his life ('Female sexuality', 1931, and 'Femininity', 1933), after he had developed cancer and when he rarely practised as an analyst. None of his theories had any anatomical basis. To a great extent Freud was a traditionalist, reinforcing the passive home-loving, reproductive role which was already well established for women. His theory of the female orgasm caused a lot more trouble. He claimed that the female child had an interest in sexuality based on clitoral excitation. At puberty her sexuality is transferred to the vagina, the seat of the truly feminine orgasm. Women who fail to make this transference were labelled 'neurotic', not only by Freud but by the whole school of Freudian analysis which followed and still influences psychiatric opinion. The writings of the Freudian analysts, male and female, adhered closely to the words of the master. Unfortunately they influenced popular culture and their ideas have been echoed in popular medical literature and women's magazines, right up to the present.

Freud saw the clitoral orgasm as infantile and a remnant of woman's masculinity. Every young girl suffers from penis envy which must be replaced by the desire for a baby, otherwise frigidity and neurosis result. ('Femininity') We are now able to see the modern woman's reluctance to discuss clitoral orgasm in its historical perspective.

Freud himself saw that there were difficulties in his theory; he admitted that the clitoris continued to function in later female sex life in a way which was not fully understood. To cover himself on this point he adopted the theory of bisexuality which 'comes to the fore more clearly in women than in men'. ('Female sexuality')

Biographers show that Freud was a man of his times, with a strong puritanical streak in his attitudes to women. In 'Future of an illusion' he condones pre-marital restraint and monogamous marriage and regards sexual repression as inevitable for social progress and civilisation to continue. But men are to be the active agents in the promotion of the civilising process. He regards intellectual women as masculine; woman's true place is in the home. Thus his normal woman must search for the 'elusive vaginal orgasm' which will expose her to the maximum opportunity for conception. In denying woman's sensuality Freud did not overcome the anxiety and fear of the primitive or the repressiveness of the Victorian.

Part 3

Woman's sensuality reestablished

Women may still be confused about their sexual response, (see part 1) but there are signs that they are gaining a new consciousness, a new awareness of themselves as sexual equals. The pill, and an increasing availability of contraception in general, helped women to explore premarital sexuality in a way that was very difficult or them formerly. But the psychological turning-point in the popular acceptance of woman's sensuality came with Kinsey's publication of 'Sexual behaviour in the human male and the human female' (1948 and 1953). The findings of the Kinsey Institute established that women as well as men were erotic and capable of orgasm, even multiple orgasms. Most of their body of knowledge was built up through the interview technique, supplemented by the cooperation of five gynaecologists who established that the clitoris was woman's most erotic organ. It was left to the work of Masters and Johnson, however, to confirm this evidence as a structure of hard scientific fact, by testing these theories in the laboratory by controlled observations.

The research into the human sexual response by Masters

and Johnson began in 1954 as the Washington University
School of Medicine, St Louis, and is still continuing. Doctor
Masters worked under the conviction that the research would
only have validity if carried out jointly by a male-female
research team, and to this end employed Mrs Johnson, a
female therapist. Until 'Human sexual response' was published in 1966 there were no large-scale scientific observations
of the female's physiological response to sexual stimulation
and her capacity for orgasm. Their research exploded the
myth of the vaginal v clitoral orgasm. Their treatment of
sexual problems showed quite clearly that not only is 'frigidity' culturally induced, but that the female's sexual potential
is in fact far greater than that of the male. 'Yet, woman's
conscious denial of biophysical capacity rarely is a completely successful venture, for her physiological capacity for
sexual response infinitely surpasses that of man. Indeed, her
significantly greater susceptibility to negatively based psychological influences may imply the existence of a natural
state of psycho-sexual-social balance between the sexes that
has been culturally established to neutralise woman's biophysical superiority.' ('Human sexual inadequacy')

Masters and Johnson exploded four myths - the vaginal orgasm myth, the myth that women are frigid, the myth that a
man's sexual performance is related to the size of his penis,
and the myth that women have to be 'in love' to enjoy sex.

The nature of female orgasm

The researchers established beyond all doubt that the clitoris
is woman's erotic organ. It is both the transmitter and the
receiver of female sexual feelings; it is the organ which trig-
gers off woman's sexual climax. Normally the clitoris is
about the size and shape of a small pea and lies above the
urinary orifice. It is almost an exact duplicate of the penis
but has a much richer supply of nerves. The clitoris contains
all the orgasm-producing nerves in the female, the vagina
being devoid of such nerves and only sensitive at the entrance.

The female response cycle is very similar to that of the male
and goes through four phases:
a) The excitement phase: Blood flows into the pelvic region
in response to physical as well as psychological stimulation.
The clitoris glans swells in response to direct stimulation or
stimulation of the mons veneris. The breasts and nipples
swell and the vagina walls begin to lubricate. The vagina
begins to expand and the involuntary muscles tense up.
b) The plateau phase: There is an increase in the breathing
and pulse rate, and blood pressure rises in response to further stimulation, which also produces further engorgement of
the whole genital area. Women who do not have orgasms are
often left at this plateau stage and consequently the pelvic
congestion, which is dispersed with orgasm, may continue for
several hours. Women who are constantly exposed to inter-

course without having orgasms over a long period often develop chronic congestion of the pelvic region which leads to gynaecological disorders.

During this plateau stage the clitoris is drawn further away from the vaginal entrance, thus the direct penis-clitoral contact advised by the older sex manuals becomes very difficult, if not impossible for most partners. The clitoris continues to respond to stimulation, either directly or indirectly through stimulation of the entire vulva area, according to the preferences of the individual woman.

c) The orgasm stage: The female orgasm only occurs if it is triggered off in the clitoris by either direct or indirect stimulation, ie by manual or oral techniques or by indirect pulling of the penis on the vulva. The latter method used alone is unsatisfactory for most women; it may take up to an hour for a woman to reach orgasm in this way, and even if the male has sufficient control to do this, the outcome is uncertain. Much more important for the majority of women is for the male to develop a range of manual and oral techniques, to ensure that the female is very near the point of orgasm before coitus occurs. Many women find it more satisfactory to have already experienced one orgasm before coitus occurs.

Masters and Johnson found that the 'missionary' or 'man on top' position which has become the cultural norm is the least satisfactory for either female satisfaction or male control over ejaculation. The female superior and the lateral coitus positions allow the female greater flexibility of movement. The rear entry position allows freedom for the male or the female herself to stimulate the clitoris manually during intercourse.

Simultaneous orgasms are neither necessary nor even desirable for the female, who needs a degree of concentration to respond to orgasm. Masters and Johnson found that orgasm produced by women themselves during masturbation was much stronger than when the male stimulated her or than an orgasm achieved during intercourse. During orgasm the clitoris throbs at the rate of two or three per second. The same kind of vaginal contractions occur during an orgasm achieved through masturbation or intercourse, but those experienced through masturbation tend to be much stronger.

The contractions felt during orgasm may extend to the rectum and may also be felt in the uterus. The fact that the orgasm, always transmitted from the clitoris, sets in motion contractions in other organs of the female, particularly the vagina, may have been the source of the confusion in woman herself about the clitoral v vaginal orgasm.

d) The resolution phase: This occurs after orgasm has reached its peak of sensation and the contractions have stopped. The woman experiences a pleasant afterglow and feeling of relief from tension. The body returns to its unstimulated state in up to half an hour; the male period is much shorter. This may not happen for hours, however, in a woman who has not passed the plateau phase.

The myth that women are either frigid or are limited to one climactic orgasm

Masters and Johnson found that, unlike the male, women do not suffer from the 'refractory' period after the resolution phase. During the refractory period the male is unable to become sexually aroused or to have another erection. This does not apply to the female, who can readily reach a second orgasm if effective stimulation is renewed following orgasm. In fact, many women are capable of experiencing up to six orgasms if effective stimulation is continued after the first, the subsequent orgasms increasing in intensity. Masters and Johnson report that multiple orgasms are more apt to occur with auto-stimulation than with intra-vaginal coition. The limit is not the woman's responsiveness but the man's erectile powers.

Multiple orgasms in the female had been reported by Kinsey and his associates. But these findings were often dismissed by male writers who even went as far as to say that multi-orgasmic women were frigid and incapable of experiencing a true orgasm. This kind of nonsense has now been laid to rest by the Masters-Johnson laboratory observations.

Masters and Johnson believe the notion of the frigid woman to be culturally induced, and their treatment programmes proved that so-called frigid women may experience intense multiple orgasms given the right conditions of stimulation and acceptance of their own sexuality. The vibrator is a useful mechanical aid to 'teach' women who are inhibited over orgasm to enjoy this experience.

The myth that a man's sexual performance is related to the size of his penis

Masters and Johnson concluded that 'the penile size is usually a minor factor in sexual satisfaction of the female partner'. The vagina is an adaptable organ and accommodates itself to the size of the penis. Most love-making positions do not allow direct penis-clitoral contact. Much more important than the size of the genitals is a sympathetic approach on the part of both partners to each other's needs and desires, communication about one's own sexual response, openness to learning effective techniques of erotic stimulation and positive acceptance of the female's sensual and erotic nature.

The myth that women have to be 'in love' to enjoy sex

The cultural myth that women but not men need 'romantic love' before they can respond sexually is still alive and influences both male and female behaviour. Sexual release is seen as a biological necessity for men but not for women. Many women feel they must be engaged or married before they are able to admit that they are capable of sexual response. This notion is culturally induced, and Masters and

Johnson's research showed that it has no physiological foundation. Given the right psychological and erotic stimulation, the female can respond to sexual pleasure and orgasm in the same way as the male and has a greater potential of response.

In the 1960s Masters and Johnson were attacked for 'taking the romance out of sex', for presenting a 'mechanistic' point of view - mainly of course by male writers. What seemed to disturb these men was not the mechanics of the male orgasm, which were already largely known, but the descrption of the mechanics of the female orgasm which had been suppressed by a chauvinist male society. Historically women have suffered from too much romance and not enough realism. Their position and future happiness cannot be harmed by injecting a little stark realism into the undergrowth of myth which surrounds their sexual position.

Orgasm neurosis or the tyranny of the orgasm

Masters and Johnson and some women in the Movement have been accused of producing 'orgasm neurosis' in the contemporary female. In fact, both groups are dedicated to overcoming centuries of female conditioning and would hesitate to impose any patterns in the area of female sexuality.

The sexual area is, however, one where we are most open to pressures and conditioning, and we live in an aggressive society where the competitive element invades every area of our private and public life. It is quite true that when women began to be aware of their potential for orgasm, a minority were not satisfied until they were having 'bigger and better' orgasms than their friends. Those who are not having orgasms feel resentful, anxious or inadequate. Others who experience orgasm on most occasions of sexual intercourse but not all feel let down and disappointed on the negative occasions. Thus the orgasm can become a tyranny, a goal to be achieved, rather than something which happens naturally when sexual pleasure reaches its climax.

When Masters and Johnson describe multiple orgasm in the female, they are describing a potential, something a woman may experience, given the right stimulation and psychological motivation. In all areas of women's liberation, there is always a gap between the potential and realisation; the individual has to deal with a social situation which exists now, with all its pressures and restrictions. As we all know, women are often tired with household chores and child care, sometimes combined with a full-time job. Economic pressures, conflicts within relationships, lack of fulfilment in a wider social context, all can and frequently do affect woman's capacity for orgasm. This points to the fact that orgasm in the female is as much a psychological as a physiological response. Her response is much less direct than that of the male, much more dependent on mood and situation. At this stage in history we are not able to evaluate whether these differences are of biological or social origin. All we know is that these differences exist for many women.

The new scientific findings about the female orgasm should not be set up as yet another standard, another imposition on the female, but as a guideline which describes the possible, a practical source of information on the female which may give her the confidence to explore and gain knowledge of her own body and to communicate her needs to others. Knowledge and confidence about her own sexuality help the female to overcome her feelings of painful inadequacy, help her to acknowledge that the sickness lies in a repressive society and not in her.

Part 4

The present scene: what lies ahead?

A clearer picture is now emerging of the female which is more complex than previously admitted, and it is a picture which undermines the rigid sex roles which society strives to perpetuate.

Masters and Johnson's research has shown that female sexuality is not necessarily connected with the reproductive act or with vaginal intercourse; in fact the female is more likely to gain full sexual satisfaction from masturbation, not intercourse. Woman's erotic organ, the clitoris, is so separated from the vagina anatomically as to make a clear-cut separation between woman's erotic and reproductive physiology possible. The male physiology does not allow this, however, the penis being a much more crude organ, being the organ of sexual orgasm, generation and urination.

It emerges that the female alone is the sex capable of separating eroticism from reproduction. This capacity in the female has been heavily suppressed by the male to maintain his dominance over the female; the female is capable of using this capacity for orgasm without intercourse as a natural form of birth control. But as we have seen, the female who is capable of free choice has always been a threat to the male ego, thus the male establishment continues to reinforce the mythology that the reproductive side of female sexuality is the norm, even though the average woman will only produce two children in her entire life.

The consequences of the continuation of this outdated attitude towards women are too serious for society to go on ignoring them and for women to be kept in ignorance of their sexual response. There are over 100,000 abortions, legal and illegal, in Britain every year. 70,000 illegitimate babies are born annually. Only one quarter of all babies born are planned by their parents (latest FPA figures). Many of these children are born unwanted. 50,000 children are received into care every year. The population is increasing by a third of a million annually; we are the second most densely populated region in the world and one of the most dependent on external resources, which are slowly dwindling as population steadily increases in developing countries. In spite of these figures the government refuses to establish a free and universally available contraceptive service immediately. Society continues to try to keep young people in ignorance of their own sexual natures, rejecting any realistic forms of sex education. When moves are made in this direction, male anxiety again raises its ugly head, refusing to tolerate a situation where women are free to choose.

The instruments of control which continue to repress women in a complex industrial society are many and varied. Some of the psychological controls are so subtle that women are often unaware that they have been applied, until they find themselves continuing the traditional role of their mothers in spite of the fact that their earlier idealism had embraced wider concepts. The male society points to the number of women graduates who have dedicated themselves to home and family to prove that woman's place is in the home. They forget to mention that men make it very difficult for women to compete in the professional world and that women graduates are not free from the conditioning of their sisters.

Moulders of women

a) The family The modern nuclear family, because of its isolation, gives the parents, especially the mother, the greatest degree of control over the developing infant. Sexist attitudes are imprinted on the developing child from the first year of life. As a result of an on-going survey of parental attitudes towards infantile sexuality, I have found that mothers tend to be more repressive towards their female children than their male children. Some degree of sexual activity is thought to be acceptable or is ignored in boys but strongly discouraged in girls. 'I mean for boys it's only natural, they can't really help it, but I wouldn't like to see my little girl touching herself. What would people think?' (Mother, 28, Brighton, two children aged 3 and 5)

Girls are more likely to be punished for their actions, if not by corporal punishment by strong social disapproval, building a firm foundation for the development of guilt and denial of sexuality later in life. Women often pass on their own guilt and anxiety about sex to their daughters.

The results of the survey show quite clearly that the mothers who tend to be most repressive of their child's sexuality are are those who come from strict religious backgrounds, those who have unhappy sex lives themselves, and those who resent the child and would have been happier without it. Invariably parents reply that they had not received adequate sex education themselves, and nearly all agreed that compulsory sex education at pre-natal clinics would be a good idea.

As the female child grows towards puberty the controls tighten around her, leaving the boy free in comparison. A girl is often prey to her mother's own fears and anxieties, and is given constant warnings about 'talking to strange men', and fantasies about the risk of rape may reach obsessive proportions. Some families still surround the menstrual period with myths and taboos, and girls still grow up feeling that 'the curse' is at best something to be hidden from the male, and at worst something dirty.

Two years ago I asked ten groups of girls at a large comprehensive school how they would react to infantile sexuality in their own child. Most of the girls wanted to restrain the child, some wanted to punish it violently; their explosive reaction seemed to be a measure of their own guilt and repression in the area of masturbation.

b) Adolescents and the educators   Adolescence is the stage when the female is bombarded by warnings and advice of a sexual nature. She is taught very effectively to deny her own sexuality through warnings about what will happen to her if she 'gives in' to the male who has the prerogative of sexual feelings. Parents, teachers and sex educators collude in the presentation of a more passive role for the female, who often emerges from adolescence unaware of her erotic nature.

'He's only after one thing' is a constant criticism levelled at boys by the adolescent female. She is denying her own sexual response, as the culture has taught her to do. Teenage girls report that their parents have 'filthy minds' and 'can only talk about one thing', issuing threats and warnings about pregnancy every time they leave the house in the evening. Girls constantly act this scene out in free drama sessions at school. These same girls said they wished that people would give them 'sensible advice' on how to deal with their real problems.

The sex education put out by books and the few schools who are brave enough to tackle the subject concentrates for the most part on the reproductive system and completely ignores the role of the clitoris as woman's erotic organ. If it is mentioned at all, it is passed over quickly as an anatomical detail so that stress can be laid on the reproductive organs. Girls are taught how babies are produced and, if they are lucky, how adults have intercourse, although books on this subject are often dangerously misleading. For example, in 'Teach your child about sex', Julia Dawkins writes, 'Your eggs won't get fertilised until you are quite grown up and have a husband' and in Kind and Leedham's 'Programmed sex information' a teenage girl could read, 'the sperm cell comes from a man, not from a boy'.

Sex education in the girls schools which I have experienced is dedicated to preparing the girl for motherhood and a relationship in marriage. If adolescent sexuality is admitted, then the girl is filled with fears of pregnancy and VD without giving her practical assistance to avoid such problems. Chastity, by implication, is the ideal method of avoidance - an unrealistic approach for girls who are already experimenting with sex and have problems facing them now. That the social ideal of chastity for women does however influence teenage attitudes if not behaviour has been shown by Schofield's survey - 85% of the girls would like to be virgins when they married, excluding girls who had already experienced intercourse. Also 64% of boys would like their wives to be virgins.

Thus the 'norm' which is projected by the adult world is sexual intercourse which girls are supposed to avoid because of pregnancy and boys get where they can. The teenage culture soon realises that sexual intercourse is being denied them; it is the only form of sexual activity ever discussed openly, thus the adolescent wants to experience what he feels is being repressed in him/her. Because there are real problems connected with this sexual act - pregnancy and disease - it is easier for society to maintain its controls on the developing individual.

Repression of pleasure

'It is always too late, and it always evades the essential point, sexual pleasure'. (Wilhelm Reich on sex education in 'The sexual revolution) Sex education and books for the adolescent uniformly ignore the subject of masturbation and sexual pleasure of the female. If it is discussed it is discouraged. The better books say it is quite normal as a sexual outlet for boys but not so widespread for girls. There is no evidence to show how widespread the practice is for girls and the authors usually forget to say that even if this is the case it is because the female has undergone a greater degree of repression than the male. They do not tell girls clearly and plainly that the clitoris is their organ of eroticism and orgasm and that effective stimulation of it brings pleasure to the girl, either alone or with a partner of either sex. The research of Masters and Johnson indicates that widespread acceptance of female masturbation and learning to masturbate to orgasm in the post-puberty period would eliminate most of the female's sexual problems.

Society's attitude to these proposals is illustrated by the establishment's reaction to Dr Martin Cole's film 'Growing up'. Their outrage was directed at the female masturbation scene; the Birmingham technical college lecturer who appeared in the scene was suspended from her post and only one local education authority has bought the film. Cole has now produced 'Understanding sex', a tape-slide package with only a fleeting mention of masturbation.

Why pick on masturbation, practiced by babes and innocents; masturbation, which avoids pregnancy and lessens the risk of disease? Why doesn't sex education encourage petting as the norm for adolescents; this would open up a whole new world of lovemaking as an erotic art for the developing adult to explore. The answer is that society as a whole is anti-pleasure, it does not want the 'controls' of pregnancy and disease to disappear. What it fears most of all is that women would have the freedom to choose their own destiny in a society where they are free from ignorance and repression.

The medical profession

'I dreamed of making London the abortion centre of the world'. (Dr Parvis Faridian, 28 February 1972, after the Department of Health's decision to close his million-pound Langham Street Clinic)

This man's attitude is typical of the hundreds of medics who make a fortune out of the women who suffer an unwanted pregnancy, conceived either through ignorance, guilt, or because contraception is made difficult for women. The medics profit from women's misery. They cling to outdated, time-consuming methods of surgery when a more humane method of abortion exists and has been successfully pioneered in the West by Dr Harvey Karman at the Los Angeles Clinic. The vacuum curettage method eliminates the trauma of hospitalisation, takes only a few minutes, and recuperation is almost immediate for women up to twelve weeks pregnant. Why is this method only being tried out in a very limited way? The rest of the medical profession studiously ignore the method. The answer is that the medical profession wants women to suffer, they want to control our bodies and most of all they want to make a profit out of it.

The history of the pill shows the same pattern - a reluctance to release the pill for general sale, while it is common knowledge that GPs issue the pill randomly with few if any checkups on the woman's health. An adequate screening process which correlates the woman's biochemistry with the hormone level of the various birth control pills has yet to be devised. Women are as yet guinea pigs in the hands of the male-dominated medical profession. (See 'Birth control handbook', available from Women's Liberation Workshop or Agitprop)

A similar attitude will be met if a couple approach a doctor for sterilisation. Most GPs suggest that the woman should have the operation, although male vasectomy is much simpler. The woman is viewed as the 'reproductive machine'.

The result of this social attitude upheld by the medics is that many women who do not desire maternity get pregnant. The findings of the Brook Advisory Centre show that women who repeat unwanted pregnancies are invariably guilty about their own sexuality and tend to be those who are getting little out of sex. Many highly educated women claim that they cannot 'enjoy' intercourse without the risk of pregnancy; some see pregnancy as reparation for the sinful sex act. Women's liberation will only be a reality when women only get pregnant because they enjoy child care and desire maternity. The answer lies in woman's sexual liberation and knowledge of her own sexual response.

The movement towards homosexuality

'If the female orgasm doesn't absolutely depend on the male penis, then women may as well have sex with each other.' (Incredulous male in a London mixed flat) 'Woman has a particular propensity to love both sexes - the clitoris aligns her to male reactions while the vagina makes her truly female. A woman is in the widest sense more double-sexed than a man.' (Dr Charlotte Wolff, MD)

Some say that homosexuality amongst women is not growing, but just being openly admitted for the first time. Certainly, female homosexuality has been less legally persecuted than male. Women have been able to live together without eyebrows being raised, but this is not because society tolerated female sexuality, but because women were believed asexual.

It is my opinion that there is a movement towards homosexuality amongst women, which will continue to grow until men completely accept women's sexual response and the inequalities of the marriage scene disappear. Women who have been heavily involved in the heterosexual scene, have been married for some years and had several children are leaving what they have found to be an oppressive situation for the gay scene. Some of these women are forming women's communes or else forming a one-to-one relationship with another woman.

I talked to three women who found themselves in this position. They had all been the victims of 'sexist battles' in marriage. They all felt they had been victims of male cultural expectations in marriage. They were given no help with child care by their partners, who saw the children as an extension of their own egos. They were all qualified to work professionally, but not only did the men require their wives to stay at home but they had to want to stay at home, to be good mothers and not threaten their male with competition in the outside world. As a consequence of these attitudes their sex lives also became a battleground, the male always seeking the dominant position. All these women claimed they had been abused because they could not agree with the 'vaginal orgasm' idea.

These women and other homosexual women I have met believe that at this stage in history it is impossible for many women to resolve their conflicts in the heterosexual relationship. The male is so rigid in his attitudes towards the female, so caught up in trying to preserve the male power structure, that he is incapable of accepting the rate of change which is occurring in woman's consciousness. He has the hierarchical power structure, built on centuries of male domination, to support his mythology and this cannot be broken down by one woman in isolation.

211

Woman herself is a collaborator in this situation. She tends to 'give in' constantly to the interests of the male. His job is the most important, his sexual satisfaction is more important than hers. Her role patterns have been so imprinted on her psyche from birth that she cannot herself adjust to an equal partnership in a heterosexual marriage. More women are taking the gay position believing that equality can only be worked out by two similar partners. These women and other homosexual women who have never experienced the hetero-sexual scene state quite categorically that the male is not necessary for woman's complete sexual satisfaction and hap-piness. They claim that they suffer most derision from their own sex, probably because subconsciously we all harbour a longing to make love to our own sex, a longing which is heavily culturally suppressed. Like the moralists, some women get their 'kicks' in debasing a situation which they envy and sec-retly desire.

Political potential of a movement towards female sexual liberation

Women need each other's support in overcoming the culturally determined male mythology about female sexuality which hist-orically has led to woman's frustration and an awful lot of misery caused by unwanted children. Rationally, our society seems ready for this change in outlook, but men, who have always feared women's freedom, will not let the changes oc-cur unless they are put under pressure from women who are united in their determination to gain sexual equality, women who are not willing to lie about their responses to flatter the male, women who are communicating openly and honestly with each other, in literature, in articles, in discussions, women who are discovering where their male-inspired hang-ups end and their real sexual feelings begin.

Women inside and outside the Women's Liberation Movement discover a unity of interest and mutual sympathy by finding that most women share their problems, their guilt and their repressions. Give your support to other women.

The political potential of the sexual area was illustrated to me by a Women's Liberation visit to a North London technical college. We faced a hostile audience of teenage girls - about 70 of them, mostly on pre-child-care courses, accompanied by about 10 hostile staff. They tore most of our arguments to shreds: equal pay, education, job opportunities, state help with child care, even contraception, were seen as issues already resolved or things that didn't concern them personally.

Out of this opposition a 16-year-old's voice was heard objec-ting to the fact that boys were allowed to have sexual inter-course and girls were not. If girls did, they were 'looked down on'. She didn't think this was fair. As if by magic, the hostility of the meeting evaporated and the girls became unanimous in agreement that this was the case and they began to reveal how much they resented it. What had been seen by the Women's Lib speakers as a 'delicate subject' not to be imposed on the girls turned out to be the only subject which really affected them now. Unfortunately, time had run out and we were not able to deal with the subject in any depth. I dedicate this tract to that girl who had the courage to stand up and air the problem in public.

WOMEN YOUR BODY belongs to YOU!

(Merseyside Women's Liberation Movement leaflet)

WOMEN AND HISTORY

Anna Davin

(Anna Davin is a member of the London Women's Liberation
Workshop)

Women's history - and therefore people's history - has yet
to be written, and to write it is part of our present struggle.
We are formed by the past, and yet know nothing about it,
because the history we were taught was the history of the
male-dominated class society, written to 'explain' (ie justify
and maintain) the status quo, to show the past as progress
towards the present, and not to suggest what might have happened instead (unless chaos) or why it didn't. We were not
shown the political skulduggery and ideological manipulation,
the economic exploitation and the social oppression by which
an adroit and rapacious ruling class maintained its grip; we
were shown economic breakthroughs and parliamentary reforms, universal advances in morals, sanitation, and education
through the judicious and paternal concern of the legislature,
and a general evolution towards the prosperous and ever-
improving democracy in which we now live.

Of course this version of the past was not necessarily worked
out by conscious propagandists - very probably it was developed by dedicated historians with faith in their own objectivity
and scholarly standards. But without setting 'standards' in a
historical perspective and recognising that historians are
formed by their background and society, and so more likely
to see certain things as interesting (or irrelevant) than others,
no-one, however scholarly, conscientious, diligent, or even
lucky, will ever achieve more than partial truth. In the teaching of history, selection (necessarily) operates from the start,
in the demarcating and labelling of periods, the spotlighting
of certain figures or institutions or places (leaving the rest
in shadow), the invention of milestones. We all had to 'learn'
about Tudors and Stuarts, electoral reform, assorted wars,
cabinets, ministers and monarchs. But we weren't taught that
selection had operated; that was all 'History', to be learnt, to
be 'done' and put behind us (tagged perhaps with marks for
the efficiency with which we had assimilated what was presented to us).

Now, when we are rejecting our present society for its inequality and exploitation and challenging not only the institutions but also the mystifications by which these are maintained,
we must challenge too, and overthrow, the mystified version
of the past through which people are taught to accept the present. That is, we must show (a) that unless cultural conditioning is recognised and rejected, the pursuit of objectivity is

an illusory irrelevance, and (b) that the nature of society affects not only the definition but also the function of history. Thus in a class society history has meant the history of the rulers, and in a male dominated society the history of men. The female population has been studied only in relation to the needs and preoccupations of the male ruling class, as part of the decorative backcloth, or as objects of 'enlightened' paternalist legislation (which 'rescued' women from heavy work in pits but not in laundries, and restricted the long hours in factories but not in kitchens). Men's activities - in war, courts, politics, diplomacy, administration, and business - were the stuff of the drama. Women's activities went unrecorded at the time, and later were excluded as an area for study by the male-oriented definition of history. Domestic work for instance, whether by housewife or servant, has been little studied: there are more books on furniture or china and silver. This exclusion - or invisibility of women's activities - then served to build up a grotesque historical stereotype of the submissive and supportive woman, which renewed in cultural terms the daily denial to women's work and life of social and productive validity.

So we now have to reject what has passed for history, to redefine the word, to discover the history which is relevant to us now. As soon as we start asking how women in the past lived, we realise how little the subject has been touched. Where they exist, contemporary novels and memoirs are likely to be as much use as history books proper, since very few historians have written specifically on women. With a little effort historians could long ago have exploded the myth of women's 'unchainging feminity' and constant role; instead by their omissions they have let it be assumed that women's life has always been the same, and only occasionally has the myth of progress been questioned. Olive Schreiner, for instance, suggested in 'Woman and labour' (1911) that through the ages woman had experienced not progress but a steadily worsening oppression, being gradually stripped of all creative and productive functions except the narrowly maternal and restricted to a smaller and smaller domestic world. Or see Engels' 'Origin of the family' (1884), which links the deterioration of woman's situation specifically to the development of capitalist society. (Ivy Pinchbeck, in a very interesting book on 'Women and the Industrial Revolution', published in 1930, is still the only historian who has done detailed work on this subject, and there is much more to be done both within the period she covered and outside it.) Looking at the past helps us to understand the present: once we see that the position of woman is integral to each society, we can understand how the changes in her position - in the nature and degree of her oppression - relate to the changing needs of the society. (Contraception and abortion become more acceptable and even government-financed when technological developments mean that a smaller labour force is needed.)

To find out about the women of the past we have to look beyond the 'famous' individuals, women who were accorded fame for their achievements in men's roles, or in areas of interest to men, or sometimes because they epitomised some aspect of the definition of womanhood current in their time. Cleopatra, Joan of Arc, Mary Queen of Scots, Nell Gwyn, Elizabeth Fry, Florence Nightingale, Marie Curie, in no way represent the mass of their contemporaries.

It is tempting to start with the material which most obviously challenges the stereotypes - with the suffragettes for instance, or with other episodes of women's resistance and revolt. When we are told that women have always been hopelessly apolitical and passive, we can look (as our informants have not) for evidence to the contrary. Then we will find, for instance, that in August 1911 in Bermondsey (South London):

'One morning... the women in a big confectionery factory suddenly left work, came out in a body and marched down the street. From factory and workshop as they passed, the workers came out and joined them as though the Pied Piper were calling. The doors of great jam, biscuit and food preparation factories, of workshops where girls were making sweetstuff, glue or tin boxes, of tea-packing houses and perambulator works, opened and gave forth their contingents, to swell the singing, laughing procession.' (From Mary Agnes Hamilton's life of the union organiser, Mary MacArthur)

These were women who earned 7s to 9s a week (girls got 3s); 14,000 of them came out, from 20 different factories and workshops, and they stayed out till wage increases ranging from 1s to 4s per week had been won. Observers were particularly struck by their high spirits: 'They went laughing and singing, through Bermondsey shouting, "Are we downhearted? No!"' It was noticeable that many of them had put on their 'Sunday best'. In spite of the great heat hundreds of them wore fur boas and tippets - the sign of self-respect.' (Daily Chronicle, 15 August 1911)

We can find women on strike and industrially militant - and when we don't we can look for reasons in the types and conditions and patterns of their work, not in the female character. Still more important, we can extend the conventional definition of political activity (as taking place in parliament and party or even unions and picket lines) and show that it is to be found wherever people combine to resist extortion and exploitation, in the community as well as at the work-place, and that in such struggles women have always been prominent. (To give a brief example, it was generally women who led the so-called 'bread riots' of the 18th century, when the hoarded stocks of millers and bakers who took advantage of scarcity would be seized and sold at the old 'fair' price.)

But it is still more important to discover first what was the ordinary condition of women. We cannot reach an effective understanding of resistance - particularly in its daily smouldering as opposed to the occasional conflagration - without understanding the modes of oppression, and how and when and why their subtle shifts occurred. We cannot even identify the less obvious forms of resistance unless we know the experience of oppression that they grew out of. Nor is it enough to know the statistics of exploitation: it is a question of making an imaginative leap, of feeling the past as well as analysing it. Unfortunately, the very nature of women's work, always tending to be seasonal, often casual, sometimes part-time, frequently in small (and shortlived) workshops, hardly ever organised, means that information about it is hard to recover. For the recent past a useful source is people's own memories. You often find out far more by talking to old people than from written records; and you can ask them questions about their childhood, family life and so on, which no records cover. Sometimes they can also tell you about their parents or even grandparents; their memories are often clearer for their childhood and early years than for the intervening years. But the documentary sources which are generally the historian's standby (and which too often determine the area of research) hardly exist until the end of the 19th century, and even then they are limited and unsatisfactory.

Women's work was invisible until some particular problem made it visible - the outcry over 'phossy jaw' and the match girls' strike led to enquiries into the work conditions in 19th century match factories, for example. But generally speaking, outside observers tended to come up with evidence which confirmed them in their prejudices (this is very clearly seen for instance in the enquiries on women in agricultural work and in mining), or to concentrate on the exceptional because the ordinary and accepted did not seem interesting.

One way of finding out about ordinary life is by accumulating information and details given incidentally in other contexts. For instance, 19th century newspapers gave detailed reports of police court cases, with not only 'facts' like name, age, occupation and address, but also material on the movements and activities of ordinary people, witnesses or those marginally involved. Or again the reports of charity and missionary societies, although full of rubbish about people's wickedness and improvidence, and how glad they are to be converted and rescued, do also sometimes give life-histories or detailed accounts of a family's circumstances. Even the enquiry of a government medical officer into an epidemic can provide interesting information. (On eating habits for example: one report from around the turn of the century shows incidentally how the children of many London families - and often the parents too - would buy food ready cooked, 'fish and potatoes' from a fried fish shop, or meat or hot pie from a cook shop, and rarely, perhaps only for Sunday dinner, sit down together to a 'family meal'.)

Generally speaking, it is easier to find out about the casualties of society (through institutional records, etc) than about
those who coped (this is true at any rate of the 19th century,
on which I am concentrating specifically); and of course many
of the casualties were women. Irregular employment, badly
paid, and the difficulty of providing against ill-health or mis-
fortune, meant that good times could never be counted on to
last. For the old and the sick, or for mothers widowed with
young children, survival was a terrible struggle often lost.
Children and the old died of cold and malnutrition; many women were permanently anaemic and had their health irrevo-
cably undermined by too frequent pregnancies and the accompanying miscarriages and complications.

Whatever sources one uses, even the bald figures of the census, it is soon clear that the generalisations and stereotypes
generally made concerning Victorian women bear as little
relation to the lives of the vast majority of them as do fashion
plates to their appearance. Their lives were not tied to the
home or sheltered, they were not timid weakling creatures
deferring to men, devoting their lives uncomplainingly to the
cult of maternity (thought there was widespread ignorance of
contraception and childbearing claimed many victims). They
were often self-supporting, and did not expect that after marriage they would give up outside employment for ever. In
short, working class women were also working women, their
toil in strong contrast to the easy life of their 'betters', and
indeed supporting it.

There is a clear connection between the cult of the leisured
lady and the growth of the middle classes. Leisure (like 'good
works') was a luxury which the poor could not afford; by so
much the more did the prosperous citizen like to 'display his
wife and daughters as symbols of his success'. ('Woman in a
changing society', Winifred Holtby, 1933) His wealth was
clearly shown not only by their clothes, but by their frittered
time, and by the number of servants (mostly women) needed
to enable them to maintain an ostentatiously idle existence.

In working class communities on the other hand, women worked all their lives, in unpaid drudgery in the home and at
badly paid jobs outside, creating by their labour (directly in
some kinds of work like sewing and domestic service, indirectly in others, through the profits employers made out of
their work and their husbands' and children's) the luxury
which their wealthy sisters enjoyed. The same men who were
fanatically protective of the womanhood of their own class
acquiesced in and depended on the wholesale exploitation of
women outside that class. The fine lady was not allowed to
open a door or carry a parcel for fear of straining herself;
but all laundry and cleaning was done by women lifting and
carrying endless heavy tubs and bickets regardless of their
health, and no protests were heard. The concern of paternalist
philanthropists was however voiced where women were seen

doing unwomanly work, which meant not that it was heavy, but that it involved for instance getting dirty and wearing trousers, like the pitbrow girls (who strongly resisted attempts to protect them from their work of sorting and loading coal as it came up from the pit), or working with men, or enjoying a degree of independence.

Young factory girls had often considerable independence, especially if they moved out of the family home and set up together. Their wages were wretched (9s a week would be typical in London); but their hours were shorter and their work conditions on the whole less cramped than those of girls in the workshop trades or doing home-work; and they despised domestic servants for their lack of freedom. Their confident outspoken manner and their uninhibited delight in dancing and joking and flaunting gay clothes shocked and fascinated outside observers. This is how a middle class evangelical, Lettice Bell, described the 'Factory Girl': 'There is no mistaking her in the streets. The long day's silence is made up for the moment she is free, by loud and boisterous laughter, and a flow of language peculiar to her and her alone. No pavement ever seems quite wide enough for her requirements, as she strolls along from side to side, arm in arm with two kindred spirits. . She is apparently born minus a sense of shyness. Why live in a free country if she cannot accost every man that looks likely to afford a hopeful butt for her sarcasm, or to stand her a drink? Amusement and drink is essential to this class; but their idea of what is amusing is often also that which is lowest and most coarse...'

Mr Lakeman, a factory inspector in the 1880s, also commented on their 'don't care style', their loud laughter and singing of music-hall songs; he complained that 'if you speak to them you are laughed at, question them and you are intruding, follow them out when work is over and they exhibit a freedom not bounded by restraint'. A more sympathetic picture is given in Somerset Maugham's early novel, 'Lisa of Lambeth', or by George Gissing in 'Thyrza' (sadly rather hard to obtain).

Country girls too were often self-supporting, and their liberty also alarmed the respectable; again the area of concern was work considered unwomanly, for instance raking manure or riding astride a carthorse, and the moral risks to which unmarried girls working familiarly alongside men (let alone celebrating with them on country holidays and festivals) must necessarily be exposed. There was a wide range of country occupations for women, as one may see from Thomas Hardy's novels. (In 'Tess of the d'Urbervilles' for example, Tess learns the basic country skills while still a child, by working for her parents and for local farmers; away from home she works successively as poultry-girl, milkmaid and field-labourer.) In town and in country there was much casual and irregular work for women; for those who had no ties would move around picking up jobs where they could, and sleeping rough or in the cheap lodging-houses which sheltered many women on their travels. In the summer work was scarce in the towns (especially London), and fruit-picking, for gangs of girls, or hop-picking, for women and children, brought many out into the country for a working holiday.

Women on their own with dependents were generally worst off, since by this period men's rates of pay were set on the assumption that they would have dependents, women's on the assumption that they would be at least partly supported. But the married woman's maintenance was hard-earned: no matter how worn down by annual pregnancies she had to keep going, washing, cleaning, and budgeting for a growing family under almost impossible conditions. She could count herself lucky if that was all, if her man was in steady and well-enough paid work to provide for them; but if his work was uncertain, or if ill-health or an employer's death or bankruptcy (or retrenchment or retirement) brought unemployment and sudden hardship, she would take for granted that she too must look for paid work. (This was liable to happen at least for a time to almost any married woman of the working classes.) A woman who could get out and leave her children might do a factory or workshop job, or find temporary work with an old employer in need of extra hands; but more likely she would get work in a laundry or as a charwoman or perhaps as a daily nurse. If she was tied to the home she would undertake one of the many varieties of homework (all sweated): all sorts of sewing, toymaking, folding books, making boxes or artificial flowers or sacks or brushes, furpulling, etc. When times were hard (and tensions rose) her earnings might even be the only money coming in: sometimes the man's only hope of work was to go off 'on tramp' in search of it, sending back irregular remittances when he could; or staying, he might in desperation seek refuge in the pub ('the quickest way out of London', as they called it) which inevitably meant a depleted family budget. And drink often led to violence, when a drunken husband might inflict the most brutal treatment on his wife, and probably go unpunished. (The punishment, a period of hard labour, was in any case of doubtful use; in giving her respite from his attentions it also left her as sole provider in his absence, and far from resolving existing problems and tensions it presumably provided a further source of resentment.) Divorce was out of reach of the poor, and particularly for women; but desertion was frequent.

Women beaten down by poverty and disaster were to be found among the down-and-outs and among those who lived from hand to mouth as street-sellers (of flowers, matches, watercress, etc) or on odd jobs: by shelling peas or walnuts at the markets, or by chopping firewood on the wharves of Bermondsey, or sweeping out shops before opening time, or washing-up at a coffee-stall or a cheap restaurant, you could earn enough for a meal or even a fourpenny doss. There were charitable doles, too, but many of these were available only for the

'deserving poor', among whom down-and-outs were not usually
numbered, having forfeited their deserts by allowing themselves to sink so low; while anyone dependent on casual work,
and lodging where she could from day to day, was by definition
not steady or deserving, though she might be good to 'rescue'.
('Rescued' girls were trained for domestic service, the only
employment for women in which demand was inexhaustible.)
Relief from official sources was hard to get and inadequate
when it was grudgingly given; and it might be conditional on
entering the much-hated workhouse. Help from any source
was often accompanied by moral judgement and humiliation;
small wonder that many women ended their desperation by
throwing themselves in the Thames.

There were however other ways of making a living. In various
forms, swindling and coining and theft could help to eke out
inadequate earnings, and they seem to have involved more
women than today. (Census figures are unfortunately of no
use in this area.) As pawnbrokers and second-hand dealers
women were effective fences; they took part in the manufact-
ure and the uttering of forged money (a thriving domestic industry); their nimble fingers were put to good use in every
crowd; in dockland and other districts they enticed victims
into quiet corners to be relieved of their valuables; in endless
imaginative disguises they conned the gullible out of 'subscriptions', 'donations', and 'loans'. It is surely significant that
today so many more women are found in mental hospitals than
in prisons: it reflects not only a change in the definitions and
expectations of the authorities, but also a generally more passive and hopeless response by women to their difficulties
(and perhaps a change in the nature of these difficulties).

Another result of the insecurity of women's economic position
(to take one of the main factors involved) was prostitution,
which was widespread in the 19th century, although reliable
information on its extent or character (as opposed to the lurid
claims of a Frank Harris or of the moral purity campaigners)
is not easily found. On the basis of Salvation Army records
it was suggested that a high proportion of prostitutes had been
domestic servants, and this rings true. Servants could be
thrown out without references or notice for being pregnant
(often by the master or son of the house or by a fellow servant) or indeed for lesser misbehaviour, and would find it hard
to get subsequent employment with no 'character'. Although
many girls went into service because it was steady and secure, such security as it afforded was hard earned, not only by
long hours and heavy work and low wages, but also by having
to submit to paternalist and moralising supervision of what
little free time was allowed, and offence to the employer could
mean instant dismissal. George Moore's novel 'Esther Waters'
vividly shows the fate of a girl in these circumstances.

It was often said that casual prostitution was resorted to by
girls in London's many seasonal trades, to tide them over the

two or three months when work was slack or non-existent, but this is not on the whole my impression. It seems more likely that prostitution itself would have been a seasonal trade, the demand declining with the summer exodus of the rich. Certainly it was very localised: there was none in respectable working class districts like Bethnal Green; it was found in low-class areas near rich ones (like Notting-dale), or in deceptively genteel ones (like St John's Wood), or round stations, or in certain central districts catering generally for the leisure and pleasure of the better-off. 'Fanny by gaslight', an interesting historical novel by Michael Sadleir, gives a convincing picture of one stratum of prostitution.

The differences between then and now, and the similarities too, are worth thinking about. One area of difference is very interestingly discussed by Richard Titmuss, in an essay written in the 1950s ('The position of women', in 'Essays on the welfare state'). He points out that until about 1911 the typical working class mother would spend fifteen years of her life in the bearing and early rearing of children; and by the time her youngest child left school she would probably be 55 years old with a life expectancy of 12 years. Today, on the other hand, he says, 'most mothers have largely concluded their maternal role by the age of 40. At this age a woman can now expect to live 36 years... Yet, at present, practically all forms of educational and vocational training, along with entry to many pensionable occupations, are shut to the woman who has reached the age of 40. Motherhood and date of birth disqualify her, while the unthinking and unknowing may condemn her in moralizing terms for seeking work outside the home.'

If women's subordination were only physiologically determined, these changes (lengthening life expectancy and a shrinking period of child care) should have released women for a much larger part outside the home. Since they have not, reasons must obviously be sought elsewhere, partly in the state of the labour market and the economy, but also for instance in another change for which Titmuss gives statistics: the amazing increase in marriage. More people now marry more times and earlier. This means fewer single women (and correspondingly a decline in status for the spinster, whose rarity does not increase her value), and more women dependent on (or merely supplementing) a man's earnings. The 'family' now makes fewer physical demands on its mother, at least in most cases, but she is no freer from it than before.

The family has clearly gone through great changes in its nature and composition, yet people still refer to it as though it were constant and inevitable, the unchanging basic unit in every human society. (One of the few works in which the history of the family is studied is 'Centuries of childhood', by Philippe Aries, who doesn't take its existence for granted or its form as unchanging, but looks at its development in relation to social change.) A similar argument is used to resist our demands: we are told that women like things as they are, it's in their nature to want to stay at home, put husband and family first, leave action and decision-taking to others, develop above all others the talents they can use in home-making: 'that's how it's always been'.

The search for women's history is not simply a question of filling in gaps, of writing ourselves back into history to restore our 'amour propre'. We need to know our past. We need to know, for instance, how long and why it has been accepted that women's work was worthless - or at least could be paid less. We need to know the forms our oppression has taken through the centuries, and how it has been reinforced by the family, and how the family itself has also changed. By showing that the role and 'nature' of women changes with each society we are helping to defeat the argument 'that's how it's always been'. Since oppressive ideology is justified by reference to a false past, it is important for us to show what the past really was, to develop an alternative to the distorted version still being used against us. Historical understanding is essential to our struggle: we must find the roots of our oppression to destroy it; we must know where we come from to understand what we are and where we are going, and we must examine the struggle of earlier generations of women to help us to win our own.

(A pamphlet which shows some of the ways in which women were involved in political action in the 19th century is Jo O'Brien's 'Women's liberation in labour history: a case study from Nottingham', published by Spokesman Publications, price 10p)

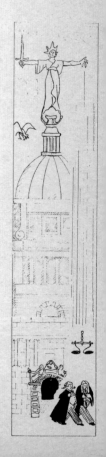

THE NIGHT-CLEANERS' CAMPAIGN

'Shrew', December 1971

(This account of the London night-cleaners' campaign was
written by the members of the London Women's Liberation
Night-Cleaners' Collective, with help from some of the night
cleaners. The campaign started with leafletting at the end of
October 1970. International Socialist Women leafletted until
Christmas, then Women's Liberation Workshop groups started
alongside them and were joined by Socialist Woman. Cleaners
have also been organising in Birmingham, Norwich, Lancaster
and Manchester. This has been especially successful in Manchester. In Lancaster cleaners went on strike for free transport, which they got, and were supported by students.)

Cleaning contractors make a lot of money out of the work the cleaners are forced to do

Instead of employing cleaners directly, many large offices in
the last few years have found it more convenient to contract
the work out to cleaning companies. This means that the cleaning company promises in the contract to provide a certain
number of women to clean so many feet of office space.

The contract is between the owner of the office and the cleaning contractor. The women cleaning don't know what it says.
So there's nothing to stop the cleaning contractor from providing much fewer cleaners than he promised. This does in
fact happen, and is rarely found out.

Night cleaning is invisible work. Who knows or cares what
goes on? The owner of the office and all the office workers
are tucked up in bed. So this and other fiddles pass unnoticed.

'Time spent on problems such as one's cleaning workforce,
recruiting it, organising and equipping it, is time diverted
from the things in which the manufacturer or businessman
is a specialist. His specialist time, effort and knowledge is
being dissipated... Well, what type of work can contract cleaners do? They clean anything and everything. Nothing is too
complicated nor too dirty.' (Contract cleaners publication)

The industry has grown by leaps and bounds since the war.
The really fast growth has been very recent, since 1965.

company	turnover		profit after tax
Industrial Contract Clnrs.	1968	850,891	57,438
and subsidiaries	1969	1,843,383	111,573
Pritchard Cleaners	1968	6,700,000	265,833
and subsidiaries	1969	10,900,000	373,761
Initial Services	1968	21,880,538	1,546,749
and subsidiaries	1969	23,017,289	1,603,614

The large firms make bigger profits than the smaller ones.
They are able to extract more profit out of the work women
do because they operate on a larger scale. The rate of

exploitation in the big firms is thus higher. Very little capital goes into equipment. The main cost for the employer is wages. So it is in the interests of the employers to keep the wages as low as possible.

Male full-time cleaners earn double the women's wages - £20.98. (£9.62 is the average full-time wage throughout the country - London rates are higher.) So it is in the interests of the employers to employ women. Male part-time workers get the same rates as women. This is why night-cleaners, who are full-time workers, are nearly all women.

On one particular building, The Music Corporation of America in Mayfair, Office Cleaning Services have a contract which costs MCA £132 per week. The labour employed consists of two women who clean the whole building, five nights a week, and whose combined wages amount to £26.

The Civil Service Union on contract cleaning

Government cleaners who are still employed directly and are in the CSU get higher wages and have to clean less space (1,000 square feet per cleaner, compared with 15,000 in contract cleaning). Consequently, contract cleaning costs are 30% lower than direct cleaning, which means that government offices are gradually going over to contract cleaning. But the 30% saving is at the expense of the women cleaners.

The CSU told the Prices and Incomes Board: 'The main reason for the difference in costs between direct cleaning and contract cleaning... is that contractors pay low wages and give poorer conditions than the government'. John Vickers, General Secretary of the CSU, says: 'In all my years in the trade union movement I've never come across conditions like those in the contract cleaning business. It's like something out of the nineteenth century'.

The 1968 TUC Conference expressed strong disagreement with the government's proposal to transfer one third of office cleaning in the civil service to cleaning contractors. In June 1968 representatives of the TUC General Council met the Chancellor of the Exchequer. Although they said they thought productivity and efficiency in cleaning could be improved, they said this should be done within the direct cleaning system by improving materials, equipment and training. They said more money would be saved in the long run this way. They questioned the government estimates and pointed out the low wages of contract cleaners, and they suggested a centralised cleaning force and incentive bonus scheme. In correspondence later, the General Council asked if the reduction of one third could exclude offices in areas of high unemployment.

The 1968 CSU motion calling on the government to make sure that cleaning contractors in the civil service should be restricted to firms paying the same rates as direct cleaning, and the General Council suggestion that the government should amend the Fair Wages Resolution, were rejected.

The Fair Wages Resolution was passed by parliament in 1946, one of the first acts of Atlee's government. It lays down that contractors to the government, local authorities and all public utility undertakings, shall recognise the right of their employees to belong to a trade union and also, in civil service jargon, says that the contractor shall pay wages not less than those paid by the best employer in the trade.

The government refused to amend the Fair Wages Resolution to cover contract cleaning in public buildings, but admitted (31. 3. 69) in principle that the wages paid in the civil service sector must be one of the factors taken into account. Although the CSU have taken cases to the Industrial Court, so far the courts have said that direct cleaning rates cannot be compared with contract cleaning rates. This means that the level of wages in contract cleaning can be held down - which of course suits the cleaning contractors.

However, it does mean that cleaners employed by contractors can get their rates raised slightly by going to an Industrial Court through the union. In this way they can get parity with other cleaners. In 1971, for example, a firm called General Cleaners was ordered by the Industrial Court in Manchester to increase the rate they paid their workers from 24p to 27.5p to cover the actual hours worked on what they called a 'job and finish' basis.

The trade unions involved (TGWU, GMWU, NUPE, CSU) said there should be a joint council of unions and employers and that the government should use its influence as a major customer to raise cleaners' rates. The Prices and Incomes Board rejected these proposals as inflationary(!), but said one union should make a determined effort to unionise. The PIB also rejected the employers' suggestion that a Wages Council should be set up. These have not in the past improved the pay of low-paid workers.

Why bother to try and unionise women?

Some people are very critical of unions. They say they are bureaucratic and only concerned to improve wages. Also, the structure of unions tends to exclude women from the executive so the particular interests of women are not considered. We recognise that unions have many limitations, and that these limitations are most obvious in the case of women workers. However, to join a union is still the necessary first step if women are going to get better conditions at work.

Cleaning is women's work

Many of the women are forced to work at night because there are no nursery facilities. This means cleaners often don't get much sleep. Over a long period this is bound to affect your health, because you are doing two jobs. Many cleaners have a lot of children, and usually quite a few young children, because this is when money is tightest in a family. All women have a very narrow choice in jobs, and women who go into cleaning for various reasons have even less choice. They are often unsupported. The PIB report published in Spring 1971 said that a quarter of the women in their survey were the sole providers of their families. About a fifth of them were from families with an income below £14 a week. More than 3% were living on the poverty line.

They are often immigrant women, which means that many jobs are closed to them. West Indian, African, Irish, Indian, Spanish, Cypriot women go cleaning because they have little chance of getting other jobs. Even within cleaning they have less chance of being promoted. Have you ever met a coloured supervisor?

There are women of all ages cleaning at night, from very young girls to old women with white hair. The PIB report found that the women in their survey tended to be under 40 (when the children are young) or over 60 (supplementing their pension). We are not certain whether this is general.

Cleaning is sometimes regarded as unskilled work that anyone can do. In general the definition of 'skilled' means privilege, and in the long run privileges only keep people divided. But in the short term even it's wrong to say that cleaning is unskilled. Cleaners have their own kind of skill. But like many of the things women can do in our society its not acknowledged.

Night cleaners are sometimes called casual workers. This is completely wrong. They are working a full working week. Some people think that the cleaners only work for pin money. This is rubbish. People who think like that should try cleaning offices for a bit. It is true that there are always women coming on for short periods, at Christmas, or during a long strike such as the Post Office strike, or when a man is off sick. But this is for the basic necessities. However there is a large group of women who work for years and years in cleaning. Indeed after 12 or 15 years it gets so that you can't work in the day even though your children have grown up. Your body has adjusted to night work.

Conditions of work in night cleaning

Long hours: 10pm to 6am generally, with slight variation. Low pay: most people get more money for doing night work. Not cleaners - they get less. Pay is around £12 a week, sometimes more, sometimes less. Wages vary from building to building. The same cleaning company can pay women different rates. When tax, insurance and fares are subtracted, cleaners can be left with only about £6. No security: cleaners can be sacked without notice. Often they don't get holiday pay.

Hard work: cleaning is physically tiring. It can be very heavy work. Sometimes it's also dirty. If someone is away you still

228

have to clean the building. When you do someone else's work
you don't get full pay, you get 'cover money'. This means you
do twice the work for about 40p extra. So it is always in the
interests of the employers to keep the buildings understaffed.

No protection: the Factory Acts don't apply to cleaners. This
means that there is no restriction on night work, that very
young girls can work all night, that cleaners who are pregnant
continue to work all night. Also, if you have an accident at
work it's very difficult to get compensation, as the cleaning
contractors are likely to deny responsibility.

The Cleaners Action Group demands

£18.75 per week wages. Sick pay. Two weeks pay instead of
notice or two weeks' notice in writing. Holiday pay - one day
for every month worked. Adequate staffing on all buildings.
Adequate cover money. Recognition of union.

Night cleaners want more pay, but there are also other demands which relate to general conditions. Until we are stronger
our best bet is through the Fair Wages Resolution.

Local demands: conditions vary from building to building.
Direct bargaining, eg over ventilation, the length of breaks,
could be effective, if there is support from other buildings
cleaned by the same contractor. Transport: at present many
of the women travel long distances to work in London. Many
live in south, east or north-east London and have to get to the
City or the West End. In Lancaster the cleaners have won the
right of free transport to work. Why not in London? Control:
any increase in wages is nearly always accompanied by a
reduction in the number of women employed on a building.
So the women pay back their increase by doing more work.
Cleaners should be able to see the contract, and the union
should be able to keep a check on the numbers employed to
make sure the employers are not fiddling numbers.

Protection and restriction: women can't afford to be against
protective legislation in general because at present women
are doing two jobs. We should try to get protective legislation
extended to men so it can't be used as an excuse to pay wom-
en less. At present, the difference between male and female
rates in cleaning is justified on the grounds that women are
not required to stretch to do high-level work. Equipment:
cleaning contractors should provide more equipment.

Leafletters report

The Shell Centre: waiting for action

Four of us from the Pimlico group and two from the Chiswick
group began to leaflet the Shell buildings last June. The campaign had been under way since the previous November. Membership of the TGWU was building up slowly but we were still
20 or so short of the 50 needed before the night cleaners could

form their own branch of the union. Shell was chosen as the next target because altogether 80 cleaners work there - 65 on the 'upstream' building and 15 on the 'downstream'.

At first we were slightly nervous. Most of us felt embarrassingly middle class. However we were very encouraged to discover that the majority of the women stopped to speak to us, and several joined within the first month. Two or three of the women who joined first have been mainly responsible for the others joining. We now have about 22 altogether in the union on the two buildings. Three dropped out the week after they joined. We have had two meetings with some of the cleaners in a cafe near the Shell buildings. We have also had a meeting in a pub with the TGWU official. He has promised to write to Shell, to ask them for a room on the premises to hold a meeting with his union members. This, he hoped, would reveal Shell's attitude to the union.

The two buildings have different contractors: Office Cleaning Services on the upstream building, and Pritchards on the downstream one. We were hoping that conditions on the two buildings would vary, so that this might provide the long-awaited opportunity for union intervention. However, the two buildings do receive the same wages, £12, although conditions do vary a little.

If the union could achieve just one small victory then we would have 'got our foot in the door', as the union official puts it, and a foot in the door with contractors is what the campaign urgently needs. At the moment, women are still joining the union at Shell, but the majority of them are very apprehensive and frightened that they will get the sack. The supervisor on the downstream building is fairly encouraging, but the one on the upstream seems to delight in provoking the women she suspects. The attitude of the supervisor to the union can be very important; the two weeks that the Shell upstream building supervisor was away was when we managed to hold the two meetings in a cafe.

At the moment we are waiting to hear the outcome of the union's letter to Shell. In the meantime we are going to show extracts from the night cleaners film at one of our houses on a Sunday afternoon.

Cooks and the Department of Education and Science: lost faith

Lucy first went out leafletting with May Hobbs and Fergus from International Socialism in November 1970. They went to Somerset House, Australia House and the ITV Centre in Kingsway. The night caretakers were mostly friendly and told them when the cleaners came on duty.

She then went to Somerset House alone, but found this rather difficult as she could only talk to one or two of the women at once, and the others would hurry off into the building. However those she spoke to about joining the union were very keen, although some of the black women were afraid they might lose their jobs. After this she went with Liz, as they could talk to many more women if there were two of them. After many weeks of leafletting and talking, they tried to persuade the cleaners to choose somebody to be the collector of their weekly subscriptions of 5p, but this failed, as nobody wanted to take on the responsibility. So they decided to collect the money themselves each week. Actually there was only one building where 8 women joined in one evening and one actually volunteered to collect the dues. They made their two buildings for permanent collection Cook's building in Mayfair and the Department of Education and Science, nearby.

The DES was a building they leafletted consistently from November to July. There were about 10 women there, 7 of them black. The supervisor was very suspicious and hostile and constantly criticised the union, telling the women they were wasting their money. Only the black women joined.

They made the mistake of giving the impression that the union would obtain wage rises and improved conditions quite soon: indeed, this was what they believed at the beginning. They had never worked with unions or been involved in any political action at all, and didn't realise the enormous amount of work and planning involved.

The women paid regularly for months; they were given the 'Cleaners' Voice' newsletter and the TGWU newspaper. The film people came along several times to interview them, much to the supervisor's resentment. The union refused to negotiate because there wasn't enough support ('enough' being at least 50% unionisation in any building before they would negotiate for wages).

They gradually realised how powerless they were to help, what with combatting union bureaucracy, hostility from supervisors and other white women, and the women's own ignorance of union affairs. They felt they had deceived the cleaners because they hadn't explained that the struggle of unionisation might extend over years. At the beginning they hadn't understood this themselves; owing to the disproportionate amount of publicity the campaign had received, they were under the impression that success was near. During the summer they went away; other people helped sporadically to collect the dues, but the women lost faith. They still see them from time to time, but they don't take their money now.

Somerset House: still paying

After the usual pattern of talking to cleaners as they went in every week, 8 women joined the union, after about two months. Two were more aware of their exploitation than others; they were not alarmed by their employers' knowing about their membership. The others were more wary, but they all talked to each other during tea-break. Some were friends anyway,

231

and in the end all joined except four cleaners on the building. The company supervisor was very rude about the women and scornful of their right to better wages and conditions. You were really back in a mid-19th century situation; joining a union, to her, was some sort of a crime.

In fact, only 2 came from Somerset House and 2 from Bush House. It seems general that night cleaners find it difficult to come to meetings; they lead busy and tiring lives. 5 women at Somerset House have 5 or 6 children. Also, many people are shy of 'a meeting'; the word doesn't necessarily mean anything to them. Of course they are aware of the companies' attitude to unions, and they don't want to lose their jobs or get victimised. Of those who came to May's meeting from Bush House, two were white, two were black. It came out later that the whites did not get on with the coloured women, and one white woman even said afterwards that she would not join if blacks were going to get higher wages. In the event, the white woman did not join, but three black women did.

So women at Somerset House and Bush House have paid union dues for six months, and they have until now been keen that the union might achieve something. But it is clear that if nothing happens in the next couple of months they will get fed up, and who can blame them?

The 'woman question' and cleaners

Why is it hard to unionise?

The cleaning contractors are completely opposed on the whole. They not only warn and threaten women but sack them on various pretexts, eg inefficiency, or go over to evening cleaning. The night cleaners work in groups of 10 or even fewer (although on very big buildings you can get 30 to 50 women employed). This makes it much harder for cleaners to organise than workers who are all concentrated together.

On the small buildings it's not too hard for the contractor to get other people in if the women complain or strike. The only hope on small buildings is to have support from women on other buildings cleaned by the same company. Help from the workers who work on buildings during the day is an important extra help.

The isolation of cleaners is made worse by the fact that they have so little time. The only night they can come to a meeting is Friday or Saturday. This means that their husband or someone else has to babysit. We've tried meeting on Saturday afternoon with the children, in an area not too far from where people live. But cleaners are scattered in different parts of London, and there's no guarantee that the women working in a particular building can all go to a meeting in the same area. We've also tried a meeting in the centre of town, with transport laid on, and meetings in pubs near the buildings before work. The main problem with these has been that the cleaners have a lot of things to do before they go to work.

As with all women at work, the attitude to the union is connected with the particular situation of women in society. Many cleaners are doubtful about the union because it doesn't have an immediate effect, and it can mean simply trouble and the loss of the bit of money they are getting at the moment. The distrust we all have as women towards other women, and the fact that the area managers are men and can be superior towards women in ways that couldn't be towards male workers combined with the brainwashing women all receive to take things from men in authority, puts some women off unions.

Even at work too, cleaners are responsible for things at home and have to think about shopping and prices; some of the women are against unions because they hold them responsible for rising prices. Also, the women who have come on for a short time feel it's not worth joining a union. There is nothing automatic about joining a union in their life, so the women who have kept on paying tend to get fed up when nothing happens, while a small minority really think about it a lot, and about the general position of women in society as a whole. But for us leafletters it is very hard sometimes to try and persuade women to keep on paying, because we know how much cleaners need every penny they earn. On the other hand, there is nothing the cleaners can do without the first step of joining a union. But first steps take such an exhaustingly long time.

It's hard to explain to people who have never been in a union before the limitations of a union. They say why bother to join at all? This is a difficulty which not only leafletters but also cleaners who have become convinced about it have faced. Cleaners are all nationalities, which splits things up more, although not as much as it could. We've found that it's more likely to be the supervisors who say things against black women. But because the work is in such small groups, black and white women often are quite close and friendly. No black supervisors, though. The supervisor works very close to the women; she is not a remote authority but a person who is either liked or disliked as a person. Supervisors vary in their attitude to the union. They can be either bitterly opposed or really very strongly in support because they know very well what the set-up is in cleaning.

Women's work

The only general characteristic of women's work is low pay. Historically, jobs which had been done by women in the home, after the growth of factories and large towns were seen as women's work. Because women were also doing housework and caring for families, and because of the way women are brought up to see the man as boss, they found it more difficult to organise to defend themselves. So women, along with immigrant labour, are useful to employers to work at cheaper rates.

As machinery and technology developed, jobs could be broken down into simple repetitive tasks. Often these became women's work. Nowadays, along with the development of industry and very expensive machines, there is more and more paper work in offices, so jobs like cleaning have increased. In these jobs labour is the main item in the employer's costs, so it is particularly important to keep his wages low. Again, many labour-intensive jobs have become seen as women's work. Because of the position of women in the society, both men and women have tended to accept this as somehow unalterable.

Because of the economic pressure on working class men to be the main provider of the family, and because in capitalism ideas of manhood are confused with ideas of dominance and power which are bound up with cash, men often have a divided attitude. They recognise the need for solidarity at work, but also fear the competition of women and immigrant workers. With women too, men often feel deep down that their manhood is threatened if women can do what they can do.

We have all been brainwashed since childhood into ideas about our own identities. Just as black people used to be taught that they were happy, smiling people who liked picking cotton and serving white people, women have been taught that they are only happy when they are submitting to men - husbands or employers - and that women are biologically suited to clean, cook, sew, type, serve, wait or handle the simplest process in a factory, but incapable of mending the machine if it goes wrong: men's work. If you're black, working class and a woman, you lose out three times over.

How can we change this?

In Women's Liberation we often get depressed because the more you think about the position of women in society as a whole, the more you realise has to be done to get any real change. Obviously you can only start with small things, and it's easy to feel you're not getting anywhere. What we have to realise when we feel like that is that to remember that small changes can have much bigger effects than we expect. Remember the Ford's sewing machinists - they encouraged women who had never worked inside a car factory.

But also, as the saying goes, 'we may not have much but there's a lot of us', and once women start communicating hope, start wondering if things have to always go on as before, learn to trust other women and become confident and proud, all that careful brainwashing gets messed up. Suddenly women won't take it any more.

It's so simple: when you really despair, or when you feel exasperated because we change things so slowly, keep talking to other women. Many of them are against Women's Liberation, but as you talk about their lives it strengthens you because all they say helps you remember why you first joined.

234

SOCIAL INSECURITY AND ANN BAXTER

(This report and analysis was written by members of Cambridge Women's Liberation)

Women with kids are supposed to live off - depend on - a man. That's the Social Security system: husband and wife are treated as one - the husband. He claims for both.

It's always the woman who gets left with the kids - that's our function. There are few nursery places for our children: even if we do find work it's so badly paid it hardly covers the babyminder, or the hours won't fit with school hours... So there's no choice. It's either a man or the Social Security. The SS is worse than a husband - they keep us at bare subsistence, watch over our 'morality', spy on us with Special Investigators, walk in at any time to check on our housekeeping, cleanliness, etc, but mostly to see if there's a man in the cupboard...

Living on Social Security means being scared to have men around, terrified to let them stay overnight, careful not to go out too often. We are forced to feel guilty, ashamed, grateful for the little we get... The SS has absolute power over us - it's hard enough to leave a husband, but impossible to leave the SS - there's nowhere else to go.

They call us unsupported mothers - and that means no-one to mend the fuses, no-one to go out with, nowhere to go, guilt, frustration, no emotional support, no love, no money.

It could mean free - not dependent on any man, making our own choices, supporting each other, mending our own fuses. We need to know how to deal with the SS - what we can claim, what rights we have: we don't have to tell them who the father is; we don't have to let them in when they come to spy on us; if we are cut off, we can appeal - most of the decisions made by the SS can be disputed at a tribunal.

Do you think you are getting what you need?

A woman living alone can claim for herself, for her children, for dependents, etc. Find out exactly how much you're entitled to. You can claim a winter heating and laundry allowance, and grants for clothes, footwear, bedding, furniture, cutlery, crockery, pram, pushchair, cot, gas/electric cooker, gas/electric fire, rent arrears, gas bill, electricity bill, hire purchase, radio, alarm clock, electric iron, lino, carpets, fares to visit relatives, to find employment, special diet expenses. You should also be getting free medicine, teeth, glasses, school dinners, milk tokens for children under 5, and orange juice for children under 2.

We can fight for these through the Claimants' Union. Claimants' Unions are unions of unemployed, sick, strikers, unsupported mothers, who came together to fight the SS for their needs as a group. The unions pool together the different experiences of all their members to fight the isolation and injustice created by the Social Security system.

Claimants' Unions demand: (1) the right to adequate income without means test for all; (2) a free welfare state controlled by the people who use it; (3) no secrets and the right to full information; (4) no artificial distinctions between so-called 'deserving' and 'undeserving'. ('The Women's Newspaper', March 1971)

The narrative

Ann Baxter lives in one of Cambridge's most neglected streets, the sort of street which has a reputation for being full of so-called problem families. Ann is an unsupported mother with five children aged from 6 to 12. She had been living on social security since she and her husband separated at the beginning of 1971, when, in April, Social Security withdrew her money on the grounds that she was cohabiting with her husband. When this was denied, two other men were mentioned, one of whom Ann had never heard of. Through her next-door neighbour, Ann contacted the Claimants' Union who, together with the Unsupported Mothers group, began to work with Ann. The first step was to appeal to the SS Tribunal to have the decision reversed, but in the meantime Ann and her children had to live on something. Ann went to SS to ask for the Emergency Allowance to which she appeared to be entitled under section 13 of the Social Security Act 1967. Social Security, on the grounds of having discretionary rights in decision-making, refused. Ann's social worker was contacted and asked to apply pressure on the SS to pay up. The social worker was not prepared to question SS's decision nor the evidence on which it was based; moreover she pointed out that she could not afford to antagonise SS since she had to work with them. After three telephone calls in which the Unsupported Mothers Group tried to communicate some sense of the urgency of the situation to the social worker, she did manage to visit Ann, bringing with her not the money or the food which she was legally able to provide, but a bag of old shoes, none of which fitted.

Ann and her children were also being harassed by the SS fraud squad. The housing department was threatening her with eviction. Her arrears dated from when her SS allowance was withdrawn and amounted to approximately £12. Ann had no money and was in danger of having no home. The Housing Department was contacted but, as with Social Security and Social Services, with no success. Legal advice was taken over SS's refusal to pay the emergency allowance and a 'mandamus' was suggested. Meanwhile, as official methods had not worked the Unsupported Mothers contemplated direct action. They and the Claimants' Union put the situation to Women's Liberation and all three groups decided to picket the SS office to demand the payment of Ann's emergency allowance. We occupied the office in the morning, talking to other claimants and handing out leaflets. Apart from a mild request that we leave, SS ignored us all day. The superficial calm and the near holiday atmosphere covered a sense of mounting tension. Sure enough, at the end of office hours the police were called in and stood by while SS officials dragged us outside. Two days later, after some local publicity about the sit-in, SS 'relented' and gave Ann the emergency allowance.

Looking back, this apparent victory was really only the beginning of our fight. With two weeks to go until the Tribunal, SS were searching avidly for more evidence against Ann. A barrister from Child Poverty Action Group was willing to represent Ann. Some of the Unsupported Mothers Group discovered that the police were also collecting evidence for the tribunal. The police questioned Ann's two eldest children and tried to question friends in the neighbourhood. They were also in touch with Ann's mother, with whom Ann had a long-standing bad relationship. The police questioning concerned: 'drug addiction' - sleeping pills; 'drunkenness' - implying that Ann's distress was due to her being drunk; 'relationships with men' - implying prostitution; and neglect of the children -implying this was due to deliberate cruelty. Our impression was that Ann's mother and brother had given this information to the police who were now trying to prove it. Also, the police informed Ann's solicitor that her husband had stated to them that he was paying her £20 a week. One other example of the police's behaviour at this point throws light on what happened to her children after the tribunal.

Paul, Ann's eldest son, had gone to stay with his grandmother. After a few days Ann went to bring him home. A row started between Ann and her mother and the police arrived on the scene. They took Paul, Ann's mother and Ann's brother to the police station. Ann was left to walk. In the meantime one of Ann's daughters got worried at how long her mother had been out and went round to her grandmother's. The police threatened to arrest Ann, and her ex-husband, if they tried to remove the two children from their grandmother's house.

The events leading up to the SS tribunal did not make us feel optimistic. The way in which such tribunals are run did not help matters. Tribunal hearings are not open to the public, and both hearsay evidence and innuendo are permissible. It turned out that Ann's husband had not told the police that he was supporting Ann; in any case he was able to show that his take-home pay, when working, was only £18 a week so he could hardly have been giving her £20 a week. The other SS and police evidence also collapsed in the tribunal. The accusations of receiving money from her husband and/or other men; drug addiction; drunkenness (based on the evidence of two empty whisky bottles); and neglect of the children. Ann's appeal was upheld at the tribunal, but the following day the SS official who had attended the tribunal denied official knowledge of the decision and refused to give her any money. She was forced to re-apply and was then given her money. Some time later, after several interactions with SS, the arrears owed to her were paid.

Two days later the two eldest children, who were still staying with their grandmother, were taken into care without their parents' knowledge or consent. The Social Services, when contacted, declared that the care order had been initiated by the police on the grounds that Ann was terrorising her children. This was based on no evidence, since the social worker had only visited Ann twice since her SS allowance had been withdrawn. The second visit was to inform Ann that her children had been taken into care and to refuse to tell her where they were. We visited every children's home in the area and everyone denied having the children. The next day we discovered they were at the second home we had visited.

After four days Ann was granted a half-hour interview with her children at the Children's Department. Meanwhile Ann's mother and brother had known their whereabouts all the time and had been given full visiting rights. Once again we decided that we had to fight publicly for Ann's rights. A large group of us picketed the Children's Department while Ann was meeting her children, and some of us went inside to argue with the social workers. Finally when we had threatened to picket the children's home until Ann was given full visiting rights the magistrates were contacted. The children were allowed to go home until the hearing of the court case dealing with the place-of-safety order.

Before the case had even opened friends were refused permission to sit with Ann; the press, as disinterested observers, were admitted. . . The magistrates seemed uncertain of the prosecution's evidence that Ann Baxter was an unfit mother. One child was taken into a home pending a psychiatric report; the other four were allowed to remain at home under a care order. The probation officer claimed that all objectivity in the case had been clouded over by the publicity created by Mrs Baxter's supporters and by the half-truths and untruths told to the court.

The disinterested observers were not present at the next assault on the Baxter family. When the hearing ended the Baxter children were all at the circus. Ann Baxter arrived with some friends to collect the children and explain the court's decision to them. While waiting outside the circus tent, they were surprised to see the county solicitor and the social worker. Preoccupied with questioning them as to exactly what they were doing, they almost didn't see Paul being grabbed by the probation officer and, with the help of six uniformed police and watched by several plainclothes men, bundled into the waiting Black Maria. Ann was left utterly distraught and the other children hysterical.

The family

If we are to understand the way in which an unsupported mother like Ann Baxter potentially threatens the present organisation of society and is therefore treated in the oppressive way we have described, we must examine the function of the nuclear family in preserving the status quo.

The nuclear family is the basic unit of our social organisation. The woman relies on the man for economic support and in return she usually stays at home looking after him and their children. She is defined by her relationship to her man. She makes it possible for him to work all day outside the home. At work the man is exploited, he is oppressed. But at home he can be seen as the oppressor - as the person with authority. The family reinforces this situation in three ways: (1) the withdrawal of the man's labour, which is his ultimate sanction in the work situation, is limited by his responsibility to his family as their main source of support; (2) the children are restricted initially to their parents' view of the world and are forced to accept it since they are entirely dependent on them. In the structure of the nuclear family we develop psychological mechanisms of deference to authority which are then transferred in our relationships to all other institutions; (3) however, since the family is increasingly the only source of real human relationships all members of the family have an additional interest in staying together over and above the purely economic.

It follows from this analysis that when a woman like Ann Baxter becomes an unsupported mother with children to care for, her first problem is to replace the man in his capacity as wage-earner. Three alternatives were open to Ann. She could have replaced her husband with another man (or men). But having just emerged from one destructive relationship, Ann, like many other women, was wary of embarking on another. In any case few men would be interested in maintaining a woman with one child - never mind five. She could have tried to get a job but again, like so many women, she was not educated to have any expectations from her work but only from being a wife and mother. She therefore had no training which would enable her to get a well-paid and satisfying job. Particularly in a depressed area like Cambridge the pay for an unskilled woman worker is low, even if she could find a job which she could combine with looking after her five children. It is not surprising that Ann turned to the third alternative - social security, getting supplementary benefit as a means of financial support.

As a claimant, an unsupported mother like Ann Baxter finds herself aligned with all other members of society who for any reason are without employment. In a capitalist society the value of an individual is assessed in terms of his productivity. Thus the unemployed man, or the old-age pensioner, suffer from the same disability as the woman whose work as a housewife and child-rearer is not considered to be productive. The unsupported mother dependent on social security highlights the position of women in general.

Success as a mother is defined in terms of being a success as a wife. A 'good home' can only be provided for her children if she is living with her husband. An unsupported mother who deviates from the accepted norms of marriage threatens them if she can successfully establish an alternative way of life. In order to preserve the full force of these norms, stepping outside the marriage structure must be seen as a failure. Therefore Social Security treat the woman as a failure, firstly, by their derogatory attitude. They also pretend to give an unsupported mother money to live on as a right, when in fact they have counter-balancing rights which enable them to make moral judgements and remove the money at their discretion.

The social services

The social services are specifically created to care for those people who cannot survive in our society. They are there to help the 'failure' (eg the unsupported mother) or the deviant individual to readjust to society; they are not working for basic social change but are trying to make the best of the present set-up. Social workers are trapped by their own ideology. When concentrating on an individual and personal effort proves insufficient (because of eg overwhelming financial need) they do not see their philosophy as being at fault by ignoring the need for social change - it is the individual who is labelled 'inadequate'. The state pays social workers to alleviate the worst situations so that things don't totally break down.

Once Ann had taken resource to a state body, Social Security, she was subject to their scrutiny and judgement. SS declares that it gives benefits to those in 'real need' but reserves discretionary 'rights', which means that in effect they define what they mean by 'real need'. All claimants are potentially seen as 'scroungers' and every effort has to be made to ensure that benefits only go to the deserving. In Ann's case SS's fraud squad was used to discover whether or not she was cohabiting. If she was living with a man then they assumed that he would support her and she would not be entitled to her allowance. This means in effect that on her own as a mother she has no real right to a direct allowance. Her job as child rearer is only justifiable if she is supported by a man and indirectly receives an allowance from him in return for serving his needs.

The housing department reinforced the position taken by SS. When Ann's allowance was cut off she could not pay the rent. Consequantly she was threatened with eviction. There was no sense in which the housing department felt they had an obligation to house Ann and her family. The service they were providing could only be obtained if you could afford it. It was

240

Ann's personal responsibility to pay the rent; the housing department did not try to put pressure on SS to pay up.

The social services department also played their part in persecuting Ann. Although the social workers' aim is specifically to help their clients rather than the more vaguely welfare orientation of, say, the housing department, they do not seriously attempt to help those clients like Ann who do not readily respond to encouragement to return to the 'fold'. According to them Ann did not 'cooperate' as she refused to stay with her husband, find a substitute for him or in general conform to middle class standards of behaviour. They said that Ann 'had been known to them for a long time'. This meant that they had given up on Ann and therefore were not prepared to fight for her with SS or the housing department. Their solution to the problem would have been to take the children into care. The only concrete help that they offered was a bag of old shoes. The social services had the possiblity of helping Ann but were trapped by their belief that personal effort within socially accepted norms would solve all. The need to preserve their professional status by placing their loyalty to the institution which paid them before their commitment to their 'clients' also limited them.

The other representatives of institutionalised authority who were directly involved were the police. Their role in the campaign was illuminating. Ann and her family, as people living in one of the most neglected and depressed streets in Cambridge, were constantly harassed by the police over TV licences, dog licences, etc. In more suburban areas in Cambridge the discovery and conviction of such petty misdemeanours does not take place. The rate of petty crime in such poor areas is high, but harassment of the above kind is based on prejudice against certain sorts of people and picking on individuals as victims. The causes of 'crime' in such areas do not appear to be the concern of the police, who see their job as being to protect members of society.

But whom do they protect? Ann asked the police to provide protection for her and her children against her husband because violent quarrels were likely to erupt when he came to the house and he would not stay away. This was refused. One night when the children were terrified by a prowler (SS investigator?) and could not sleep, Ann phoned the police; they did not arrive. If a middle class mother had phoned the police with the same complaint, would they not have turned up? As an inhabitant of Ross Street, Ann was not only victimised but protection was actually withdrawn. The availability of protection from the police depends in part on one's social class and in part on the degree to which one is challenging the status quo in any given situation. Thus, although the police did not respond to Ann's summons, they did respond when her mother asked for help. Ann and her mother were often in conflict and the police were willing to arrive on the scene of any domestic quarrel. At this point Ann's mother was seen as supporting the status quo and her daughter as the 'deviant'. The police made use of the antagonism which is often found between mother and daughter by turning the mother into their ally against the daughter; in this way they obscured the similarities in their oppression as women, and particularly working class women. This was dramatically manifested in the court case over the children where mother gave evidence against daughter. The authorities should have been on trial, not Ann. But the police exist to reinforce the power of the authorities; they cooperated with Social Security at the tribunal, and when they lost the tribunal, the police continued their persecution of the 'deviant' using other weapons - the children - and with the collusion of another institution - the social services. The court order putting the two eldest children into care arrived together with notification of another court case which would probably have resulted in the other children being put into care. Such court cases are usually a formality as all the institutions represented are on the same merry-go-round. The mother is on her own - a victim.

As in any society the 'deviant' is an anomaly. In this case Ann was hounded and brought to trial in order to reinforce the values of our society. Her plight was not used as a means to comment on those values and to try to change them.

After the crises of the Baxter family were over it became clear that if the results of our battles with the various authorities were to be consolidated, some form of long-term support had to be provided. The follow-up work had to be done in such a way that in every situation the necessity and therefore the ultimate objective of social change was maintained without alienating the department and losing the opportunity for influencing individual social workers. This has not been easy to achieve. We managed to have a member of Women's Liberation appointed as a voluntary social worker, and later another WL woman joined her. However this in itself created certain problems. Both of these women were middle class and they had to be constantly wary of being used by the social services in a traditional role of middle class go-between, mediating between the working class individual and the authorities, thus allowing the social workers to perpetuate their own patronising attitudes towards 'clients' and belief in the system. The voluntary social workers had to be constantly on their guard to see that they did not find themselves doing the bidding of the authorities. We hoped that they might be able to radicalise the policy of the social services by working on the inside. Each time the voluntary workers were able to effect a change, eg having the client attend all conferences concerning her situation, we hoped that this would provide a precedent making it possible to demand this right for all clients in the future. We hoped that the volunteers could use the influence of their middle class status in the interests of change rather than colluding in the workings of the present

242

system. They did make headway in this direction, and the Unmarried Mothers Group is still struggling in a similar way with the social services.

Through our analysis of the role played by the various social services and the voluntary social workers we can see the basic contradiction between the stated aims of the social services, eg to help an unsupported mother, and their real aims, to help clients live respectable lives, ie to put as top priority tidiness, punctuality, deference to experts and, above all, not to blatantly flaunt the rejection of conventional sexual morality. If the unsupported mother cannot or will not conform she is forced into accepting a situation of hardship in which she shares her problems with all unsupported mothers, whatever their class. The only way in which she can hope to improve her situation is to unite with other women in a similar position. She has usually not chosen to become 'unsupported', yet her situation confronts her with the possibility for political awareness and collective action. The possibilities of this struggle have a very real significance in terms of the wider aims of Women's Liberation. The struggle to bring up a family without a father in the marriage situation contains the embryonic threat to our present organisation of society in which both the ideology of marriage and economic dependence are used to keep people in their 'place'. The alloted 'place' of the majority of women is that of being trapped in their home as wife and mother and with little opportunity to control their own lives and choose how to lead them.

Political awareness of the Women's Liberation Group

Our views on the political significance of fighting alongside an unsupported mother should by now be clear. Much of this understanding was acquired during the action rather than through abstract discussion. We feel that through action the rather vague theories we voiced before were solidified and reaffirmed; through action we also became aware of many pitfalls involved in implementing our theories which had not previously occurred to us.

The following is an attempt to state our current political position as it developed from our original amorphous ideas: as members of Women's Liberation we did not wish to impose our theories and leadership on the working class and use them as political tools. We do not want blind acceptance of political dogma but a real understanding which we felt we had gained from starting where we were at in our own personal lives. We felt that no revolution would be successful unless it came from the people and their consciousness and awareness in their own terms. If the revolution does not come about through a democratic process with equal participation and responsibility in rights and decision-making we will never have a truly socialist society. This theoretical principle was clear to many of us before the campaign but in the midst of

243

action it took some hard knocks.

Here are some of the hurdles we discovered: as a predominantly middle class group there existed certain real barriers to communication with working class women. We have middle class values in terms of the weight we place on education for our children. We know that work can be creative; we have a future towards which we can work because of our education and privileged situation in society. We can also pose non-materialistic values because we have had the security of a well-endowed background or position; some became excruciatingly aware that they had employed working class women to do their shit-work and were guilty of exploiting the women with whom they wished to unite in collective action; we realised the disadvantages of being reasonably articulate and having worked out a political theory which was incomprehensible to working class women because of, firstly, the language we used and, secondly, our emphasis on needs many of which were meaningless to them because of the difference in backgrounds.

The danger of there being such wide gulfs in experience, expectations and behaviour was that it was difficult not to fall into the trap of expressing what we felt was right or best on a political level but in so doing being guilty of lack of understanding. Such patronising and dominating attitudes would only succeed in alienating people, ruining any hope of democratic activity by taking away the autonomy of the very women who along with ourselves we hope to unite with. We did not want to collude in a dependent relationship with either a husband or any authority. The problems of having a more developed theoretical position and more ideas concerning the necessity of collective action and how to carry it out than working class women were also manifested in the group itself, where some women were at times clearly seen as leaders and others as followers.

Despite all these barriers (which we must face in order to overcome them) we were all able to identify with each other as being of the same 'caste'. We discovered that as women we could surmount anything, class, racial barriers, as we are all oppressed in a similar way. Society is structured in terms of sex roles which are used as a basis for the division of labour. We all have the same roles, the same problems; male chauvinism, being dependent on men or on a man, abortion and contraception, child-rearing. The unsupported mother, in particular those who are without training and qualifications for a job, crosses class boundaries in the economic sphere and has the same difficulties in being isolated, a single parent and suffering the general victimisation of the woman on her own.

We found that through relating to other women in both groups and in Ross Street at the personal or micro- level and trying constantly to put our democratic principles into operation in in that sphere (of personal relationships through identification of others in the same caste) that we could combine both

personal politics and political activity on the macro level in
a constructive way. Our actions were not in contradiction to
our political theory and vice versa. Hopefully, when we combine in collective action over the common goal of setting up
an adventure playground we shall be saying 'we' and 'us'
instead of that ominous 'us' and 'them'. (This project has already had several ups and downs over the problem of well-
intentioned individuals 'taking over' from the mothers. But
developing awareness of this as bad politics has led to constant re-assessment of strategy and confirmation that the
way one goes about things is as important as what one is
trying objectively to achieve.)

As well as the contradictions we faced in the action itself,
we also found that it brought to a head many of the contradictions in our own personal lives. Many of us when faced with
irate partners had to admit that arrangements previously
thought of as satisfactory were not so when the roles were
reversed. We were forced to ask ourselves whose life the
nuclear family was structured around. If as a group we had
remained concentrating on our own domestic scenes such
personal issues would not have been raised so significantly
or convincingly. Our partners would have continued to do a
few more duties, sew on a couple of buttons and take care of
the children more frequently without the necessity of change
in the basic structure of sexual roles emerging. We now feel
that full-time commitment to changing our personal lives is
a rationalisation for inaction. Group meetings themselves can
be seen as cathartic and instead of being preparation for further action can lead to further inactivity. Through action we
demonstrated and achieved more on the personal level; it
certainly was not deliberate; it was certainly unavoidable.
We now know that to be politically active and relate to others
in the present social structure based on the nuclear family
is virtually impossible. We felt convinced that alternatives
had to be found. Since the campaign some of those involved
have formed a commune and others are planning similar
structural changes in their living. In effect we discovered
the necessity of having a simultaneous commitment to external political activity and changing one's personal life.

One of our chief concerns during the campaign was that we
were concentrating on an individual case as opposed to taking
action for all unsupported mothers and all claimants. Quite
frankly we fell rather blindly into supporting Ann with political zeal based more on anger and identification than on a plan
for an extended campaign aimed at broadening the issues. Intellectually we know the importance of not putting all our energies into a rescue operation for one individual, thereby
neglecting the necessity for all claimants to unite to undermine the system. We saw the danger of success with an individual through personal effort making us feel that perhaps
the system is all right and that perhaps with a few changes
here and there it would function satisfactorily. It was clear

to some of us then and to all of us after the campaign that one cannot change society just through working with one individual.

Another difficulty in working with an individual case was that naturally one could never sacrifice the individual for the cause or even for a political principle. It was even possible that in our concern to rescue Ann from her desperate situation we were used as tools to reinforce the status quo. In carrying out a rescue operation for one person one can easily miss the opportunity to mobilise others and unite in collective action. Ideally an individual case can be used as propaganda. We achieved this within the Women's Liberation group, where consciousness was raised, but failed on the whole to get much sympathy from the general public. This was caused by lack of organisation on our part due to our inexperience, particularly in dealing with publicity. However the Unsupported Mothers Group is still growing and along with the Claimants' Union has made some impact on Social Security. Claimants, including unmarried mothers, have now a very good chance of receiving what they are entitled to if accompanied to the SS offices by another claimant. If this fails we fight for rights at tribunals and have access to help from the Child Poverty Action Group.

Through helping Ann and getting her back onto her feet it has become apparent that Ann can mobilise others; she has got women together to work on the adventure playground and taken other unsupported mothers to SS; and she and friends from Ross Street participated in the recent abortion campaign. From the activities of the voluntary social workers in this particular case a group is emerging of people who are willing to work with an institution in order to raise the consciousness of others working there by creating the realisation that radical change is essential. We feel this to be a viable strategy if one does not lose sight of the long term political goals.

We therefore discovered that working politically on an individual case does not necessarily mean that one sacrifices the goal of radical change. What matters is that one has worked out the best strategy to attain one's long term objective, rather than working entirely within the perspective of the needs of the individual. During the campaign, just as many reached political awareness, so other more convinced revolutionaries reassessed possible strategies.

But above all the personal involvement and identification with Ann and the living out with her daily the oppressive and brutal acts of the institutions against her led many of us for the first time to comprehend how efficiently, thoroughly and cruelly the system operated to crush those who did not conform. We saw how the system used Ann by labelling her inadequate to reinforce its own inhuman and evil values; without this involvement on a personal level we would not have felt the anger and courage we did; we would not have understood the power of the system; we would not have united so strongly in collective action against the authorities. We would not have been so aware of the danger of authoritarianism in ourselves; we would not have been so aware of the oppressive structures of our own nuclear families. The action radicalised many who were basically untouched by theoretical discussion and reading. It became evident to all that although Ann had been supported in fighting the authorities, had won her case and regained her five children, she still has to support them on £14.50 per week in inadequate and overcrowded conditions and in a barren environment. Her situation, along with that of other unsupported mothers, is still basically the same; there is still the constant threat of victimisation and the struggle to maintain herself and her children in nearly intolerable circumstances. We still have a long way to go.

Ann's case can be seen as representing a devastating comment on a system which calls itself democratic. The only solution for her and the many others is to unite with all the oppressed and to work with them to raise consciousness and mobilise forces to undermine and destroy the present system, in order to build another. Through personal involvement came political awareness which resulted in collective action. This is the only way that we can win.

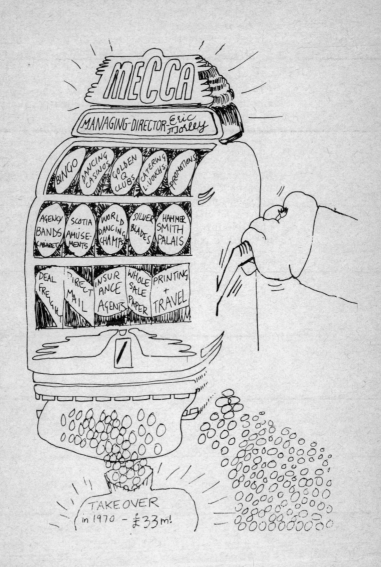

MISS WORLD

(This was written by the women who took part in the demonstrations against the Miss World contest in 1970 and were arrested. Their trial took place in summer 1971. The article first appeared as a pamphlet, 'Why Miss World?', available from the London Women's Liberation Workshop)

'I felt that the event symbolised my daily exploitation. I saw the contestants being judged by men, and I know what it feels like to be judged and scrutinised every day when I am just walking down the street. I saw women being forced to compete with each other and being judged by men. I felt for them. I had no intention of hurting them or attacking them in any way. We did not throw anything on to the stage when the contestants were there. We threw missiles on the stage when Bob Hope was speaking. In the same way we threw nothing when the Miss World contestants were going into the Cafe de Paris. This was a conscious decision. We regard these contestants as unfortunate victims of the male capitalist system. This system, that makes money by persuading women to buy goods such as false eyelashes. We are sick of all this line about beauty. We are not beautiful and we are not ugly. It is a big capitalist con.'

The first Miss World contest took place in 1951. It coincided with the Festival of Britain, a centenary of the Great Exhibition, which celebrated the Nation's brave post-war recovery and demonstrated its continued technological inventiveness. Technological innovations are essential to capitalism. They stimulate production and thereby increase profits - provided that new markets are secured both at home and abroad.

At the Festival Hall on the South Bank leading manufacturers displayed up-to-date items of interest for international consumption, with the firm intention of putting Britain once more 'on the map'. On the North Bank, at the Lyceum, Mecca Ltd presented their new invention - an international beauty contest. The organiser, Eric Morley, lamented the fact that 'in those days some countries hadn't even heard of beauty contests'. So of course he congratulated the company bosses for 'shrewdly anticipating the public appetite for such an event'. The 'event' has made Mecca into a £20million enterprise.

In 'The Miss World story' Morley tells how he 'made it' and, like most tales of entrepreneurial heroism, it's a matter of transforming petty thieving into respectable big business. Prior to the Miss World contest, Mecca ballrooms throughout the country had been running contests of the 'outright' (ie outdated) type. Local girls paraded in bikinis, or stars and G-strings, and were disqualified by the audience jeering at their under-or over-weight statistics'. (These contests were were probably derivative of carnival culture, and as such at least had more vitality than the slick, hence more insidious, prefabrication of Miss World.)

The new brand of contestants, unlike those of the 'outright' type, were seen as National Representatives selected in order to stand up to international competition. To start with, Morley looks for what he calls 'basic material': girls between 17 and 25, ideally 5' 7½", 8 or 9 stone, waist 22-24", hips 35-36", 'no more no less', a lovely face, good teeth, plenty of hair and perfectly shaped legs from front and back - carefully checked for 'such defects as slightly knocked knees'. Then with the 'basic material' plus the aid of cosmetics and a deportment school, he manufactures the 'perfect product'. It is a sound capital investment since overheads are low. First of all, raw material is practically free. Morley proudly affirms that he refuses to pay the girls travelling expenses, gives them only board and lodging and a small allowance. Secondly, labour, represented by performance, is unpaid except for the winners' £2500. Mecca makes up for this in the long run since Miss World is obliged to sign a contract for future appearances. The contestants were forced to make so many appearances that as early as 1952 they threatened to go on strike. Obviously this wasn't in the 'public interest' and the girls weren't even accorded the sparse dignity of union-style negotiations. Morley, giving himself a man-sized pat on the back for his expertise in 'human relations', settled, or rather pre-empted the dispute by rushing out and buying each girl a teddy bear!

'Human relations' under capitalism means the art of exacting services from a subordinate without provoking a consequent sense of injustice. Applied to women, 'human relations' means exaggerated paternalism or diluted chivalry. The first approach insists that women are like children and therefore respond to scolding or pampering. As Morley said of the dissident contestants' reactions to his teddy bear ploy, 'they are all sweetness and smiles again'. The other approach senses the injustice of women's inferior social position but suggests that polite gestures are sufficient compensation. The Miss World contestants caricature the alienating effects of selling one's labour - they are literally engaged in selling 'themselves'.

Married women are banned from the contest because, Morley explains, 'it might make a woman dissatisfied with her life as housewife and mother... husbands ought to have their brains tested if they allow it'. As for the contestants 'reputation', this is ensured by chaperones who 'rule the girls like Holloway prison warders'. Respectability ultimately has a class connotation, he continues, 'this contest is no longer degrading, because unlike the 50s when it was the sort of thing girls of the so-called lower classes did... now we have daughters of some titled people, a number from wealthy families or of public school education'.

There is no question of 'fixing' the contests, but to get the 'right' girls you have to get the 'right' judges. They must look

for more than a 'busty girl with a sweet face'. Competition is
no longer with the girl round the corner, but with the girls in
the sunsilk ad. Mecca make a substantial sum by selling the
rights to televise the contest. This means that the entrant had
better be able to read a script, speak into a mike without stut-
tering, and generally look good on TV.

Over 27 million people watch the Miss World spectacle. They
see racism carefully concealed behind the 'family of nations'
facade; Miss Granada can become Miss World, make obliging
remarks about the British hospitality, and consequently pacify
2 million underpaid immigrant workers. A Miss White South
Africa and a Miss Black South Africa make it possible to pretend, at least for an evening, that apartheid is not so definitive.
Miss India, during her reign as Miss World, entertained American troops in Vietnam and 'received cheers in spite of being
coloured and wearing a sari' (Bob Hope). The Miss Third
World trend reflected the 'wind of change' - a view of the
world as a happy family of united nations engaged in peaceful
competition rather than violent confrontation. (This ideology
served to obscure the anti-imperialist struggles at home and
abroad. In fact, post-war retention of foreign markets has
meant that Britain has had to intervene in, or at least condone
the repression of national liberation fronts in places like the
West Indies, South Africa, India and the Arab Gulf - even today
RAF planes are bombing the small villages of Dhofar held by
the NLF.)

Miss World viewers also see sexism masquerading as a celebration of a Venus de Milo (cameras zoom in on a copy of the
famous Greek statue), the timeless heritage of antiquity, the
symbol of transcendental beauty. However, Miss World beauty
is far from transcendental, it is profoundly temporal, out of
date in less than a year. At the same time the promotion and
proliferation of the image through advertising persuades women to 'transcend' their 'basic material'. The consequence
of this 'transcendence' is the expansion of the domestic market. For example, by the mid-60s the annual expenditure for
clothing and cosmetics had reached £174million for the teenage group alone. At the same time 70% of all girls aged between 15 and 19 left school and only one in a thousand from
working class families attended university. Women are not
expected to 'achieve' anything and even if they want to there
are few jobs that offer a real opportunity for promotion or
economic security.

Beauty contests epitomise the traditional female road to success. For many women, entering one is like doing the pools -
a kind of magic individual solution to the 'economic problem'.
Mecca's economic problems aren't centred on subsistence but
on accumulating profits from finals, heats, rights, ads, bingo
and bets. What's in it for the contestants? According to Morley
'the adventure and excitement of living for a few days in luxury
hotels and travelling first class', with of course 'the fringe

benefits of marriage to wealthy or attractive men and memories worth treasuring for ever'. This is a scrap-book life of women's magazines, the condition of all women which is assumed to be innate and unalterable. As one journalist put it, 'We were obliged to be realists about women... their concern is not with ideas or principles but with persons and things. Their main interest is their feminine role'. Eric Morley underlines the limitations of this role and the farcical escape which it offers when he says that Miss World is 'something of a cinderella'. But now women are asking why she didn't seize the magic wand and save herself from running home in rags.

The demonstration

The Miss World competition is not an erotic exhibition; it is a public celebration of the traditional female road to success. The Albert Hall on the evening of November 20th 1970 was miles away from the underground world of pornography. The atmosphere was emphatically respectable, enlivened by contrived attempts at 'glamour'. The conventionality of the girls' lives and the ordinariness of their aspirations were the keynotes of all the pre and post-competition publicity, eg the example of Miss Granada (Miss World): 'Now I'm looking for the ideal man to marry'. Their condition is the condition of all women, born to be defined by their physical attributes, born to give birth, or if born pretty, born lucky, a condition which makes it possible and acceptable within the bourgeois ethic for girls to parade, silent and smiling, to be judged on the merits of their figures and faces. (Bob Hope: 'Pretty girls don't have those problems', ie the problems that plain girls have in finding a husband or making a successful career; WL girls must be plain, because only plain girls would have an interest in attacking the system.)

Demonstrating against Miss World, Women's Liberation struck a blow against this narrow destiny, against the physical confines of the way women are seen and the way they fit into society. Most of all it was a blow against passivity, not only the enforced passivity of the girls on the stage, but the passivity that we all felt in ourselves. We were dominated while preparing for the demonstration by terror at what we were about to do. To take violent action, interrupting a carefully ordered spectacle, drawing attention to ourselves, inviting the hostility of tousands of people was something that we had all previously thought to be personally impossible for us, inhibited both by our conditioning as women and by our acceptance of bourgeois norms of correct behaviour. It was a revolt against the safeness of our lives, the comfort of continual contact with like-minded people. The fact of joining WL shows a level of awareness of women's condition. But it's also possible within the movement to become sheltered by the support and understanding of a group and/or friends. In the Albert Hall we were back in the previous isolation of the outside world, surrounded by people, men and women who were there to take part in the oppression of women - and who were outraged and bewildered by our challenge to it. The outside world is mystified, and consequently often hostile, but WL cannot for that reason fear communication with it. Women must be confident enough to challenge the distortion or indifference of the press and transcend their own feelings of vulnerability.

The seating arrangements in the Albert Hall were completely different from what we had expected. For example, Sally and I found ourselves unexpectedly isolated on the other side of the hall from most of the others; we had only managed to fill the two extra seats at the last moment; Laura found herself downstairs instead of upstairs. We had reduced our grandiose plans to the simplest strategy of aiming for the jury and the stage with the comic array of weapons with which we were armed. We got into the hall amazingly easily; we thought, what with the Young Liberals' propaganda, the bomb scare and strict security that a group of unescorted girls would never be allowed in. Once seated, Sally and I realised that the hall itself wasn't nearly as vast as our heightened imaginations had led us to believe. Above all we saw how ludicrously accessible the stage was, and that our only possible plan could be to make for the stage. Our feelings ranged from complicity with the audience - a mixture of people backing their own national candidates, overdressed couples on a night out and the odd family outing - to an intense feeling that we stood out, and that everyone was staring at us. The conspiratorial non-acknowledgement of each other in the ladies' and the intermission - silent solidarity. Mostly it was the feeling of being caged in, surrounded by superficially 'nice' but basically hostile thousands.

In the hall, Sally's and my conversation fluctuated wildly between frantically whispered consultations of mutual encouragement and overloud comments about the show, the judges, the girls, anything 'ordinary' and unsuspicious. We tried our best to laugh at Bob Hope's jokes, in a pathetic attempt to feel one with the audience at last. But as joke after joke fell flat, we were even isolated in our effort at normality. Suddenly the signal which we had been waiting for so anxiously came, at the perfect moment. It was our robot-like response which surprised us most of all. When the moment came it was easier to act than to consider; in the scuffle with the police, it was anger and determination that prevailed. As I was lifted bodily out of the hall, three Miss Worlds came running up to me, a trio of sequinned, perfumed visions saying, 'Are you alright?' 'Let her go'. When the policeman explained we were from WL and demonstrating against them, I managed to say we weren't against them, we were for them, but against Mecca and their exploitation of women. 'Come on, Miss Venezuela, we're on', and the trio disappeared. Then I was dragged off and taken to a room where, to my relief, I saw that Sally and the two girls who gave the signal had already been detained.

How was it, with so many odds against us, that the demonstration was successful? The spectacle is vulnerable. However intricately planned it is, a handful of people can disrupt it and cause chaos in a seemingly impenetrable organisation. The spectacle isn't prepared for anything other than
tators. Bob Hope made more connections than we ever hoped to put across: his continual emphasis on Vietnam revealed the arrogance of imperialism behind the supposedly reassuring family of nations facade. The press, searching for sensations, turned a small demonstration into headline news. Let's leave the last words to Bob Hope: 'They said we were "using" women. I always thought we were using them right. I don't want to change position with them. Why do they want to change position with me? I don't want to have babies, I'm too busy'.

We threw smoke bombs, flour, stink bombs, leaflets, blew whistles, waved rattles. Bob Hope freaked out, ran off the stage. We got thrown out by Mecca bouncers: Sally was arrested for assault (stubbing her cigarette out on a policeman). Jenny was done for an offensive weapon (a children's smoke bomb). Some went on to the Cafe de Paris, where the Miss Worlds were having dinner: two more arrests - Jo and Kate for throwing flour and rotten tomatoes at the Mecca pimps. Maia was arrested for abusive language (telling a policeman to fuck off): her charge was dismissed early on in the case.

The Miss World action and the trial which followed was the first militant confrontation with the law by women since the suffragettes. It is over 60 years since Annie Kenney and Christabel Pankhurst received 3 and 7 days in Strangeways for addressing the crowd outside a meeting of the liberal candidate Winston Churchill in Manchester. Previously they had been roughly thrown out of the hall for causing a disturbance when they asked the platform for a statement of its position on the question of votes for women. This first illegal action of the suffragettes was followed three years later in 1908 by the celebrated trial of Mrs Pankhurst, her daughter Christabel and Mrs Flora Drummond. They appeared at Bow Street charged with conduct likely to cause a breach of the peace, and received 2 and 3 month sentences. The witnesses included Lloyd George and Herbert Gladstone, whom they had sub-poenaed. The Pankhursts conducted their own defence. Their cross-examination of witnesses, the speeches they made in court amounted to a brilliant exposure of male prejudice and of the legal system. In the course of the trial we re-discovered the political importance of self-defence, both as a means of defending our self-respect and as a means of consciously rejecting the image of female acquiescence. Self-defence is a public demonstration of our refusal to collude in our own repression. It is an expression of the politics of women's liberation.

We each reacted differently to thinking about the trial

I was coming face to face with the law and it looked like this. .
I was scared - scared to assert myself in the face of the law
of the land. Why shouldn't I try and get off with a light sentence? Admit I was guilty. A lawyer could defend me better
than myself. Small charges - first offences. Easy way out -
play it straight, get a lawyer, employ an expert to represent
me and say It better (what? why?), implying get it over with,
plead guilty... Why?

Because that's a whole contradiction to a whole action which
was Joyful... So what's the point of adopting a new clean-
clothed, safe, tamed, timid, intimidated Woman Image, if it
means standing in a public dock box and mouthing the words. .
'I am guilty... of insulting behaviour'. It's not true, and saying
we caused a breach of the peace... insulting whom, and whose
peace are we breaching?

Defend what? What are we defending? Questions, questions
are forming all the time... What are we defending? We will
be on trial. What for? Individual acts or Women's Liberation?

All our lives we had been letting other people defend us, speak
for us, lead us, apologise for us. This was a chance to change
that, to speak for ourselves, break through our passivity...
and that led to challenging too the role that lawyers played,
in society. Experts, well-oiled in legal jargon, ready to defend
any person's acts against the system, but never to step over
that line and challenge the basis of the Law. This was confirmed by various lawyers reactions, like a woman barrister
saying 'I can defend Women's Liberation, but not your actions'.
And 'Be prepared for a psychiatric report'. And another,
'Just think of me as a mechanic with a garage of legal information'. 'Out of the garage and into the streets', we chorused
to him.

So we began to think what do WE want out of the trial, and
who are we?

And by thinking of ways of challenging we begin to feel confidence from working together, knowing that we can emerge
from Conditioned Responses, remembering the joy and strength
of that togetherness feeling in the Albert Hall, jumping from
the seats, racing down the aisles, shattering the Spectacle of
Beauty and saying What the fuck is all this about? What is
happening to Woman?

And realising how a scream can be a public event - meaning
let's make public, let it out, the stifling feelings, keep no more,
making secret safe silent shameful... private, let's change,
challenge, bring into the open, expose, abolish... the Private,
privates, Property, Screams, War-cries... becoming weapons
that mean transforming the guilt-defences - passivity - soft -
inexpressed - sacrificial thoughts that are static.

And remembering in the court room the first time we came
up (to be remanded on bail) the emphasis on being and keeping

silent... the peace... acceptance, restraint, order, suppress,
pain, tears, pills, tranquilizers, sleep, peace, calm, soft passivity... keep calm, accept society, and silence in court... the
lawyer will speak, the magistrate will answer... the Soft
Process continues... knowing that the 'common prostitutes'
we spent the night with in the cells when we were remanded
will follow us in and plead 'guilty' - because it's easier - the
policeman said so, so why bother to question what 'guilty' or
words or 'justice' means... 'just get it over with quick love'.

And remembering and realising... I wanted to scream, make
some sound, some Human Noise to shatter the silent static
procedure, the soft mysterious process that envelops...
'werenotgonnatakeit... We're not gonna take it'.

Suddenly the roaring horror of my own passivity hit me in the
face. The years and years of lack of faith in myself were all
rearing their ugly faces and jeering at me - you, defend yourself? they said - you must be joking! Who do you think is
going to take someone like you seriously. You'll be smashed
and spat upon, you won't even be able to open your mouth to
say a thing in court, you'll be so scared.

That's right, I thought, that's myself speaking after all. But
the only trouble was that that was the part of myself I didn't
like at all. It was the part of myself that was always making
excuses for myself, always backing out of things, hiding behind
an image of helplessness and lack of confidence. I didn't want
to be like that. I wanted to escape from all that, throw it away,
and I knew that the only way I was going to do that was by
defying it and saying 'no, I'm not like that. I can stand up in
that court and speak for myself along with the other women,
and fighting the weakness I feel by myself'.

These were our thoughts, fears, hopes, that we went through
before the trial. And it was getting nearer that.

We wanted to go further than defending ourselves. We wanted
to ATTACK...

... the law that had arrested us, the court that was sentencing
us, and show that it was part of a system based on the protection of private property interests. We wanted to break down
the structure of the court itself and the isolation of being on
trial as an Individual, feeling intimidated by the Court, the
Law, the Science, the Mystery.

That meant challenging the court at every point: by speaking
to each other in our own language that would be understandable to anyone; by speaking to witnesses ourselves, as they
were the women we demonstrated with; and explaining that
way why we wanted to stop the contest; by using the court to
talk to other women and to create a space in the court. How?

We started the trial by trying to make the actual courtroom
less formal - by demanding the right to have friends as legal

advisors (for the three of us without lawyers). We found a previous case (McKenzie v. McKenzie) gave a precedent for this - which meant sitting with friends, instead of sitting alone in the dock.

We asked for our 4 cases to be heard together. We started by pleading 'not guilty' - 'we've been guilty all our lives as women and we won't plead guilty any more'. We challenged the Bench and the Magistrate - explaining that as they had a 'vested and pecuniary interest in the verdict' (ie paid male) they had no right to judge us. For a man shall not be judge in his own cause.

So we did it, and the reality was a tremendous feeling of exhilaration and joy. We were fighting back on our own terms, refusing to be humbled by the court, laughing in its face, feeling tremendous confidence and trust in each other.

They spun it out over 5 days, with as much as a month and a half in between, but in spite of that, the confidence of the women on trial built up and up until the court was being held on our terms: we were beginning to say what we wanted to and learning and showing what justice is - a farce. The Magistrate was patronising and stifling. He became Daddy, dispensing wisdom to his naughty but intelligent daughters. So we ignore him effectively by continuing to talk to each other and our witnesses about our lives... 'What do you think of the Magistrate?' we ask. 'He is irrelevant'. Finally his patience gets thin, because... Daddy is not fair or honest... he is angry.

The Sick comedy turns really sour as the power is turned on. Witnesses were dragged out of the witness box. On the last day but one three women (all of them witnesses) were detained outside the courtroom by Special Branch and CID.

But the show goes on... justice must be <u>seen to be done</u>. When Jo (6 months pregnant) tried to leave the courtroom to get a lawyer for the three women, she was thrown to the ground by six pigs. In the fight that followed one woman was arrested for assault, and the three were dragged off without being arrested or charged, and held at Barnet police station for 9 hours before they were released. They were interrogated about the bombing at Robert Carr's house on January 12, the bombing of a BBC van the night before the Miss World contest, their politics, their friends, their kids ('who does he belong to anyway?'), their sexuality ('you're butch, aren't you?').

The four defendants spent that night in Holloway, and were interrogated about the bombing the next day before they appeared in court. They were scared - not surprisingly - they were told they would have to go up to Barnet for further questioning as soon as the trial was over. The fact hung over them as the magistrate refused to allow them any more witnesses, and finished the case in 2 hours. The 'star' witness, Morley, chairman of Mecca and the brains behind the contest, was conveniently refused as a witness. The defendants were not allowed to put their case. The court was packed with police as usual, and only 15 people (including a Special Branch man who had been there every day) were allowed into the public gallery. Justice was seen to be done. Also, as usual, Nina Stanger, the lawyer defending one of the women, was completely ignored, treated like shit, and in general put down by the magistrate. Women lose out in every situation, but few areas are so obviously a man's world as the courts. Legal games depend on ego battles, and Nina didn't stand a chance against Daddy Rhees. The defendants were allowed two minutes to sum up. The fines came to £80, and each woman was bound over to keep the peace for two years or forfeit £100.

After

In Holloway, I see that the Miss World contest was but a drop in the ocean of Capitalism's mess - a sordid spectacle saying Look-but-don't-touch, Stimulate-but-can't-have, Provoke-but-don't-protest. Exposing it because we related to it was the beginning of a rejection of our culturally privileged positions. But freaking-out at the phoney glamour of this sort of spectacle is only a start, because it's still a limited and middle class response. The same with the trial. We challenged the court process by freaking out, but when the reality of the sort of power we are against came out of the game we began to feel really threatened and unprotected by our armour of educated wordgames - they will only stretch so far. Realising that we are privileged when we meet women in Holloway who are much more the victims... one girl in there for 2 weeks on remand for being in possession of a stolen licence... but then there's a woman this week in the papers, on homicide, for pushing a dummy down her own child's throat, because a whining husband was demanding his supper, and she not being able to cope... Miss World was a drop in the ocean.

The plea was an understatement, saying Daddy was inadequate to judge as a man, when we realised he wasn't a human being, he was/is merely a tool. As Daddy he was comparatively harmless. A Wet Liberal merely being Masculine and pompous. But he revealed himself often as the capitalist pawn and finally exposed himself as a tool of a powerful oppressive capitalist and imperialist Way of Life, whose liberal laws as applied mean separation and repression.

Beauty and the bovver girls

The Miss World demonstration was conceived as a propaganda action. We calculated that groups of girls emerging from the gloom of the auditorium waving football rattles, hurling 'weapons', shouting slogans and being dragged out would create enough of a counter-spectacle to disrupt the show. As predicted, the media encouraged by Bob Hope's hysterical reaction, moved in - the screens of 7 million viewers erupted with streamers, leaflets and chaos for several minutes and the following day we were splashed all over the front pages of the popular press. We had indeed drawn attention to ourselves, but we had disastrously underestimated the ability of the press to 'interpret' events. The pre-contest planning meetings had unanimously rejected the use of any slogan or action that could possibly be construed as an attack on the contestants, or that might lead us into any violent confrontation. So we were naive enough to assume that although reaction might be hostile, the important issues would clearly emerge and other women would understand what we were doing. This was a miscalculation.

It was Bob Hope's impression of us as ugly bomb-throwing drug-addicts that received generous coverage. Our purpose in demonstrating and the politics of the Women's Liberation Movement were entirely ignored. Instead the focus was placed on our freakish personalities, our connections with left-wing extremisim, etc etc. We had made, it seemed, yet another contribution to the bra-burning, man-hating horror image of Women's Liberation.

As the trial escalated into police harassment of witnesses, suppression of the defence and intimidation of the defendants, publicity continued, undirected by us, and developed into a smear campaign. 'We're not beautiful, we're not ugly, we're angry', read one of our leaflets. The Special Branch led by Det. Chief Sup. Habershon, apparently under heavy pressure from the government, jumped to the conclusion that there must be some connection between Women's Liberation and the Angry Brigade. This (desperate) speculation on the part of the police had the full support of the capitalist press: 'Ford bomb: women's lib quiz by police' (Evening News, 20. 3. 71), 'Angry Brigade woos women militants' (Evening Standard)

The reality was rather more prosaic. We were neither vengeful harridans embittered by the sight of a pretty face, nor a tightly-knit terrorist unit. Few of us had any previous political experience: most of us met for the first time over the demonstration. Some came from different WL groups up and down the country, others were on their own. We did anticipate the possiblity of some police intervention. What we did not anticipate was the scale of confrontation with the forces of the state that the Miss World action unleashed. Events overtook us, and we found ourselves in a situation where it was difficult if not impossible to resist media manipulation and distortion.

The fact that about 100 girls demonstrated was almost immediately forgotten by the press. Interest focussed - at least until the link-up with the Angry Brigade - exclusively on the 5 defendants. Our immediate reaction was alarm; we felt isolated, over-exposed and even faintly ridiculous. Once the first shock of arrest etc had died down, all our time and energy was spent on the trial. If a journalist approached us, they were rapidly passed on to someone else. As a result, only the most persistent were given interviews and WL lost a crucial opportunity for communication.

The Miss World action was a reaction against humiliation, powerlessness. It wasn't part of a plan - we hadn't worked out clearly where out oppression comes from, how the system runs on it, why we are used, how we can change it. So there was nothing to fall back on. As far as we could see the demonstration had had no effect. (In fact, the Women's Workshop membership doubled in the month after and a year later women were still talking about it as something that started them thinking about their oppression.)

For us, out of that vacuum, we began to build ways of acting together which will make a movement over years instead of flash and disappear. We've worked more in the communities we live in - fighting for nurseries, playhouses for our kids, working with unsupported mothers in Claimants' Unions, meeting in small groups. Some of us have tried to live in collectives, some have worked with GLF. Most of it has been slow, painstaking organising compared with the Miss World demonstration - but it's in the home, around sexuality, kids, that our oppression bites deepest, holds hardest. The 'left' have always said the economy, our exploitation, has to be changed first, before our lives, our oppression. We say both have to be changed at once - the struggle against internalised oppression, against how we live our lives, is where we begin, where we've been put. But we can't end there: it's through that initial struggle that we understand that we can't live as we want to until the power structures of society have been broken. Women's oppression cuts across class, but our roles serve capitalism, and are caused and dictated by it. We're needed as wives and mothers to breed and feed the producers, serve and clothe the work force; as sexual objects to relieve our providers after the day's alienation; as prostitutes for a safety-valve for the family.

Women's liberation is impossible without the destruction of the class system - and a middle class women's movement can't do that. It's only the oppressed and exploited people who have the strategic power to overthrow capitalism. We need an organisation which recognises our particular oppression and gives us a framework to meet in and work out a common direction. The small groups that there are now must become fighting units. We can't afford to be afraid to criticise each other: the only real sisterhood is fighting side by side.

APPENDIX

Reading list

In addition to the references mentioned throughout the book, the following are useful general reading, though only the first three relate specifically to the present Women's Movement.

'Women's estate', Juliet Mitchell, Penguin 25p
'Dialectic of sex', Shulamith Firestone, Paladin 50p
'Sexual politics', Kate Millett, Abacus 60p
'The second sex', Simone de Beauvoir, Penguin 75p
'Patriarchal attitudes', Eva Figes, Panther 40p
'The female eunuch', Germaine Greer, Paladin 50p
'The feminine mystique', Betty Friedan, Penguin 40p

A comprehensive bibliography is 'Women's Liberation and revolution', compiled by Sheila Rowbotham for her own book, 'Women: resistance and revolution' (due out in early 1973). The bibliography is available for 15p from: Falling Wall Press, 79 Richmond Road, Montpelier, Bristol BS6 5EP. They also publish other women's liberation literature.

As well as the groups listed below, particularly the London Workshop, another organisation which has a large selection of women's liberation and other radical literature is Agitprop, 248 Bethnal Green Road, London E2 (01-739 1704)

Groups

The following is a selective list, of groups which have been going for some time. They will act as contacts for other groups in their area: if you write to the group nearest your area they should be able to put you in touch with a more local group. They will also provide information about publications, newsletters, meetings, campaigns and actions.

London & South-East

Women's Liberation Workshop, 3 Shavers Place, London SW1
Jen Murray, 25 Montpelier Crescent, Brighton, Sussex

Essex & East Anglia

Cambridge Women's Centre, 48 Eden Street, Cambridge
Sheila Bell, 16 Cabbell Road, Cromer, Norfolk
Pamela Lucioli, 45 Lonsdale Road, Stevenage, Hertfordshire

North-East

Caroline Freeman, 44 Old Elvet, Durham

Yorkshire

Lee Sanders, 71 St Ann's Lane, Leeds 4

(list continues)

North-West

Merseyside Women's Liberation, 2 Rutland Avenue, Liverpool 17
Merseyside Women's Liberation, 218 Upper Brook Street,
Manchester

Midlands

Catherine Hall, 65 Prospect Road, Moseley, Birmingham 13

South-West

Philippa Hills, 96 Elvaston Way, Reading, Berkshire
Ellen Malos, Garden Flat, 1 Apsley Road, Bristol BS8 2SH

Scotland

Pearl Mitchell, 3 Sinclair Road, Torry, Aberdeen

Wales

Diana Sidwell, Old Gardeners Cottage, Pent-y-goytre, Llanfair-
Kilgeddin, nr Abergavenny, Mons.

Ireland

Irish Women's Liberation, 7 Fownes Street, Dublin 7

*   *   *   *